Secrets of Success from
the Application Process
to Landing the First Job

# Law
# School
# Lowdown

Ian E. Scott, Esq.

J.D., Harvard Law School

**BARRON'S**

*This book is dedicated to my*
*daughters Olivia and Victoria*

*All inquiries should be addressed to:*
Barron's Educational Series, Inc.
250 Wireless Boulevard
Hauppauge, NY 11788
**www.barronseduc.com**

ISBN: 978-1-4380-0317-7

Library of Congress Control Number: 2013018094

**Library of Congress Cataloging-in-Publication Data**
Scott, Ian E.
    Law school lowdown : secrets of success from the application process
to landing the first job / Ian E. Scott, Esq., J.D., Harvard Law School.
        pages  cm
    Includes bibliographical references and index.
    ISBN 978-1-4380-0317-7 (alk. paper)
    1. Law students—United States—Handbooks, manuals, etc.    2. Law—Vocational
guidance—United States.    3. Law—Study and teaching—United States.    I. Title.
    KF283.S37 2013
    340.071'173—dc23                                                      2013018094

PRINTED IN THE UNITED STATES OF AMERICA
9 8 7 6 5 4 3 2 1

# Contents

# Introduction

Law school can be a fun, rewarding, and educational experience. It can also be confusing, daunting, and stressful. With all of the late nights, stress, and uncertainty though, I still have the following sound advice for my two daughters: "You can be anything you want to be when you grow up, as long as you go to law school first." This advice to my next of kin really sums up my opinion with respect to law school and the law school experience, so you should expect a bias from this book.

I started this book in my second year as a student at Harvard Law School when I repeatedly heard myself saying, "If someone would have told me this, I could have saved myself so much time, money, and stress." As I navigated through the tough first year of law school, a law review competition, moot court tryouts, finding summer and full-time employment, learning to do well on law school examinations, deciding whether to transfer to another law school, the second and third years of law school, and the bar exam, I realized that the questions did not stop but instead increased. I also noticed that year after year, new students were asking me the same questions that I had asked when I was in their shoes, and they were looking for practical advice from people who could help them avoid mistakes that would cost them time and money they did not have.

As I accumulated more and more questions during law school, I started to write down the questions and responses, and those questions and answers turned into this book. As I started writing this book when I was a student and finished the book just after I graduated from law school and sat for the bar exam, the practical money- and time-saving advice was still fresh in my mind as I wrote each section. I had to learn the hard and expensive way, but you will benefit from my experience.

If you have not yet decided to go to law school, this book will explain what you can expect so that you can make an informed decision on whether or not law school is right for you. If you have already decided to go to law school or are already there, this book will provide you with money- and time-saving advice that will guide you through your remaining years and the bar examination. The helpful tips in this book start from the law school application process and cover every important aspect of law school, right through to preparing for and sitting for the bar examination. There are even some pointers on what to do while you are waiting for your bar exam results.

In terms of specific topics, this book will answer questions regarding some common law school myths, your chances of finding a job after law school, the Law School Admission Test (LSAT), the law school application process, selecting a law school that is right for you, how to do well on exams in your first year of law school, what you should consider when looking for summer employment in your first year, whether you should transfer to a different law school after your first year, how to make it onto law review, how to become part of a moot court team, how to effectively select courses and navigate through your second and third year of law school, the full-time employment and recruitment process in your second year, what it means to work in a large law firm, what to expect in your second-year summer job in a law firm or public interest organization, how to obtain fellowships and scholarships, the part-time law studies experience, how to publish articles in journals, how to prepare for the bar exam, and much more.

The advice given will answer questions that you will have as you go through the law school process and provides you with answers before it is too late. Some tips may save you $40 while other may save you thousands. Other tips will eliminate hours of needless research. What you will get here is practical, targeted, and specific tips on how to effectively navigate through the various parts of law school and the bar exam. After reading a tip in this book, you will never walk away wondering what I mean. Each tip is a Eureka type tip and will often represent a light being turned on where there was darkness previously. In many cases, when you share this advice with friends, you will immediately see the appreciation and gratitude on their faces. You can rest assured that you will walk away from every chapter armed with one or more important pieces of information, answers to your questions, where to get additional information, or the important follow-up questions to ask. This book is the best law school investment you will ever make.

## Finding a Job After Law School

Deciding if you should go to law school can be tough, and the decision is made harder by all of the bad press that law school has been getting lately. Many say that there are too many lawyers, and with over $150,000 of tuition at stake, many more advise that students should find another profession.

In addition, by now you should have heard about the controversy surrounding how some law schools report statistics on job data. If you have not, you should know that for some schools when you see a statistic that says ninety-five percent of students have a job after graduation, this may simply mean that they are "employed" and the percentage often includes people who are working at fast food restaurants or bars, collecting census information, cleaning houses, and, well, you get the picture. A friend told me that when he started law school and was setting up his cable television subscription, the customer service operator told him that she was a former law student from the school he was going to attend. Thus, the operator was most likely included in that school's job data stats.

This reporting has led to a wave of protests and even lawsuits, as students argue that they were misled and that if they would have known how dismal the job market was, they would not have spent over $150,000 to go to law school. In an attempt to address the misleading job data, the American Bar Association has developed general guidance on how law schools should report employment data and now publishes statistics—by school—on how many students find jobs. However, this has not stopped some critics. For example, one individual on a popular blog who wanted to dissuade some individuals from applying to law school called for comprehensive reform and an advertising campaign "similar to a proactive public health education on HIV" before students "ruin their lives." (I found this description a bit on the dramatic side, but who am I to judge.) Here are a few points on this topic and my opinion on whether or not you should go to law school.

First, I fully support accurate reporting of job statistics, and students should make an informed decision as to whether or not they want to attend law school. The legal profession is based on ethics and has many professional responsibility requirements that, clearly, law schools and lawyers should follow. Law schools should not wait for regulations to force them to accurately report their statistics, and all of them should take the steps that some law schools have already begun to take to make sure their data is accurate.

While law schools should make sure that their data is accurate, I also think students have a responsibility to perform some research about the job market so they are comfortable with their decision to become lawyers. This task is much easier now, as more data is being provided to students and pressure will continue to be applied to law schools to accurately report data.

I also feel that students should not give up on a dream to become a lawyer because of a current or future poor job market. The fact is that, in any poor economy, many graduates in all fields have and will continue to have a tough time getting a job, and this should not stop an individual from going after the profession they desire. If you go to law school and want to become a lawyer, you should do it because you have a passion for law and want to become a lawyer. If this is the case, you will likely find a job (eventually) as long as you keep plugging away at it. I have many friends who went to lower ranked schools, and it is true that many did not have jobs immediately after graduation (legal or other), but after a couple of years, I connected with many of them and saw that many were able to find jobs in a legal field. This is not always the case, but the job market is one thing that no one can guarantee. In order to arm yourself with the information you need to make a decision, though, you should check the American Bar Association's statistics on job placement and ask critical questions about how each of the pieces of data were compiled.

Putting jobs aside, another good reason for you to obtain a law degree is that it will help you in many other fields. I also have an M.B.A and to tell you the truth, I have found my J.D. much more helpful. Law school improved my ability to think and express myself in an effective manner and this occurred even after already obtaining a B.A. and an M.B.A, working in an Investment Bank for over ten years, and obtaining a Certified Public Accountant (C.P.A.) designation.

I suppose that one good thing about the controversy surrounding law school job statistics reporting is that it may create a large group of lawyers who go to law school for the right reasons. Presumably those who are unsure or think that they will not make enough money will decide to do something else.

# The Top 12 Myths About Law School Exposed

Before I started law school, I had an idea in my head of what it would be like. This was primarily driven by a number of myths that I had heard repeated over and over again. Here are the top 12 law school myths exposed and the reasons they are myths.

| | Law School Myth | Why Is It a Myth? |
|---|---|---|
| **1** | *Your first year of law school is similar to your first year of college.* | *The two are like day and night, and for many, law school is considerably more work. Two key differences are the amount of time you will spend preparing for each and every law school class and the Socratic method (described below) of teaching. Also, be prepared for one exam to determine your entire grade in law school.* |
| **2** | *Your second and third years of law school are as tough as your first.* | *After year one you get to select your own courses and make your own schedule. Also, since your first year enables you to get used to the way things are done, these two years are much easier than the first.* |
| **3** | *You will not find a job after law school.* | *A job in any field is not guaranteed, but many who stick with it find jobs in law related fields or a field of their choice after law school. At times it takes longer than you may think, and there is a clear positive correlation between highly ranked law schools and finding the job of your choice. Check the American Bar Association website to get current job statistics by school.* |

**4** A law degree is as good as a money printing press.

No way! Some lawyers make lots of money, and some do not. If you are going into this profession for the money you should rethink why you are becoming a lawyer. According to the American Bar Association, lawyers at top firms in New York are paid just over $160,000 per year, but a public interest lawyer will be lucky if he/she makes $44,000 per year. Lawyers in smaller firms—two to ten people—make an average salary of $54,000.

**5** The grading system in law school turns students into monsters.

Perhaps many of you have seen the movie Paper Chase, which reflects students sabotaging other students. This is not the case in law school, and most students are quite collegial. Many meet their spouses in law school and develop lifelong friendships.

**6** Professors are more interested in publishing rather than teaching.

While publishing is an important part of a professor's job, most love to teach and love the subject matter of the courses they teach. Try engaging them and it will usually pay off.

**7** You will fail out of law school.

Law schools grade on a curve based on other students' grades, and typically the lowest mark that a student who does the work will receive is a C. There are, of course, exceptions, and some schools apply grading systems similar to those used during college. Nationally, only four percent of people leave law school because of poor grades.

**8** You have to be an excellent public speaker to do well in law school and become a lawyer.

This is absolutely not the case. In order to be an effective lawyer and law student, you must write well, but public speaking is not a requirement. I have found that most people who get the highest grades in law school classes are those you do not hear a word from all semester.

**9** Most lawyers work in a courtroom

This is only the case in the movies. Ninety-nine percent of lawyers will only enter a court room if they are on jury duty.

**10** You can surf the Internet and still pay attention in class and do well.

Surfing the Internet in class = mediocre grades in law school + irritated classmates and professors. Also, why pay almost $50,000 per year to surf the Internet?

**11** Law school is full of theory, and you will not get any practical training.

There are many excellent clinical programs in law schools in which you get to represent actual clients. Also, more and more law schools are introducing practical "lawyering" courses in the first-year curriculum.

**12** You can make up for bad grades in your first year during your second and third years.

Although this is number 12, it is the number-one myth about law school. Your future as a lawyer is often based almost exclusively on your grades in first year. Make the first year count.

## What the Author Can Teach You

I hope you will take my advice for several reasons. As a recent Harvard Law School graduate, I can provide sound advice and suggestions on how to improve your chances of getting admitted to or transferring to the school of your choice and how to do well in your first year of law school and beyond.

Second, I also have direct experience with all of the topics that I discuss in the book. For example, I transferred from a part-time program to Harvard Law School's full-time program, so I can discuss my experience attending different law schools, the transfer process, and part-time programs. Also, I was selected for both law review and moot court membership in my first year, so I can share my successful perspective. In addition, I was also able to publish a fifty-page paper in a law journal while in law school, so I can describe the process and give you pointers on how to put together and publish your own work. Finally, I successfully completed two state bar examinations and will walk you through what to expect and how to improve your chances of success on any bar exam.

Third, I can also provide sound advice on the job market. During the summer of my first year, I worked in a public interest (not-for-profit) job at the United Nations High Commissioner for Refugees. During the summer of my second year, I was offered and accepted a position with a large top Wall Street corporate law firm. Moreover, I very successfully completed the rigorous on-campus recruitment process at Harvard. Even though I ended up taking a job at a large firm, I spent months during this recruitment process researching legal employment opportunities in small firms, government agencies, and not-for-profit agencies. As such, I can also provide sound advice regarding job possibilities in a vast number of areas. My perspective in this regard is also unique, as I am a "mature" student with an M.B.A., a Certified Public Accountant (C.P.A.) designation, and over ten years of investment banking experience. My age and work experience afford me the benefit to provide insight on finding employment and the culture of various types of organizations.

Fourth, I started this book while a student at Harvard Law School and completed it just after I finished law school, so all of my advice is being recounted with the experience still fresh in my mind. As such, all of the things I wish that I knew beforehand were all still fresh in my mind when I wrote this book. This law school success book will not bore you with general academic summaries or broad generalizations, as I am aware of the issues you are struggling with and the information you want to know.

Finally, this book will answer your questions. During law school, I often had questions on all of the topics discussed in this book. While I ultimately found answers to all my questions, it was often through a process of trial and error, or after extremely time-consuming research. You will receive practical time- and money-saving tips that will help you on a daily basis in law school.

I wish that I could have had the benefit of these tips when I started the law school process, as it would have been a great help.

## How Is This Book Different from Other Law School Guides?

There are several ways this book differs from other law school guides. Besides having the perspective of a recent Harvard Law School graduate, this book differs from other law school guides because some others will give you generic general advice like, "maintain a healthy body and mind." While this advice is sound, it does not go a long way toward giving students what they need to succeed. This book differs from other guides because it focuses on specific practical advice that you will be able to use immediately, and the book will answer real and specific everyday questions you may have.

Another difference between this guide and other law school guides is that many other guides focus on procedural aspects of law school, such as how to register for the Law School Admission Test (LSAT) and how to complete the law school application. As useful as this information is, it is often readily available on the Internet.

In contrast, this book covers some procedural aspects but focuses mainly on signaling and alerting you to key pieces of information and advice that you will not readily find elsewhere. Each tip will save you money, time, and aggravation.

In addition, unlike many other law school guides, this book will provide you with several real-life examples. For example, I have included the personal statement that I used to get into Harvard Law School, along with other successful personal statements from friends who were also admitted to Harvard Law School and other schools. Also, I have included a copy of an effective résumé and letters of reference that I used to get into Harvard Law School. In addition, I have included a highly graded legal writing memo that I wrote, my successful law review competition submission, my completed law school application, and much more. Moreover, the book refers to several website sources for additional information on topics of interest.

Finally, buying this book will give you access to a real, live person to answer your questions. For the first five hundred copies sold, this book comes with the author's e-mail address, which you can use to submit a personal code and ask the author a question. As you read the book and find that you need one-on-one advice while in law school, just use your code to contact the author. How is that for virtual reality?

## *Follow the Light Bulb Tips to Success!*

This book walks though the various aspects of the law school process before, during, and after law school. It starts at the law school application process and ends with the bar examination. In each section, I point out tips that will save you time, stress, and money. Speaking of tips, it is an excellent time to provide you with the first and arguably one of the most important, practical tips.

*Grades in your **first** year of law school will have a significant impact on your options after you graduate. As such, your first year is the time to focus on grades and not the time to think that you can make it up the following year. You should be aware that, for most people, your future as a lawyer is almost exclusively defined by your grades in the first year. For example, most full-time law firm jobs, research assistant positions, and law review/journal positions are determined almost exclusively based on your grades in your first year. Moreover, if you wish to "upgrade" and transfer to a different law school, the school you wish to transfer to will make its decision based on the grades you obtain in the first year. Poor grades in year one can mean the difference between a job that pays $40,000 per year (or no job) and one that pays over $160,000 per year.*

The advice that you should get good grades may sound obvious, but when you start law school, you are under the incorrect assumption that employers will wait until you are done with law school and look at your grades and rankings over the three years.

The exact hiring process is further described below, but understand that, for most jobs in large law firms, employers make their hiring decisions at the beginning of your second year of law school. As such, employers can only look at the grades from your first year. As most people do not have much, if any, work experience, your grades are a significant contributing factor toward a law firm's decision to hire you, and large law firms typically do not hire students after graduation or in the third year of law school. For example, my interview and ultimate offer and acceptance of a job with a top Wall Street firm was made based on my transcript from my first year of law school, and the firm did not ask for another transcript until after I had graduated. By the time I graduated, I had already received and accepted their full-time job offer.

Exactly how to get these good grades is a tough question, and this book provides you with valuable tips in the section "How to Get High Grades in Your First Year and Beyond" in Chapter 2. While grades will be discussed further in subsequent chapters, it is important that you understand when you start your first year the importance of doing well from the beginning. Unfortunately, many students wish that someone had told them during their first semester that they did not have five other academic semesters to make up for a lousy first semester or year.

Once you read the entire book, keep it and refer to it as you are going through your first year. Then read it again when you are looking for summer employment and starting your second year. Pick it up again when you are going through the on-campus recruitment process for employment in your second year and when you are looking for a law firm or public interest job. Then read it one more time when you start your third year. Finally, read it after or during your third year to help you prepare for the bar examination. You will be happy that you did!

# 1. The Law School Application Process

The application process for law school is extensive, and there are many pieces that must be successfully combined in order to get admitted to the law school of your choice. The application process starts with a Law School Admission Test (LSAT), and the next step is a comprehensive application that requires you to answer several questions and pull together information such as a personal statement, a résumé, letters of reference, and transcripts. Most people apply to over ten law schools at one time, so the information that you submit to each school will often be the same or similar. It is important to ensure that your application is accurate, complete, and well thought out. A good way to ensure this is to get a mentor or advisor as soon as you start the application process to assist you with the application process. The mentor should be someone you trust and someone who has life experience; this person can be a friend, family member, lawyer, or non-lawyer. A mentor is an excellent resource to bounce ideas off of, and a different perspective can only improve your application. For example, you may discuss with your mentor who you should ask for letters of reference. Moreover, as the law school application process is long and detailed, it is a great idea to have a second set of eyes looking over the material you submit. Lawyers are sticklers for detail, and small errors can cost you admission to a good school.

# The Law School Admission Test (LSAT)

## *What Is the LSAT?*

The first step in the law school process is sitting for the Law School Admission Test (LSAT). This is a standardized test that is supposed to test your reading comprehension and analytical ability, among other things. Surprisingly enough, it is a key factor that is used to determine which law school you will go to. I use the word "surprisingly" because, even in my final year of law school, I still did not really see the relevance or predictive ability of the test—although the Law School Admission Council (LSAC) indicates that there is some correlation between grades in your first year and LSAT score.

According to the LSAC website:

*"The LSAT is designed to measure skills that are considered essential for success in law school: the reading and comprehension of complex texts with accuracy and insight; the organization and management of information and the ability to draw reasonable inferences from it; the ability to think critically; and the analysis and evaluation of the reasoning and arguments of others."*

Although the LSAT is designed to measure skills that are considered essential for law school, the test does not have any "law" questions on it and does not require any legal analysis. Also, one of the three tested areas that deals with logical games has little to do with what you will do in law school or as a lawyer. While the predictive ability of the LSAT can be debated, it is used as a key indicator for admission to law school, and there is no way of getting around that.

So what can you expect when you sit for the LSAT? The LSAT consists of five thirty-five-minute sections of multiple-choice questions and a writing sample. Only four of the five sections are graded, but you will not know which section is the section they are using as a practice test. There are three types of multiple-choice questions in the LSAT: reading comprehension, analytical reasoning, and logical reasoning.

The reading comprehension section will give you a number of long and somewhat complex passages to read, followed by five to eight questions to answer for each passage. The questions test your ability to read quickly while paying attention to detail. In addition, this section tests your reasoning ability by asking questions for which you have to deduce the answer from the text that you have read. This part of the exam is the section that is most related to law school, since in law school you will often read cases and then have to spot legal issues and answer questions about what you have read. That being said, the passages that you will read on the LSAT will relate to general topics such as economics or science and are not law related. Also, in law school, part of the learning process is to quickly spot legal issues, and most law students really learn how lawyers spot issues when they are in law school.

The logical reasoning section requires the reader to read a fairly short passage and then answer questions about it. Often the question will make you think critically and draw a conclusion, or reason through a problem by making inferences or using analogies. The multiple-choice question that is presented after the short passage will usually take one of the following forms: Which of the following, if true, undermines the argument? What is the flaw in the above argument? This section is somewhat similar to the reading comprehension section, except the passages are shorter and the questions focus more on pattern recognition and analogies based on relationships rather than quickly assimilating relevant facts.

The analytical reasoning section is often referred to as the logical games section and can be very tricky. Also, this section is the furthest away from the tasks that you will perform in law school or as a lawyer. The questions look at your ability to understand how relationships are structured and ask you to come up with logical conclusions about the structures or how that structure might relate to other structures. You will have to use deductive reasoning that stems from the fact pattern in the question and select an answer that best follows the pattern you have deduced. Many people have a tough time with this section, and it is often referred to as the most difficult part of the LSAT. While difficult for many, though, some minds are wired this way, and for those people this section is very simple.

The LSAT also requires you to write a brief passage at the end of the exam, but this is not graded. The sample is, however, forwarded to law schools for their review. The writing sample often will not impact your admission, but it could be used when a law school is not sure about you or, if you are a borderline case, the law school may read the writing sample to decide whether or not to admit you. As such, you should do your best and take it seriously.

## How Do I Sign Up for the LSAT?

Prior to sitting for the LSAT, you must register with the Law School Admission Council (LSAC). This is a nonprofit corporation whose goal is to provide admission-related services for law schools and students. The LSAC services more than 200 law schools in the United States, Canada, and Australia. The key functions that the LSAC performs are as follows: registration and administration of the LSAT, collection and categorization of letters of recommendation and electronic applications to law schools, and transcript processing. You should spend time on the LSAC website, as it is very helpful. You can find the LSAC website in our "Useful Resources" section.

LSAC administers the LSAT four times a year at designated centers throughout the world, and the LSAT is required for admission to virtually all law schools in Canada and the United States, and to some other law schools around the world.

The fees for the LSAT are around $136, and you will have to pay another $68 if you miss the deadline and sign up late.

*You should sign up for and sit for the LSAT as early as you can. Most law schools require you to take the LSAT the December prior to the year you want to start your first year, so you should plan accordingly. Also, if you want to be eligible for early admission to the law school, you will have to sit for the LSAT even earlier. Moreover, the LSAT fee gets more expensive if you wait too long and register at the last minute. Sign up early and save yourself almost $70.*

*The LSAC will waive the LSAT fee if you can prove that you cannot afford to pay for it. In order to be eligible for this, you have to request it. Check the LSAC website for details.*

## How Important Is the LSAT?

Your score on the LSAT is a significant factor that will dictate which law schools will admit you. Even a 4.0 grade point average (straight A grades) will not necessarily get you into a top law school if you have a poor LSAT score. As such, take it seriously and study accordingly.

*Take the LSAT early, but only when you are ready. Your score will strongly influence which law school you are admitted to, so take it seriously. Also, if you sit for the exam twice, some law schools will count your highest score, but many will average your scores. Even if they say they will only count your highest score, the law school will still see your lower score, and a poor score will not ever be helpful.*

## How Do I Prepare for the LSAT and How Important Is Preparation?

There are many courses that you can take to prepare you for the LSAT. I paid over $1,000 for a month-long course, and it was very helpful. Signing up for a course—even an online course—or using a good guide will increase your score for sure. In fact, some companies will often provide a money-back guarantee if you get a lower score on the actual exam than on your first practice test. This is somewhat misleading, though, as it is virtually impossible to get a lower score than your first attempt, as your first attempt is done without any preparation.

A preparation course is a great way to get you ready for the LSAT, as the course will stress some exam "tricks" and you will also do several practice tests in exam-like conditions. Moreover, the course will force you to stay focused and set a fixed schedule for you to devote to exam studying. If you are not disciplined, a preparation course is highly recommended.

**TIP** *Take an LSAT preparation course if you can afford it. Taking one of these courses can be expensive, but it will improve your score on the LSAT.*

The key to doing well on all sections of the LSAT is **practice**. You should complete hundreds, if not thousands, of questions prior to the exam to become very familiar with the patterns of the different questions. Of course, though, part of doing well on the LSAT will be your aptitude for doing well on this type of standardized test. Notwithstanding this factor, you will always be able to improve your score with practice.

*How do you do well on the LSAT? Practice makes perfect, and the key to success is to do as many practice exams as you can under timed conditions. I cannot stress enough that if you take timed exams and then calculate your score, you will have a good idea of how you will score on test day. Do not expect your score to increase much from your practice scores. When I sat for the LSAT, I scored within two points of my final practice exam, and many students have recounted the same experience to me. Practicing and focusing on the areas on which you are scoring poorly is the only way to improve your score.*

Taking a preparation course is one option, but because they are expensive, you can try other options. First, the LSAC website provides some free information that includes sample tests and official guides, along with supplemental questions and explanations. Finally, Barron's has an LSAT preparation guide with sample questions and practice tests that many find useful, and it is relatively inexpensive.

*If you cannot afford an LSAT preparation course, a study guide will give you all of the information you need. They are a fraction of the cost, but you must ensure that you are disciplined enough to work through the material in a systematic manner. Also, you will have to do several timed exams under exam conditions so you will need the willpower to do this by yourself. Finally, the LSAC provides some free preparation material, so you should take advantage of that. If you feel that you have the discipline to do this on your own, you could prepare for the LSAT for $100 instead of over $1,000.*

### How Is the LSAT Graded and What Does my Score Mean?

The LSAT is scored on a scale of 120 to 180, and the average score is around 150. In order to get into a top law school, though, you will need to score well over 160. Over the years, the LSAT score for the bottom twenty-five percent of the entering class for Harvard has been around 170, and this score puts a candidate around the top two percent of those who sit for the exam yearly. The LSAT score for the top twenty-five percent at Harvard is around 175, which is the top one percent of candidates. A score of 154 would place you in the sixtieth percentile, which means that you scored better than sixty percent of the candidates.

After you have completed the LSAT, you will have two of the primary indicators that will determine which schools to start considering. That is, your grades and your LSAT score. There are actually websites that will allow you to input your GPA and your LSAT score and "predict" which schools will accept you.

You can try one of these tools if you want, but I would not advise it as it may discourage you from applying to certain schools. It is true that even schools like Harvard will always admit some students who did not think that they had a chance based on their LSAT or GPA. If you use these websites and then avoid applying to some schools based on their predictions, you could miss out on some great opportunities. As such, if you use these tools, my advice is to use them with extreme caution.

---

 *Be careful if you use law school predictor tools that tell you your chances of getting in to certain law schools is low. They may give you an idea of what a law school is looking for in terms of GPA and LSAT score, but the predictor alone should not discourage you from applying to a law school if you have some other positive things going for you. Remember that the predictor is a mechanical tool, and it does not know you and does not take into account*

*all of the subjective aspects of your application. Every year there are people who apply to top schools like Harvard and Yale and are shocked when they are accepted. I was one of them!*

Now that we've covered the LSAT, in the next section, I will explain how to effectively apply to law school.

## Completing the Law School Application

After a comprehensive review of the LSAC website, you will see that one great thing about applying to law school is that the LSAC makes the administrative part of the application an electronic and streamlined process.

Even though the LSAC streamlines the law school application process, you still have to pull together a significant amount of information. In order to ensure success, your application must be effective, thorough, and complete. The application process can take several weeks or months to complete, and you should get your mentor (a friend, family member, or faculty advisor) to review and edit all aspects of it. Moreover, as you will be very familiar with your own application, it is a great idea to get fresh ideas from others who can suggest changes or alternate approaches. My mentor reviewed key aspects of my application, like my personal statement, and provided me with valuable feedback.

The LSAC acts as the central repository for all aspects of your application. This includes the application form, your personal statement, your transcripts, and letters of recommendation. After you have completed all of the application requirements, the LSAC will electronically submit your application and the other key pieces of information to each law school, and each school will electronically confirm receipt of the application. Some law schools will accept a paper application, but this is an inefficient way to apply to law school. As such, this summary will focus on the electronic application only.

## *What Are Some of the Questions on the Law School Application?*

Most students apply to several law schools at the same time. As such, on the LSAC website, you may first complete a common application form that asks general questions that almost all law schools will ask. This form covers basic information such as your name, address, schools attended, degrees earned, work history, volunteer work, social security number, and several questions related to any possible disciplinary sanctions or criminal convictions you may have received. Once you have completed the common information form, the information is automatically transferred to the law school applications for the specific schools to which you wish to apply.

Take a minute and look at my application to Harvard Law School to get an idea of the types of application questions law schools ask. (My redacted, completed Harvard Law School application is shown on the following three pages.) While common information is not segregated on the application, it would be all of the generic factual information that is listed. The purpose of the common application form is just to avoid having to enter the same information on multiple applications.

The operational aspect of selecting a law school to apply to is quite easy, as the LSAC website lists all of the over 200 law schools, and you simply point and click to access the application for the specific law school. As noted above, once you access the application, you will find that the individual law school's application has been populated with the common information. You are then required to answer the other specific questions that the school may have. You can, of course. modify any of the common information that was transferred to the application from the common form.

Each school will have more specific pieces of data that they are interested in obtaining. For example, one of the many questions

# Transfer Application for Admission to Harvard Law School ■ Juris Doctor (JD) Program

IMPORTANT INSTRUCTIONS: Please complete this form fully. We rely on you to summarize information about your background on this form. If you do not, we may assume there is no relevant information in your case. You should feel free to attach additional or more detailed descriptions, or, if applying electronically, use an electronic attachment, but it is important to provide as much information as possible on this form. **Please do not submit this form before April 15.**

Full Name  Scott                                            Ian
(Last)                                               (First)                                          (Middle)
(Please be sure that this name is *exactly* the same on all application and LSDAS materials.)

| | |
|---|---|
| LSAC account no.: | **Present Mailing Address** (Address to which you would like correspondence sent.) |
| Social Security No.: | Street  120 West 21st. Street Apt. 213 |
| Date of Birth: ☐☐☐ MM/DD/YY | City  New York |
| Place of birth:  London, | State & Zip  NY  10011 |
| Country of citizenship:  Canada and UK | Telephone: (cell no. preferred) |
| If you are not a U.S. citizen, are you a permanent resident?  ☐ Yes  ☒ No | Country (If U.S., leave blank) |
| | E-mail (valid until 9/1/08)  ian.scott@brooklaw.edu |
| | **Permanent Mailing Address** (Address through which you can be contacted at any time.) After what date should we use this address? ____ MM/DD/YY |
| Have you applied for admission to HLS in a prior year?  ☐ Yes  ☒ No | Street  Same as above |
| | City |
| If so, which year(s)? | State & Zip _____  Telephone:  -  - |
| | Country (If U.S., leave blank) |

High school name, location, and year of graduation:  Pickering High , Ajax                                    08/85

List all colleges, universities, graduate and professional schools that you have attended:

| School | Dates of Attendance | Degree | Date MM/YY | Major | Rank & Class Size |
|---|---|---|---|---|---|
| University Of Toronto | | MBA | | Accounting | |
| University Of Toronto | | BA | | Accouting & Economics | |
| | | | | | |
| | MM/YY-MM/YY | | | | |

List and briefly describe non-academic activities that have been important to you:

| Activity | Description or Position | From MM/YY | To MM/YY | Avg. Hrs. per Week |
|---|---|---|---|---|
| Junior Achievement | Instructor | 09/07 | 12/07 | 3 |
| Big Brothers | Mentor | 09/07 | 05/08 | 7 |
| Low Income Tax Clinic | Tax Preparer | 09/00 | 06/07 | 5 |
| Immigration Watch | Court Observer | 01/08 | 06/08 | 2 |

If you were employed during the academic year as an undergraduate, list the positions you held:  I held various teaching assistant positions during my undergraduate and graduate years.  During my first year of Law school, I worked fourty hours a week at CS.

No. of hours per week:  Fr. Yr. _____  Soph. Yr. 10 _____  Jr. Yr. 10 _____  Sr. Yr. 15

List full-time employment, including summer employment, beginning with the most recent:

| From MM/YY | To MM/YY | Employer | Position | Reason for leaving |
|---|---|---|---|---|
| 03/99 | 04/08 | Credit Suisse | Director | Left to attend Law School |
| 03/94 | 03/99 | Bank of Montreal | Senior Manager | Another Opportunity |
| 09/91 | 03/94 | Ernst & Young | Manager | Another Opportunity |

LSDAS E-APP  page 1 of 3

List your important scholastic or academic honors including scholarships, fellowships, prizes, honor societies, etc..

Ontario Graduate Scholarship - Full Graduate Scholarship, Dean's List - Brooklyn Law School, 2007/2008, Moot Court Honor

Society – Appellate Division, Dean's Merit Recognition Scholarship - 2008/2009, Cali Award for Excellence for the Future Award in

Criminal Law, Edward V. Sparer Public Interest Fellowship, Brooklyn Law Review.

List all dates you have taken the LSAT (MM/DD/YYYY): 28/02/2004

Date(s) registered with LSDAS (MM/DD/YY): 09/01/04

| Names of the two people submitting recommendations for you | (1) Letter enclosed with this application form. Date letter and form sent (MM/YY): | (2) Letter will be sent directly to HLS. Date you requested recommendation (MM/YY): | (3) Letter will be sent to LSAC. Date you requested recommendation (MM/YY): |
|---|---|---|---|
| Indicate a date under (1), (2) or (3) for each letter: | | | |
| 1. | | | 05/08 |
| 2. | | 05/08 | |

## PLEASE ANSWER ALL QUESTIONS AND SIGN THE FORM BELOW. IF YOU DO NOT, PROCESSING AND CONSIDERATION OF YOUR APPLICATION WILL BE DELAYED.

1. ☐ Yes ☒ No  Has your academic career been interrupted for one or more terms?

2. ☐ Yes ☒ No  In an academic setting, have you been subject to disciplinary sanctions, or are charges pending?

3. ☐ Yes ☒ No  Have you ever been expelled, suspended, placed on probation, or given an academic warning?

4. ☐ Yes ☒ No  Have you been convicted* of a felony?

5. ☐ Yes ☒ No  Have you been convicted* of a misdemeanor within the last five years?

6. ☐ Yes ☒ No  Are any charges pending which, if you were to be convicted, would require your answer to either of the two previous questions to be "yes"?

If you have answered "yes" to any of the above questions, you must provide details on a separate sheet or electronic attachment.

*without the conviction later being vacated.

(Optional)  How would you describe yourself?

☐ Asian/Pacific Islander
☒ Black/African-American
☐ Mexican American/Chicano
☐ Puerto Rican
☐ South Asian
☐ White

☐ Other Hispanic (specify) _____

☐ American Indian/Alaskan Native: Tribe (specify)_____

☐ Other _____

## NOTE: THIS APPLICATION AND ALL SUPPORTING MATERIAL MUST BE RECEIVED PRIOR TO JULY 15.
Address: Admissions, Harvard Law School, 1515 Massachusetts Avenue, Cambridge, MA 02138

By signing this application or transmitting it electronically, I certify that the information presented in my application is accurate, complete, and honestly presented. I also certify that any information submitted on my behalf is authentic, including letters of recommendation, academic transcripts, and certifications. I understand and agree that any inaccurate information, misleading information, or omission will be cause for an investigation of misconduct in the admissions process, rescission of any offer of admission, or for discipline, dismissal or revocation of degree if discovered at a later date. I agree to notify Harvard Law School of changes to information or of new information pertinent to this application for admission.

Signature: _____          Date: _____

LSDAS E-APP page 2 of 3

## Transfer Application for Admission to Harvard Law School ■ Juris Doctor (JD) Program

## Statement Form

Name _Scott_      Ian
(Last)      (First)      (Middle)

LSAC account number: ☐☐☐☐☐☐☐☐☐☐☐

Social Security Number: ☐☐☐■☐■☐☐☐

### Personal Statement

Please present yourself, your background and experiences as you wish in a brief personal statement. You should include your reasons for applying for transfer admission. A need to be located in the Cambridge area may be relevant and should be discussed. If applying electronically use an electronic attachment.

To provide a context for writing your statement, we offer the following observations. The personal statement can be an opportunity to illuminate your intellectual background and interests. You might do this by writing about a course, academic project, book, artistic or cultural experience that has been important to you. The personal statement can also be an opportunity to clarify or elaborate on other information that you have provided in the application and to provide information about yourself and your achievements that may not be evident to the readers of your application. Because people and their experiences are diverse, you are the best person to determine the content of your own statement. It is for you to decide what information you would like to convey and the best way for you to convey it. Whatever you write about, readers of your statement will be seeking to get a sense of you as a person and as a potential student and graduate of Harvard Law School.

We understand that it can be difficult to discuss oneself on paper, but our experience is that written statements are valuable in the selection process. Candid, forthright and thoughtful statements are always the most helpful.

The Committee makes every effort to understand your achievements in the context of your background and to admit a diverse student body. After completing the application form and personal statement, you may feel that there is other information that may help us in these efforts. If so, please include it with your application. Any information that you believe may be helpful is appropriate.

Limit your statement to two pages, typed, double-spaced, minimum 11 pt. font, and 1 inch margins. Put your name and signature on the statement and attach it to this form, or use an electronic attachment and sign the Certification Letter.

### Interests (Optional.) If you have a strong interest in one or more areas of law, please indicate below.

Potential Careers/ Jobs

☒ Academia/ Law Teaching
☐ Clerkships
☒ Government/ Public Sector
☐ Private Sector/ Law Firms
☒ Public Interest/ Non-Profit
☐ Other/ Non-Law (list)

_____

Areas of Interest

☐ Administrative Law/Regulation
☐ Antitrust
☒ Civil Rights/Civil Liberties/Law and Race
☒ Constitutional Law
☐ Corporate/Commercial/Business Law
☐ Criminal Law/Procedure
☐ Cyber Law/Law and Technology
☐ Employment/Labor Law
☐ Environmental Law/Land Use
☐ Family Law/Child Advocacy/Education
☐ Financial Institutions/Securities Law
☐ Gender and the Law
☐ Health Law/Biotech/Bioethics
☒ Human Rights/Humanitarian Law
☒ Immigration/Asylum Law

☐ Intellectual Property/Patent/Copyright
☐ International Law (Public)/Law and Development
☐ International Trade/Finance
☐ Jurisprudence/Law and Philosophy
☐ Law and Economics/Behavioral Economics
☐ Legal History
☐ Legal Profession/Ethics
☐ Local Government/Urban Planning/Urban Issues
☐ Negotiation/Mediation/ADR
☒ Public Interest/Public Service/Social Justice
☐ Public Policy/Politics
☐ Real Estate/Property
☐ Sports/Entertainment/Media Law
☐ Tax/Estate Planning
☐ Trial Advocacy/Litigation

on the Harvard application is whether or not you had parents or relatives that attended the school. For the most part, the questions on the specific law school forms relate to factual data, but in some cases, the questions can be a bit more explanatory in nature. For example, you may be asked to describe an incident that was very formative in your life and relate why that was the case. Take a minute to look again at my completed application as an example.

Almost all applications also ask about any arrest record or criminal history you may have. While an answer of "yes" in this area is not going to help your application, it will not necessarily preclude admission. I am personally aware of at least two people who had indiscretions or run-ins with the police in college, and they were still admitted to law school.

The key thing to remember here is not to lie or omit anything. If you lie or omit information, you not only run the risk of expulsion but you also risk not ever being able to become a lawyer. Always keep in mind that once you are done with law school you have to answer similar questions prior to being admitted to any state bar. Moreover, the law school or the state bar may verify everything that you put down on your application. If there are inconsistencies and you are caught in a lie, you may not be admitted to the bar even though you have completed three years of law school and passed the bar exam.

At the end of the day, law schools recognize that people make mistakes, and they will look at the reasons the event occurred, how long ago it occurred, and the corrective actions taken by you. All of these things will be considered before they make their decision, and they will be fair—so do not worry. The important thing is to be honest. This concept of honesty really applies to all parts of your law school application and your conduct in law school generally, so remember that now is not the time to lie.

Even though the information in the application is factual and somewhat repetitive, it is important to ensure that your application is accurate, complete, and consistent. As such, it is important to get someone to proofread the application and another person to review your documents for consistency. Lawyers (and most, if not all, people on the admission's committee will be lawyers) are sticklers for details, and having an error on your application is like having an error on your résumé that someone notices at a job interview.

Also keep in mind that once you complete the common form electronically on the LSAC website, the information you input will be used to populate all of your applications. As such, one small error may follow you to ten or fifteen law schools. It would be a shame to have a number of law schools all see the same glaring error or inconsistency, and there is really no reason for this to happen. Even a minor error on an application can mean the difference between acceptance and rejection.

While you are preparing your application, always keep in mind that some of the best law schools have a very low acceptance rate (Harvard's rate is around eleven percent of the thousands of applications they get), and this means there are many people with your qualifications applying. If they are comparing two pretty equal people and one has a typo in his or her application, the choice will be clear. On one of my last proofreads of my application to Harvard, I noticed an error that I am sure would have cost me my acceptance. I was lucky that I caught it. Do not let a silly error ruin your chances.

## Résumé

Another important part of any application is a résumé. Take a minute to review the format of the résumé I completed shortly after my first year on the next page.

Note that the law school résumé has a very distinct and concise format, and my résumé follows the standard law school format. While you do not have to necessarily model the résumé after this

## EDUCATION

**Harvard Law School,** Juris Doctor Candidate, June 2010
    *Honors:*      Human Rights Journal, Primary Editor

**Brooklyn Law School,** First Year, 2007–2008 (Transferred to Harvard Law School)
    *Honors:*      Dean's List
                   Invited to join Moot Court Honor Society—Selection based on appellate brief
                   and oral argument
                   Invited to join Brooklyn Law Review—Selection based on grades and writing
                   competition
    *Awards:*     Dean's Merit Recognition Scholarship—2008/2009
                   Cali Award for Excellence for the Future Award in Criminal Law
    *GPA:*         3.954
    *Activities:*   Research Assistant—Constitutional Law, Tax Clinic, Junior Achievement
                   Program Mentor

**University of Toronto Graduate School,** Masters of Business Administration (M.B.A.), May ****
    *Honors:*      Ontario Graduate Scholarship

**University of Toronto,** Bachelor of Arts with Major in Commerce and Economics (B.A.), May ****

**Canadian Institute of Chartered Accountants,** Chartered Accountant Designation (C.A.), June ****

**American Institute of Certified Public Accountants,** Certified Public Accountant Designation
(C.P.A.), June ****

## EXPERIENCE

**United Nations—High Commissioner for Refugees**, New York, N.Y.
**Summer Legal Intern**             May 2008–July 2008
    Researched and assessed proposals related to asylum and human rights issues. Wrote legal
    memorandum for discussion with senior policy makers. Researched international human
    rights law and applied the law to immigration and asylum cases in third world countries.

**Credit Suisse Investment Bank**, New York, N.Y.
**Director**                      March 1999–April 2008
    Researched and assessed accounting pronouncements and prepared comprehensive comments
    for appropriate regulators. Assessed the impact on the bank and developed accounting policies
    and procedures for use by business units. Conducted training presentations to large and small
    banking groups to ensure difficult accounting literature was understood and properly implemented.
    Evaluated and reviewed new bank products, including derivative and treasury products, assessed
    implications for the bank, and provided accounting opinions as appropriate.

**Big Brothers**, New York, N.Y.
**Volunteer Mentor**           September 2007–April 2008
    On a biweekly basis, mentored a 15 year old student from an underprivileged group during the
    academic term focusing on educational, vocational, and cultural activity programs. Taught job
    skills, reviewed homework, discussed relevant topics and engaged in other recreational activities
    to enhance the student's self esteem and educational opportunities.

**Bank of Montreal, Toronto**, Ontario
**Controller, Global Treasury Group**     December 1996–July 1998
    Provided comprehensive finance support to the treasury business lines including, the Derivative,
    Money Market & Foreign Exchange business lines. Finance support included, planning, forecasting,
    and analysis of results.

when you apply to law school, you should follow the general rule that your résumé should not be a book. Most law school résumés are one page, and that is likely sufficient for someone who does not have much work experience. I had over ten years of work experience and was able to fit it on one page. A good sample résumé for someone applying to law school is on the next page.

While it is clear that you want to show the admission's committee what you are made of, you have to remember that some law schools have thousands of applications and tens of thousands of pieces of paper. As such, you have to say what you mean in an effective and concise manner. One page is sufficient to do this, and certainly a résumé should not exceed two pages.

**TIP** *Make sure that your résumé is concise, and try to keep it to one page. This is consistent with the law school format of résumés and will help keep the admission's office focused on your key accomplishments. Most people will stop reading after one page, and a poorly organized résumé will take some of the great things that you have done off the table.*

## Transcripts

Your application will also include your transcripts from all of the post–high school work that you have done. This will include both college and any graduate work. You will have to get your educational institutions to send your official transcripts to the LSAC, and the LSAC will organize them into the appropriate format for the law school.

Regarding deadlines, do not miss the law school deadlines and ensure that you understand what the deadlines mean. For example, some law schools set deadlines for *completed* applications, which

# SUSAN SMITH
555 Holder Street. Apt. 24
NY, NY 11201
222-222-2222
susan.smith@gmail.com

## EDUCATION

**Brown University**, Master's in Philosophy, *magna cum laude*, May 2009

| | |
|---|---|
| Awards & Honors: | Dean's List 2008, 2009 |
| Activities: | Debate Club Chairperson, Volunteer at Homeless Shelter |

**CUNY University**, Bachelor of Arts in Environmental Science, *cum laude*, May 2007

| | |
|---|---|
| Awards & Honors: | Dean's List 2005, 2006, 2007 |
| | National Science Foundation Award, 2005 |
| | Science and Public Policy Award, 2004 |
| Activities: | President of Student Council, 2007 |
| | Chess Club |

## EXPERIENCE

**Teacher's For Life**, Brooklyn, NY
*Teacher*   August 2001—June 2004
Instructed 6th graders in Life Science, Physical Science, and Math. Successfully implemented conflict resolution and behavior modification to maintain classroom management and enhance learning.

**Law Offices of Charles Jones**, New York, NY
*Paralegal*   2004–2007
Assisted a group of lawyers with legal briefs, wills, and other legal documents. Drafted legal documents and conducted client interviews.

**United Nations Human Rights Commission**, Washington, DC
*Intern*   Summer 2004
Assessed human rights conditions in various third world countries and assisted policy makers with recommendations and different courses of action.

**The Legal Aid Society**, Newark, NJ
*Intern, Housing Division*   May 2005–February 2006
Participated in representation of defendants who had landlord/tenant issues and assisted with litigating these matters in court. Conducted initial client interviews, interviewed witnesses, investigated alleged facts, and assessed evidence. Strategized theory of case with staff attorneys and researched and drafted motions.

## LANGUAGES

Fluent in Japanese and Spanish.

means that all letters of recommendation and transcripts must be *received* by the law school by a certain date. I have come across people who thought that as long as they sent their application (without transcripts or letters) to the law school by the deadline, they would still be considered; however, they were wrong.

*Make sure that you understand and adhere to deadlines. Law schools have many applications and are often unforgiving when it comes to missing a deadline. At a minimum, a missed deadline will not help your application. At a maximum, it could be the reason that you are not accepted to the law school of your choice. Moreover, even if the law school decides to review your application, the late submission will not help your application. Also, remember that you should register and pay for the LSAC to assemble and send your material at least six weeks before your first law school application deadline. It takes a few weeks to process a transcript or letter of recommendation, so do not be one of the many who are frantically running around at the last minute trying to pull everything together.*

## Letters of Recommendation

Most law schools also require a letter (or letters) of recommendation. Each school will provide specific guidance on what they are looking for and the letter can be general or specific. A general letter is a "To whom it may concern" letter. The letter will, of course, say great things about you, but it will not talk about a particular school you are applying to and can really be used for any school. While general letters are sufficient, they are not as good as a specific letter.

A specific letter is a letter that addresses the dean or admission's office of the school to which you are applying. It also relates your experience or talent to the reasons you should get into that particular school. If you can, try to get a specific letter from someone who was a former student at that law school; it is an added bonus and will give your letter additional weight.

Regardless of the type of letter you get, they are all usually sent to the LSAC, and the LSAC will send them to the school along with your application. There are also instances where the recommender sends his or her letter directly to the law school. You can easily check the status of your letters (whether they have been sent to the school) on the LSAC website.

### Who Should I Select to Write a Letter of Recommendation?

In general, the more letters you have the better, but all letters should be relevant and come from someone that knows you and can speak to why you would succeed in law school.

The best letters come from your old college professors who can speak to your intellect and your ability to do well in law school. The professor should of course know you and be familiar with your work, and this usually means that you had the professor for a semester or you have performed research for the professor. An unhelpful or non-relevant letter from a professor would come from a professor who is a friend of your parents who you have never met. This type of letter is useless and will not get you very far. Similarly, if you know a professor but have never been in his or her class, the recommendation will only serve as a character reference and this is generally not what the admission's office is looking for. What they are looking for is a letter that will demonstrate that you will do well in law school, and this letter must be from a person who is in a position to give a reliable opinion about this.

Another good letter is a letter that comes from a lawyer who knows you and can speak to your scholarly potential. This is especially the case if the person will be able to illustrate why you will do well in law school. Another great source is a past or current employer, especially if the employer can write about your analytical skills, problem solving ability, or scholarly ability.

I have included several letters here that were written for me that I used to get into law school.

## *Example Letters of Recommendation*

*Reference Letter 1:*

*To whom it may concern:*

    *I am writing to provide Ian Scott with my highest level of recommendation. I understand that he would like to pursue a law degree, and I think that given his logical mind and his intellect he would definitely excel at this.*

    *I met Ian when he joined Credit Suisse First Boston as a Vice President in April 1999, and he worked directly for me for three years from March 2000 to March 2003. Ian's performance during that time was exceptional. He displayed strong technical and analytical skills, and his oral and written communication skills are outstanding. He thinks strategically and acts pragmatically.*

    *During the three years that Ian worked for me, one of his significant accomplishments was the management of the implementation of a complex initiative. The bank was converting its accounting standards from Swiss Accounting Principles to U.S. principles, and Ian led this project in the Americas managing approximately ten staff over a period of two years. The implementation required Ian to utilize his professional accounting skills and knowledge and he was able to show his technical accounting proficiency by interpreting the accounting standards as well as applying them to complex business transactions. Due to the large number of complex issues, the position required advanced problem solving skills, which Ian possesses. Ian's understanding of the subject matter was so in depth that he often developed and taught complex training courses to international audiences. He always received positive feedback for his teaching abilities. In particular, he could take complicated topics (for example, derivatives and securitizations) and break them down for various audience levels so that they would understand it. In fact, when the project was done, several groups attempted to recruit Ian into their group.*

At the end of 2005, I had the pleasure of putting Ian forward for a promotion from Vice President to Director. The promotion process is an extremely arduous, competitive, and difficult process, and Ian was successful on his first attempt. He received positive feedback from all of his sponsors and has done an excellent job since his promotion. Ian significantly and consistently exceeded expectations across all areas of performance and was rated as outstanding "1—the highest performance rating" over the last two years.

In closing, I would like to reiterate that I give Ian the highest recommendation. Ian doesn't work directly for me anymore (he is working on the implementation of a Securities Exchange Commission legislative requirement), but I'm sure he will succeed in whatever he does. I wish him the best of luck, and it has been my pleasure writing this letter for him.

Please feel free to contact me if you have any questions and I would be happy to discuss Ian with you.


### Reference Letter 2:
TO WHOM IT MAY CONCERN:

Please accept this letter of reference on behalf of Ian Scott, whom I have personally known for the past three (3) years. Based on my numerous contacts and conversations with Ian, I believe I am in a position to comment on his interest in a legal career.

I am currently a Support Magistrate in ****** ****** Court, a position I have held for the past 13 years, and during almost my entire legal career I have worked in the public sector. Ian had expressed to me his desire to attend law school and upon graduation engage in the practice of public interest law. This is the same view I had when I entered law school over 30 years ago and which I have followed through with since graduation. Ian's demonstrated compassion for others and those in need would be very useful in any area of public interest law he might pursue, and I trust in his sincerity to follow through with such. He is highly intelligent and motivated, as shown in the fact that while attending law school he has continued in his full-time employment.

I therefore would give Ian my highest recommendation and support him in his pursuit of a legal education and career.

*Reference Letter 3:*

*Dear Sir or Madam,*

*I have known Ian since 1996, when the both of us were colleagues in the Accounting and Corporate Financial Information Systems department at the Bank of Montreal. Ian was the Senior Manager of the Accounting Policy group while I was a Manager in the Accounting Risk group. What impressed me about him was that he always maintained a very professional and personable manner, and his articulate explanations conveyed a depth of understanding of the issues that was unusual, given the number of people that he managed and responsibilities that he had.*

*It was based on that positive impression that I did not hesitate to join Credit Suisse First Boston in New York as a Vice President and work for Ian in the Strategic Change Management group. I worked directly for Ian for three years, and it was during that time that I gained firsthand experience of his strong mentoring and managerial skills.*

*From both a personal and professional standpoint, working for Ian was the most rewarding and fulfilling experience in my career to date. As a mentor and manager, Ian provided unparalleled support, guidance, and interest in developing his team members' potential. He always had a strong and in-depth knowledge of industry topics and utilized this strong business knowledge on a day-to-day basis. He provided guidance at the outset to communicate his expectations and implemented a stringent review process to facilitate the completion of the tasks. Also, in cases where his clients did not explicitly acknowledge his staff's contributions, he would go out of his way to ensure that the work was recognized and appreciated. Ian always inspired me to do my best work and also provided sound advice that I could trust.*

*From a client service perspective, Ian always exceeded his clients' expectations. Ian had an uncanny ability to perceive his clients' needs, even when they couldn't articulate or sometimes even know what they needed. Whether he was presenting to senior management on project progress and findings, or explaining a technical detail to an analyst, Ian was always able to convey the message to his constituents to their full satisfaction. It is that skill, and his talent, drive, and motivation, that continue to give his clients, justifiably so, the confidence that their needs would be successfully met.*

*For the last few years, Ian and I have had several conversations regarding his interest in law school and his desire to dedicate his efforts to public interest work. Even though Ian has to date dedicated his career to investment banking, this did not come as much of a surprise given his commitment to others and his ability to put others before himself. He has always strived to ensure that minorities are heard and has been a strong supporter of the underdog.*

*In the workplace, Ian has been very active in diversity as well as employment equity initiatives. He serves as an excellent role model for the success of diversity in the corporate environment, where there still continues to be a lack of adequate representation of diversity in senior management. He shows strong integrity and doesn't hesitate to speak up to ensure that a balanced view is considered. He is able to exert his positive influence in a subtle yet effective manner, such as actively seeking out the opinions of those people whose voices would otherwise be ignored or belittled due to their not fitting the senior management corporate "mold." He also ensures that in his senior participation in the hiring and promotion activities, there is a fair consideration of diversity candidates. In summary, he exhibits admirable traits of strength in character and is an active advocate for equality and fairness in the workplace.*

*It is my privilege to know Ian, and I believe and am very proud to say that he will be a strong asset to the public service arena.*

### Reference Letter 4:

*Re:   Ian Scott—Candidate*

*I am writing to you in support of Ian Scott's candidacy as a transfer into the Harvard Law School. As a Harvard alumnus, my excitement at learning that he was applying was probably second only to his. His professional experience to date, together with his unique interests, dedication, and intellectual acumen make him in my view an ideal candidate for the rigors of Harvard's law curriculum.*

*I've been privileged to know Ian at an interesting point in his journey. When I met him a few years ago, he was just beginning to reflect on where he'd arrived in his career and, even more important, what would be the best strategy to position him for future goals, with law school quickly surfacing as the most viable path. His is a keen mind—one that both grasps concepts quickly and possesses the penetration to analyze them on many levels simultaneously, necessary for success both as a student at Harvard and later as an attorney.*

*Perhaps the quality that I admire most in Ian is his strength of character and the dedication that he brings to any pursuit. He is a passionate change agent with a rare understanding of the complex mix of historical, social, economic, and political factors contributing to present global challenges, and which likely contain the key to lasting solutions.*

*I am presently vice president of education for the National Association for Multi-ethnicity in Communications (NAMIC), a trade association whose core mission is to champion multi-ethnic diversity in the communications industry. I consider myself first and foremost a process facilitator whose primary task is to create the space where learning can flow organically from the group dynamic. I envy individuals like Ian who possess the mental prowess to transform seemingly random, disconnected inputs into a structured reality with measurable impact. As a lawyer, he will rely heavily on this ability— rendered even more powerful when this essentially intellectual trait is accompanied by true heart.*

*Ian Scott's intellectual gifts are a given, and I've no doubt whatsoever that he will parlay his stellar track record at Brooklyn Law School into equally as impressive accomplishments at Harvard Law School.*

Each of my letters was selected to cover an area that I thought would interest the admission's committee. Namely, one came from someone who attended Harvard, another came from an employer, another came from a judge who could speak of my scholarly ability, and the others came from professors whose classes I did well in. Each person was strategically selected, and the selection worked well for me.

*You should select your recommenders strategically, and it does matter <u>who</u> you select to recommend you to a law school. First and foremost, the person should know you and be able to speak to your academic or scholarly potential. This usually means old professors or past employers who are in a position to give an opinion about how well you will do in law school. Lawyers who know you well and who are familiar with your academic potential are also good sources. Finally, if you can find alumni from the school you are applying to that you know well, their letters will help you as long as there is a basis for their opinion regarding your academic potential.*

## Who Should I NOT Get Letters of Recommendation From?

Letters from personal friends, family, people who do not know you well, or other sources who are not work- or school-related are not helpful and will generally be disregarded.

You should also ensure that the person who is writing the letter of recommendation is going to give you a good letter, and your goal should be to get a recommendation that you are sure will be *glowing*. Even a mediocre or lukewarm recommendation can hurt you, as you can rest assured that most letters of recommendation for law school candidates are glowing. I cannot tell you how many cases I have heard of where someone asks someone else to write a letter and ends up getting slammed. Make sure that the person likes you and has good things to say about you. Also, there is nothing wrong with asking that person to see the letter. However, it is not appropriate for you to write the letter and have the recommender sign it, as this is not ethical behavior. The letter should be the recommender's words and should reflect what he or she thinks of you and your abilities.

*When you ask someone to write a letter for you, ensure that you give them an out so that they do not feel pressured. A letter that is written with obligation will not shine, and you are better off finding someone else.*

## The Personal Statement

The final and *very important* part of the law school application is the personal statement. For most law schools, this is a significant aspect of the application and at times can be the compelling and most important reason that someone is admitted. Usually the personal statement is a two-page single-spaced document that is a description of what you have done and why the school should admit you over other candidates. Every year, there are students admitted to Harvard and Yale who thought that they did not have a chance, and if a student thought he or she did not have a chance, it was likely because their grades and LSAT scores were not the best. If the student was still admitted with poor grades or a poor LSAT, it was probably because of his or her excellent personal statement.

To give you an idea of what an effective personal statement looks like, I have included the statement that I used to get admitted to Harvard Law School. My personal statement is included on the following pages, and examples of other successful personal statements are also included in this chapter.

## What Does a Good Personal Statement Look Like?

### Example of my Personal Statement That Got Me Admitted to Harvard Law School

#### PERSONAL STATEMENT—IAN E. SCOTT

*While my background to date has focused primarily on banking and finance, last year I made the important decision to change this direction by pursuing my dream of becoming a lawyer and working to help others. As a mature student with an M.B.A., a C.P.A. designation, and over ten years of senior management investment banking experience, the decision to change careers did not come easy. After a year of law school, though, I am more confident than ever that I made the correct decision, and I could not be happier.*

*During my first year at Brooklyn Law School (BLS), I attended classes four nights a week in their part-time program and worked forty hours a week full-time at Credit Suisse as a senior director. Although the demands of my job were extensive, I was able to place in the top 7.5 percent of my class with a 3.954 GPA. In addition, I was placed on the Dean's list, received a Dean's recognition scholarship, received a CALI award in criminal law, received a public interest fellowship, was selected by the Moot Court Honor society, was selected as a research assistant for Constitutional law, and was selected for Brooklyn Law Review. I believe this successful year was a function of my genuine love of the subject matter combined with the deliberate choice to pursue something that I knew I would naturally excel at.*

#### Why I Am Interested in a Public Interest Law Career

*As a visible minority, I have always struggled with the issue of inequality and fair treatment in our society. Over the last few years, I have not only thought about the topic but have also examined my own actions to address the issues. I concluded that I was not doing enough and took steps to make more of a contribution to under-represented groups. There are two related reasons for my decision. First, I think equality and*

28

*fairness are necessary and important. Second, bringing about this type of change and the impact it has on people's lives is something that gives me an enormous amount of personal satisfaction and fulfillment. Although my investment banking career was quite lucrative, the personal satisfaction associated with doing something worthwhile and noble was missing. I am now one of those fortunate individuals who will be able to spend a lifetime doing what I love. I recently taught a junior achievement seminar for high school students where the topic was selecting a career. One maxim from one of the exercises was, "Select a career that you love and you will never have to work another day in your life." As I repeated this to the students, it brought a smile to my face because I realized, I am leaving behind the draw of wealth and doing something that I truly believe in. This is the reason I decided to leave a career as an investment banker and become a public interest lawyer.*

### Experiences That Have Shaped my Interest in and Commitment to Public Interest Law

*One experience that has shaped my interest and commitment to public service law is the lack of diversity and the large amount of discrimination in the workplace. While my former organization has made some progress in this area, there is still work to be done. I have worked in the investment banking industry for fifteen years, and my experience as a minority has taught me that even if you are smart, talented, and driven, it is difficult to succeed. People are discriminated against in the workplace for a variety of reasons, and I am often surprised at just how blatant the discrimination is and that it is tolerated. What has been especially painful to me is to see people who have worked hard but gave up due to systematic letdowns. In order to address the problem at my workplace, I was always active in diversity as well as employment equity initiatives and committees and often acted as a voice for people who were not very well represented. I am proud that I was able to use these committees to successfully bring about some change in the organization and plan to continue this work as a public interest lawyer.*

### The Areas of Public Interest Law I Am Interested In

*My interests are firmly routed in bringing about equality in the world, and as such, I am interested in human rights and immigration law. To this end, I was awarded a Sparer Public Interest Fellowship at Brooklyn Law School and currently work as a summer intern at the United Nations High Commissioner for Refugees, where I examine international immigration and asylum law as it relates to countries where human rights violations are occurring. In addition, I would like to practice law to contribute to the black minority struggle that I identify with, and other areas where people are treated differently based on irrelevant factors. As such, I would also like to focus on areas where there is discrimination in the workplace based on race, gender, or sexual orientation.*

### Why I Would Like to Attend Harvard Law School

*I would like to attend Harvard Law School for a number of reasons. First, Harvard's diverse student body is extremely appealing to me. As a mature African-American male, diversity is an important element for me in terms of my own comfort level and in terms of my view that diversity can bring about change in the world. In addition, the truly global and international nature of the student body would afford me the opportunity to share different experiences and learn from a talented, diverse group. I am confident that my age, race, and business experience will add a unique perspective to the already diverse group of students. Second, the Bernard Koteen Office of Public Interest Advising and the Mandatory Pro Bono requirement prior to graduation both demonstrate Harvard's strong commitment to playing an important role in under-represented communities. As described above, I would like to pursue a public interest law career, so Harvard's exceptional public interest program, which includes a wide range of courses, clinics, and opportunities for hands-on experience, are key factors for my strong interest in Harvard Law School. Third, Harvard Law School is an internationally renowned institution with an exceptional faculty. I would welcome the opportunity to learn from this distinguished and diverse group that represents the* leaders in the development of legal research and theory on important areas like Constitutional law, gender studies, and human rights.

### Professional Accomplishments

After my M.B.A., I decided to pursue a professional designation and obtained my Chartered Accountancy (C.A.) designation. I passed my accountancy exams on my first attempt and scored in the top 5 percent in all of Canada. As a result of my high score, the Canadian Institute of Chartered Accountants offered me a scholarship to pursue a Ph.D. in accounting studies. While I did not pursue that opportunity, teaching is something that has always appealed to me, and I would like to pursue this once I have gained some legal work experience. As I anticipated the possibility of living in the United States, I wrote the corresponding accountancy exam in the United States and was awarded a Certified Public Accountancy (C.P.A.) designation. After this, I was afforded the opportunity to work in one of the top four accounting firms (Ernst & Young) where I performed audits of large banks. After this, I worked at a large retail bank in Canada and held a number of positions there over a five-year period. I then moved to New York and joined Credit Suisse (CS) as a vice president and within three years I was promoted to director. I worked at Credit Suisse as a senior director up until April of 2008, when I decided to pursue law on a full-time basis.

### Commitment to Personal Development

Although my academic and professional accomplishments have required a fair amount of focus, I have always attempted to maintain a balance between professional development and more personal aspects of development. To this end, I have fulfilled a number of personal goals including extensive travel, living abroad, and learning a new language. Since college, I have visited forty countries and one hundred and fifty cities that span across every continent in the world except for Antarctica. This includes extensive travel to numerous countries in North America, Europe, Africa, Asia, Australia, and South America. I consider travel an integral part of my life, and I always try to immerse myself in the culture *and language to enhance the learning experience. At a young age, I knew that in addition to travel I wanted to live and work in other countries. As such, after establishing a career in Canada, I left my job and moved to Spain to study Spanish. At the end of a six-month period, I received an award of distinction and am now fairly fluent in the language. After this, I moved to New York and was hired by Credit Suisse, where I have worked for the last nine years. In addition, in 2006, I had the opportunity to live and work with Credit Suisse in Zurich for six months.*

*The pursuit of my dreams has always been the driving force that has allowed me to challenge myself and change. Law school is part of this evolution, and I really hope that I will be able to continue this growth with Harvard Law School.*

## Detailed Examination of my Personal Statement

### How Should the Personal Statement Be Organized?

Now let us spend some time looking at my personal statement. When I developed it, I used topic headings to separate major areas. These topic headings provided clarity and indicated when I was moving away from a particular topic. Also, the headings told the admission's committee that I had answered their questions, as some headings aligned with what Harvard asked to see in the personal statement. Moreover, since any committee will read thousands of applications, it is important to compartmentalize topical areas so a reader can focus on what he or she feels is important. Many readers get bored quickly, so headings keep them focused.

I also found it useful to select an area of legal focus to which I could tailor my personal statement. In my case, it was public interest law, and I included three sections: why I am interested in a public interest law career, experiences that have shaped my interest and commitment to public interest law, and the areas of public interest law that I am interested in.

I rounded out the statement with a section on my professional accomplishments and my commitment to professional development. These subject areas not only allowed me to focus on specific areas but also personalized my statement and provided information to the committee, like my travel and interests, which were not in other parts of my application.

## *What Makes an Effective Personal Statement?*

I started my personal statement with an introduction to give the admission's committee a snapshot of who I was. I felt this was important, as I have a unique background in that I am a "mature" student and also an accomplished professional accountant with extensive investment banking experience who made a conscious decision to change my career. As most law students go to law school immediately after college, I hoped to alert the committee that I was different. If you have some aspect of your application that can really make you stand out, lead with it so that you grab the committee's attention and make them want to read on.

*While my background to date has focused primarily on banking and finance, last year I made the important decision to change this direction by pursuing my dream of becoming a lawyer and working to help others. As a mature student with an M.B.A., a C.P.A. designation, and over ten years of senior management investment banking experience, the decision to change careers did not come easy. After a year of law school, though, I am more confident than ever that I made the correct decision, and I could not be happier.*

After the brief introduction to establish who they were looking at, I included this:

*During my first year at Brooklyn Law School (BLS), I attended classes four nights a week in their part-time program and worked forty hours a week full-*

*time at Credit Suisse as a senior director. Although the demands of my job were extensive, I was able to place in the top 7.5 percent of my class with a 3.954 GPA. In addition, I was placed on the Dean's list, received a Dean's recognition scholarship, received a CALI award in criminal law, received a public interest fellowship, was selected by the Moot Court Honor society, was selected as a research assistant for Constitutional law, and was selected for Brooklyn Law Review. I believe this successful year was a function of my genuine love of the subject matter combined with the deliberate choice to pursue something that I knew I would naturally excel at.*

Here, my purpose was to let the admission's committee know that during my first year, I worked full-time and was still able to do well in law school and participate in a significant number of areas in law school. This paragraph was important because it very nicely links together everything that I accomplished in the first year. While this information is also in other parts of the application, it is spread out and the committee may not readily make the link that I did all of this while working forty to fifty hours a week. Notice that even though my grades were great, I only spent one sentence on them since the admission's committee already had my transcripts.

My personal statement is then broken out by headings with the first and second as follows:

### Why I Am Interested in a Public Interest Law Career

*As a visible minority, I have always struggled with the issue of inequality and fair treatment in our society. Over the last few years, I have not only thought about the topic but have also examined my own actions to address the issues. I concluded that I was not doing enough and took steps to make more of a contribution to under-represented groups. There are two related reasons for my decision. First, I think equality and fairness are necessary and important. Second, bringing about this type of change and the impact it has on people's lives is something that gives me an enormous amount of personal satisfaction and fulfillment. Although my investment banking career was quite lucrative, the personal satisfaction associated with doing something worthwhile and noble was missing. I am now one of those fortunate individuals who will be able to spend a lifetime doing what I love. I recently taught a junior achievement seminar for high school students where the topic was selecting a career. One maxim from one of the exercises was, "Select a career that you love and you will never have to work another day in your life." As I repeated this to the students, it brought a smile to my face because I realized I am leaving behind the draw of wealth and doing something that I truly believe in. This is the reason I decided to leave a career as an investment banker and become a public interest lawyer.*

### *The Areas of Public Interest Law I Am Interested In*

*My interests are firmly routed in bringing about equality in the world, and as such, I am interested in human rights and immigration law. To this end, I was awarded a Sparer Public Interest Fellowship at Brooklyn Law School and currently work as a summer intern at the United Nations High Commissioner for Refugees, where I examine international immigration and asylum law as it relates to countries where human rights violations are occurring. In addition, I would like to practice law to contribute to the black minority struggle that I identify with, and other areas where people are treated differently based on irrelevant factors. As such, I would also like to focus on areas where there is discrimination in the workplace based on race, gender, or sexual orientation.*

These two paragraphs are somewhat related and accomplish two important things. First, I explained why someone who worked in an investment bank for so many years all of a sudden wanted to go to law school and do public interest work. If I had a passion for law that related to banking instead of public interest, I could have also used this paragraph to explain that. The second thing that I did was tell the committee what type of person I was—that is, a person who wants to help others. This just happened to be who I am and why I went to law school, and it came from the heart. Even though a corporate banking narrative may have been easier for me to sell, I felt it was important to discuss my interests passionately, and this would have been hard to do if I was making it up.

Do not get me wrong; people can be passionate about banking and finance, too, and all admission's committees realize that the world needs corporate lawyers as well as public interest lawyers. What I am trying to say is that what the admission's committees are looking for are valid and believable explanations of your reasons for wanting to become a particular type of lawyer.

## Considerations if You Are a Minority?

If applicable, a personal statement can also be used to highlight minority status along with any factors in your life that you have used to overcome obstacles or discrimination. This is often an important element in an application, as some law schools apply a point system in which points are awarded for gender, race, sexual orientation, age, nationality, and other factors in order to ensure a diverse first-year class.

While minority status can generally be a positive thing on your application, if minority status does not really have much to do with your decision to go to law school or you do not think that it will shape you in any particular way, you do not have to write about it in the personal statement.

Keep in mind that the committee will see that you are a minority, as they will ask this as an optional question on the application. The commentary in your personal statement will only help if you can speak from the heart intelligently about why this makes a difference in your case. Some statements can sound phony or contrived, but this is usually not the case if you really mean what you say and you think that this part of you is something that the committee should know about.

## *Should the Personal Statement Be General?*

It is also important to be as specific as possible and relate things that you have done to things that you say. For example, when I wrote about my love for public interest in my personal statement, I linked my discussion to my summer job at the United Nations High Commissioner for Refugees, my volunteer work, and my award of the Sparer Public Interest Fellowship. Be as specific as you can; the more examples you can give the better. Talk is cheap and action gets reaction.

## *What Else Should Be Included in the Personal Statement?*

The second-last-paragraph of my personal statement highlighted my professional accomplishments. While the application asks for your degrees and where you worked, it usually does not ask you to describe what it is you did or what was involved in each of the degrees that you obtained. Moreover, a section like this gives you the ability to highlight where you ranked or placed in certain areas in school and in the workplace.

### *Professional Accomplishments*

*After my M.B.A., I decided to pursue a professional designation and obtained my Chartered Accountancy (C.A.) designation. I passed my accountancy exams on my first attempt and scored in the top 5 percent in all of Canada. As a result of my high score, the Canadian Institute of Chartered Accountants offered me a scholarship to pursue a Ph.D. in accounting studies. While I did not pursue that opportunity, teaching is something that has always appealed to me, and I would like to pursue this once I have gained some legal work experience. As I anticipated the possibility of living in the United States, I wrote the corresponding accountancy exam in the United States and was awarded a Certified Public Accountancy (C.P.A.) designation. After this, I was afforded the opportunity to work in one of the top four accounting firms (Ernst & Young) where I performed audits of large banks. After this, I worked at a large retail bank in Canada and held a number of positions there over a five-year period. I then moved to New York and joined Credit Suisse (CS) as a vice president and within three years I was promoted to director. I worked at Credit Suisse as a senior director up until April of 2008, when I decided to pursue law on a full-time basis.*

In the final paragraphs, I not only conclude my personal statement but I also tell the committee something about me that was not apparent on the application. This could be any unique feature you have to indicate why you stand out. For example, you could be a musician or you could speak 10 languages. For me, I outlined my commitment to personal development outside of school and work, which included extensive travel, learning new languages, and living in different countries outside of my comfort zone. Again, examples are key.

### *Commitment to Personal Development*

*Although my academic and professional accomplishments have required a fair amount of focus, I have always attempted to maintain a balance between professional development and more personal aspects of development. To this end, I have fulfilled a number of personal goals including extensive travel, living abroad, and learning a new language. Since college, I have visited forty countries and one hundred and fifty cities that span across every continent in the world except for Antarctica. This includes extensive travel to numerous countries in North America, Europe, Africa, Asia, Australia, and South America. I consider travel an integral part of my life, and I always try to immerse myself in the culture and language to enhance the learning experience. At a young age, I knew that in addition to travel I wanted to live and work in other countries. As such, after establishing a career in Canada, I left my job and moved to Spain to study Spanish. At the end of a six-month period, I received an award of distinction and am now fairly fluent in the language. After this, I moved to New York and was hired by Credit Suisse, where I have worked for the last nine years. In addition, in 2006, I had the opportunity to live and work with Credit Suisse in Zurich for six months.*

*The pursuit of my dreams has always been the driving force that has allowed me to challenge myself and change. Law school is part of this evolution, and I really hope that I will be able to continue this growth with Harvard Law School.*

## What Are Some Tips for an Effective Personal Statement?

Based on this review of my own and other successful personal statements, I have boiled the suggestions down to the following things you should consider when developing your personal statement to ensure that it is effective:

1.  Do not simply regurgitate the same information in your personal statement that is in your application. For example, the admission's committee already has your grades, so there is no need to spend more than a sentence on this unless you are explaining poor grades in a term or year. You only have two pages, so do not waste it on things that the committee already knows.

2.  Be honest and do not exaggerate when developing your personal statement. Lying is a bad way to start law school, and every document you submit to law school is kept as a record. A blatant lie can come back to haunt you, and you will see that there are several professional responsibility requirements that you have to meet as a lawyer. If you are caught in a lie, it could bar you from ever becoming a lawyer. If you are caught after you are a lawyer, you could be disbarred.

3.  Spend a sufficient amount of time developing your personal statement. It took me over a month to complete my personal statement for Harvard, and in my opinion, this was the main reason that I was accepted there. If I spent less time or did not take the personal statement as seriously, I would not have been admitted.

4. Ensure that your personal statement is well organized and concise. A good way to do this is to either to follow a chronology of your life or to effectively use subheadings. Admission's offices read thousands of statements, and if they cannot understand what you are saying or they get bored, you will not be accepted.

5. Include as many examples of your actions that support your assertions in your personal statement as you can. Words are nice, but actions that show you can back up the words are better. For example, in my personal statement, I express an interest in public interest and point to at least four concrete examples of volunteering and other activities that support my assertion. Examples make your comments more believable and give weight to them.

6. Review what the law school is asking to be included in the personal statement. Often, an application will ask you to write about very specific things in your personal statement, and you have to ensure that these things are addressed and highlighted. For example, Harvard's application, among other things, asked that the personal statement for a transfer student address why he or she wants to transfer to Harvard. Even though the answer to this question may be obvious, it was important to dedicate a sufficient amount of discussion to this topic because the school expected to see it.

7. Try to make your personal statement as specific to the school that you are applying to as possible. Law school websites are quite comprehensive so you can learn a significant amount from them. Also, make the statement as personal as you can by talking about yourself. Avoid generic or vague statements like "I would be an excellent candidate." This type of statement may be your opinion, but the committee needs to know why this would be the

case. Moreover, do not rely on or use pre-packaged personal statements that you can purchase. Also, exaggeration and some statements can sound phony or contrived but this is usually not the case if you really mean what you say and if you think that a certain aspect of your life should be shared with the committee.

As law schools read thousands of applications, cookie cutter personal statements will be very easily identified and will be discarded.

## Sample Personal Statements

Here are some sample personal statements that were used by different students to get admitted to law school.

### PERSONAL STATEMENT—STUDENT 1

*I was 12 when Tajikistan declared its independence from the USSR. The leaders of my country did not know that they would be unleashing a nine-year civil war resulting in fifty thousand deaths and a half a million refugees; but that is what ensued. My family was glued to the TV screen watching the news from Dushanbe, the capitol. My father always kept the living room dim. The warm glow of the tube revealed my little brother sneaking under the table, close to me. "What's happening, brother?" he whispered, "Earthquake?" I didn't know how to respond. I thought maybe it would be better if he associated the images of bodies being wheel-carted around with an earthquake. I didn't want to scare my little brother, but I was terrified. I kept my stick sword next to my bed for a week. Just in case.*

*The situation got worse quickly. Tajikistan, already one of the poorest soviet republics, saw most of its population descend into abject poverty. My parents were simple music teachers, so my family was no exception. Often we had little more than bread and butter for dinner. Sometimes we skipped meals altogether. Education had to be de-prioritized. After my high school graduation*

*I was rejected from the local law school because we could not scrape up enough money for a bribe that was required for everyone who was not a relative or a friend of a school official. That was when a friend told me about an exchange program that sent kids from former Soviet republics to the United States. For the next month I became completely obsessed with the program. My knowledge of English was at best marginal, so I borrowed some American books, loaded up on Metallica and Bon Jovi tapes, and began my own English bootcamp. I knew that there was almost no chance that I would make it out, but this was my only opportunity to escape the extreme poverty and the numbing pain of watching my country fall apart.*

*On the day of the first testing round, my mother and I took the bus to Khujand at six in the morning. A testing official told me that over 200 kids took the test at that location. I was one of fifteen that made it through. I had a week to prepare for the second round, a three-hour standardized test. I had never taken a standardized test before. In addition, half of the test's questions were based on an audio recording, and my only exposure to spoken English was Metallica and Bon Jovi. I shifted uneasily in my chair as the proctor collected the papers. When I came out of the room, my mother gave me a kiss and said that she knew that I passed. I did. A few months later, amazingly, I passed the final round. Because of the hostilities, the exchange program closed its operations in Tajikistan shortly after I left.*

*My American high school, Plainfield High, was located in a suburb of Indianapolis. It had only two African American and no Asian or Latino students. My ancestors are the Mongol Tatars of the Ottoman Empire. I have yellowish-brown skin, black hair, and dark eyes. Add to that a significant language barrier and considerable cultural differences and it is easy to see why I had difficulties fitting in. The problem was exacerbated by my often aggressive reactions to being teased about my inability to speak English. I worked diligently to improve my English and social skills. This eventually paid off as I was able to make a few very good friends with whom I am still in touch today. My English skills steadily improved through college. Although I started at Indiana University with a substantial number of B's, I graduated in the top fifteen percent of my Business School class. After college, I quickly rose through the ranks at an insurance software company, ending up managing the customer service department, an unlikely feat for a foreigner who could barely speak English several years ago. I continued working on my writing and reading skills, which ultimately resulted in a substantial scholarship to attend the University of Miami School of Law. This was a proud moment for my parents, neither of whom received a college education.*

*Today, after successfully completing the first year of law school and thereby earning an opportunity to work in one of the nation's top law firms, I often find myself thinking about the meaning of the American Dream. How could a poor kid from the Soviet Union, coming from nothing, with barely enough English to ask for directions and not a cent in his pocket, end up with a prospect of attending the nation's most venerable law school? Because of this concept of the American Dream, I do not believe that my unexpected and surprising progress stops here. Admission to Harvard Law School would mark another incredible milestone in my life. Of course, I see great value in the general quality of instruction at Harvard. But more specifically, I find the Berkman Center's work in the Internet field very intriguing. Likewise, I am thrilled about the high degree of excellence in the Tax program, featuring such exciting professors as Anne Alstott and Alvin C. Warren. I also feel that the larger-size student body at Harvard allows for greater diversity of perspectives and opinions, which is so central to a well-rounded education. But probably the most important reason for my application to Harvard Law School is the fact that my wife—who, among other things, is a crucial component of my success thus far—was recently admitted to the Harvard Graduate School of Education.*

*A wise man once said that life's challenges do not disappear; rather, they change shape. In my experience, these challenges can be overcome by a mixture of patience, hard work, adaptability, and a bit of good luck. I realize that I still have a long way to go, and I am looking forward to Harvard Law School as my next great challenge.*

### PERSONAL STATEMENT—STUDENT 2

*During my first and only year as a middle school math teacher with the NYC Teaching Fellows program, a creative dramatics group visited our faculty meeting to impart theater-related classroom management. These young dramatists, known for having no control of classrooms when they visited, told a group of veteran teachers that merely "validating" students would stop bad behavior. When the principal castigated us for not trying this method, I raised my hand and asked whether this approach was not simplistic. Later, when I whispered a brief response to a colleague, the main presenter publicly took me to task. I quietly asked, "Shouldn't you be validating me?" The entire room went silent. Afterwards, my fellow teachers praised me for standing up to the condescending visitors and judgmental principal. I had found my voice and couldn't stop using it.*

*Like many new teachers, I found the New York City school system to be a theory-espousing bureaucracy that ignored students' problems and treated teachers as less than professional. While I was counseled by my fellow teachers to smile and nod, I became emboldened when I realized early on that I did not plan on a career as a teacher. I could make myself heard in circumstances where considerations of job security might silence others. As I took increasing advantage of this freedom over the course of the year, I learned the extent of my desire to speak up for what is logical and right and to challenge capricious authority.*

*Teaching Fellows were obliged to take a class at a local college about teaching math in urban schools. My frustration with the class boiled over when one of my classmates demonstrated solving a problem (the square root of $i^4$) incorrectly. My professor and some of my classmates congratulated this teacher on his smooth delivery of the material. I raised my hand to explain why both his math and the underlying logic were flawed. My professor and some of my peers admitted they weren't sure of the answer, but claimed that the correct mathematical solution wasn't important. In their view, the teaching mattered more than the accuracy of the math. This notion was anathema to me. I leapt up to the board and wildly gesticulated as I drew my proofs, but I failed to see any light of comprehension in people's faces. I went home angry and frustrated with my inability to explain the solution clearly enough. So after a consultation with my engineering-major college roommates, as well as my own research, I developed two intelligible proofs for the problem, typed them up in a three-page document, and at the next session handed it out to everyone in class. My professor begrudgingly admitted that I was right, although we had a discussion in which I asserted that if, as math teachers, we claimed the math itself "wasn't important," our students would inevitably wind up feeling the same way.*

*I continued to challenge errors of analysis. At one faculty meeting toward the end of the year the principal handed out a set of statistics that showed the number of student "incidents" (usually fights) and where they took place. With a smirk, she claimed that there was now numerical proof that teachers were failing, because most of the incidents took place in classrooms. I inquired whether, given that our students spent an overwhelming percentage of their day in classrooms, it made sense that most of their fights would take place there. She stammered an acknowledgment, but her eyes were full of malice when a line of teachers came over to me afterwards with congratulations ranging from "I was thinking the same thing!" to "I thought she was right until you spoke up."*

*My fellow teachers and I faced more than verbal criticism. Official written observations of a teacher's lesson by an administrator hung over the faculty like a dark cloud. Our administration was renowned for wielding them with abandon as instruments of terror. One assistant principal especially known for unfairly harsh written observations of lessons—and little knowledge of math—wrote a particularly acerbic observation about one of my math classes (to the point of "12:16 P.M., one student was staring at the wall for a couple of seconds"). The tone was doubtless inspired by two previous interactions with this administrator: one about a particularly dangerous student who was threatening the welfare of his classmates but being ignored by administration, and another about a brilliant student who was denied entry to the honors class. I constructed a point-by-point response to her report, explaining why a number of her criticisms were either inaccurate or flew in the face of instructions I'd previously received from her or other administrators and questioning the support she provided. This response landed me in deeper disfavor. However, "the letter" garnered me fame among my co-workers, and the acknowledgment from one dean that I could have a job as a literacy teacher if math didn't work out. I felt that I had struck back at this system of fear by showing the administration that the pen could defend as well as terrorize.*

*I saw my own feelings about authority reflected in my reaction to my students. While those who took my word as gospel made my life easier, I had a particular fondness for students on the opposite end of the spectrum. I admired those students who challenged new concepts that didn't make sense to them, and who unhesitatingly pointed out when I was hypocritical, boring, or unable to*

45

*explain an idea properly. They were using their brains and their instincts, and I was proud of them. And my students, who somehow found out about every development involving school higher-ups, looked at me with a new respect for challenging people whom they knew to be unjust and incompetent. Veteran teachers told me that I was a hero and a champion of a mistreated faculty. As flattering as it was, I knew they were wrong. I was far from a hero. I had made some snappy comments and gained some anecdotes, but at the end of the day I would be gone and they would still be mistreated. I want to continue to use analytical thinking and my eagerness to challenge unjust authority, but I want to do it on a broader stage with a more noble end result. I know that obtaining my J.D. is the best way of doing just that.*

## *PERSONAL STATEMENT—STUDENT 3*

*There was a time when my mother and her family enjoyed an idyllic Cuban life. My grandfather was the Chief of Police. He was known as "El Coronel," The Colonel. It was a designation of deep respect bestowed upon him by the grateful citizens of Havana for his years of faithful service. My family was committed to their country as true Cubans, and they were blessed for their sacrifice. They enjoyed acres of land on a beautiful countryside estate, living at the center of Havana's social and cultural scene. Then communism descended upon Cuba. My family was ripped from their homeland and forced to leave everything behind. My mother, then in her late twenties, fled to Puerto Rico by way of Miami, with a single suitcase and five dollars. My grandfather chose to stay, working for an oppressive government as a common laborer on the very land he had spent his entire life nurturing and protecting as his own. Still, my family never considered themselves victims. Instead, they rebuilt their lives. My parents created a new home in the United States, raising seven beautiful children, who now have families of their own. From their watchful care have risen engineers, business owners, corporate executives, and servicemen dedicated to the defense of our liberties. My family claimed victory in the face of tribulation.*

*Tragedy struck again when my father was taken from my family, succumbing to a long and painful battle with Leukemia when I was only six years old. My mother raised me alone, and never allowed the term "victim" to enter my vocabulary. Instead, she taught me to honor the principles of hard work, sacrifice, and perseverance, and instilled in me the qualities that were passed along to her by El Coronel. I put these characteristics to use in the professional world, as a sales counselor for one of the largest residential real estate developers in the world. During this time, I built fiduciary relationships with new homeowners. I guided them through the emotional process of purchasing a home, one of the most significant decisions a family will make. I learned to counsel, to listen, and to dedicate myself to their needs. These valuable skills are difficult to learn in a classroom or from a textbook, yet will undoubtedly prove themselves useful as an attorney. Like my grandfather before me, I was rewarded for my hard work. I received regional awards for my accomplishments as a salesperson and, even more meaningful, national recognition for service to my clients. I have tasted the joy of victory as a professional.*

*Soon after, our nation entered one of the darkest economic downturns in its history. Once-powerful corporations buckled and collapsed, and I was laid off from my position after years of dedicated service. Millions of other Americans lost their homes, their life savings, and were forced into poverty. There are very real victims of this recession, but I refused to allow myself to become one of them. I transformed my misfortune into opportunity, and returned to Arizona State to complete my Biological Sciences degree, to which I added another undergraduate degree in Economics. I excelled in two classes at the Sandra O'Connor College of Law as part of a special program at ASU. I have experienced the life of a law student in a very tangible way, and I have been victorious in the classroom.*

*I know I face may obstacles to fulfill my calling in the law, challenges that will provide more opportunities to surrender and count myself a victim. I know the facts and figures regarding the hardships facing law school graduates. I am aware of the competitive nature of admissions, the high cost of attendance, and the shortage of entry-level positions. I have not chosen law because of the nebulous promise of worldly success, the desire for significant financial returns, or the prestige associated with a tilted profession. Instead, I embrace the conviction that I am meant to pursue it. My greatest intellectual gifts, a passion for research, synthesis, and writing, along with my professional experiences align*

47

*perfectly with the requirements of an attorney dedicated to the service of the law. I will pursue this goal with every ounce of strength I have, as long as I have to, until I have brought it to fruition. I will not be a victim. I am a victor.*

### Conclusion: Personal Statement

The website of the office of admissions at Yale Law School emphasizes that a good personal statement "provides a coherent narrative of what has brought you to this point and a great personal statement goes a step further by relating the things they have chosen to mention to something that is larger than themselves." I am not entirely certain what this means but I guess this is a fancy way of saying that the personal statement should tell the person reading it why you should be selected over the thousands of other candidates. Whatever it means, though, I cannot stress enough how important your personal statement is, and this advice holds true regardless of how high your grades or LSAT score are.

---

*Your personal statement is an extremely important part of your application, so spend the requisite amount of time on it. Remember not to repeat information that is already on your application; be honest and sell yourself. Make sure that you follow all of the tips outlined above, and get someone to edit and suggest changes to your statement. Once you have finished, put it down for a week and then reread it with a fresh mind.*

---

If you need help with your personal statement, there are many guides and aids you can purchase. In addition, there are several companies that offer personal statement services that help students get into top schools. Also, you can get personalized advice from the author of this book who runs a blog at *www.lawschoollowdown.com.*

While guides may be helpful as examples, you should tailor your personal statement to yourself, and you should not copy or simply regurgitate another person's personal statement. After all, it is a "personal" statement.

## Choosing a Law School

With over 200 law schools to choose from, your decision on which school to attend can be daunting. There are a few key things to consider that can focus your selection and make this part of the process a bit easier. Before we get started looking at specific factors, keep in mind that many options are better than few, and remember that many schools compete for good candidates.

---

 *Apply to as many schools as you can if you think that there is even a slim chance you may go there. It is better to keep your options open, as your plans may change later. In addition, if you get accepted to a school that offers you a scholarship, you can often use this offer to get the same or a better scholarship at another school. Also, law schools do not interview students prior to their acceptance, so the most you have to lose is the application fee.*

---

Some students with good grades only apply to two or three of the top schools, and this is a risky approach since you may not get in. Keep in mind that there are many students with excellent grades and LSAT scores that do not get accepted to top schools so you should ensure that you at least have other options if you do not get accepted to your first choice. You do not have to accept an offer from your second or third choice, but at least you will have the option available to you.

While you should apply to several law schools, it would not be practical or financially feasible to apply to them all. As such, we will now look at a number of factors that you should consider when selecting a law school.

## How Are Law Schools Ranked and Are Rankings Important?

### How Are Law Schools Ranked?

When deciding which law school to go to, you should ask yourself whether the school rankings are important to you. In the United States, schools are ranked based on a number of factors and each school falls into a tier ranging from first (the highest ranked) to fourth (the lowest ranked). The top fifty schools fall into tier one, the next fifty tier two, and so on. Some of the factors that determine the rankings include student to professor ratio, number of students admitted, average grades and LSAT scores of the entering class, and the makeup of the faculty.

As you can see if you review the history of the top law schools, Yale has consistently been ranked the number-one law school in the country and Harvard usually holds the number-two spot. At times, Harvard and Stanford battle it out for the number-two spot, but when I wrote this book, Harvard had secured its place as the second best law school in the country.

These rankings can be helpful but should only be used as a guide. For example, it would be silly to select a school ranked thirty-six over one that is ranked thirty-nine just because of a three-point difference. However, you might think twice about accepting an offer from a school ranked ninety if you have an offer from one that is ranked ten.

You can also easily find LSAT scores and grades of the top and bottom twenty-five percent of the people who accepted offers of admission at each school but these are not cut off scores. They are instead average scores of the top and bottom twenty-five percent, so again just use them as a guide.

As stated above, do not discount a top school because you feel your grades or LSAT are poor. It is true that your chances of getting in may not be great, but Harvard, Yale, Stanford, and many other schools look at the total picture. Since this is a very important point, I will write it again—every year there are students at these top schools who were accepted and thought that they did not have a chance. In fact, I was one of those people. Even though I did well in my first year of law school prior to transferring to Harvard, my LSAT was average. Also, I was coming from a part-time program at a school ranked in the mid-60s. I really thought it was hopeless, but I already had most of my transfer student applications prepared for other schools where I thought I had a better shot. As it turned out, I am happy that I was not discouraged and that I still applied to Harvard.

---

**TIP** *Apply to the top-ranked schools if you have a special or unique quality, even if your GPA and LSAT are not that great. This does not mean that you should apply for the sake of applying. If you do apply, you should have done something "special" that you can sell to the committee. Grades are important, but they are not always everything.*

---

At Yale Law School, the number-one law school, applicants with GPAs around 3.5 (B+) and LSAT scores in the 150–155 range (very average grades and mediocre LSAT score) have been admitted. Even with these average scores, they were accepted to the best law school in the country and arguably the world. I will make a cross-reference here to the importance of the personal statement, since with these lower scores the personal statement is what will bring out the special qualities of these students to the committee.

## *Are Law School Rankings Important?*

Make no mistake about it: rankings matter and have a significant impact on your job prospects. As such, if there is some basis for your acceptance to a top law school, you should apply. Even if you decide not to go, you at least have the option of selecting them, and once the application deadline passes, this option will vanish. The obvious advantage of these schools is the name recognition. In particular schools often seen in the top five—Yale, Harvard, Stanford, Columbia, NYU, and Berkeley—all have worldwide recognition, and therefore, the degrees are more easily transportable outside of the United States. As such, international career opportunities may be a significant factor when looking at these schools.

The name recognition associated with these schools and other highly ranked schools will also significantly impact your job prospects in the United States. First, employers heavily recruit from top schools and extend offers to students irrespective of their class rankings. Some of the top schools—for example, Harvard—do not even provide employers with class rankings in any year. In fact the top two schools, Yale and Harvard, use a modified pass/fail grading system so it is very difficult to distinguish students. (At Yale it is almost impossible.)

I spent my 2L (second year at law school) summer at a top Wall Street firm in New York, and there were at least fifteen other Harvard students there out of ninety-five people selected for summer employment at that firm. If there were fifteen who accepted, they likely made summer job offers to many more students as many would turn down the job and go to another firm. Students from top schools usually have multiple job offers. In contrast, there were two people from Brooklyn Law School there, and those were likely the only two (or perhaps two more) who received offers. Also, these two students from Brooklyn were at the top of their class, and I know one graduated summa cum laude—the top one percent—at her school.

While I do not think it is a great policy, it is clear that top firms significantly limit how many students they will take from second-tier schools and if you are not in the top ten percent of your class, you can forget about working in a large firm unless you have some other connection. This really is an unfortunate part of the recruitment process, and some firms will not even recruit at many second-, third-, and fourth-tier schools. For example, if my memory serves me correctly, Wachtell (the most prestigious law firm according to the rankings) did not recruit at many lower ranked schools.

For a school ranked twenty-five to fifty (so still top tier), employers will often advertise that only the top ten to twenty percent of the class need apply. In addition, the employers select the students they want to see and limit the number of interviews to twenty to twenty-five people out of a class of almost five hundred. The selection process is based almost exclusively on your first year grades and this process ensures that only the top of the class get interviews.

In contrast, at Harvard, the students select who they want to interview with through a lottery system, and the employers are unable to impose restrictions that bar interviews. In addition, grades are still important for top firms, but as long as you are in the top two-thirds of your class, you will likely get a job offer at a large firm.

Finally, instead of interviewing a mere twenty-five students, the large firms conduct hundreds of interviews at top schools. Even if you do not get an interview with a firm through the lottery system, you may contact the firm and they will gladly arrange an interview with you. In some cases, the firm will even contact you for an interview if you were not selected through the lottery system. This happened to me twice during the job search process. Firms often compete for top students, and if you go to a top school, firms will actively try to recruit you. The job search process will be more thoroughly discussed in a subsequent section; the point of discussing it here is to illustrate how important rankings are.

To vividly illustrate the potential impact of ranking, I offer this account. When I was at Brooklyn Law School and awaiting a decision from Harvard regarding my transfer, I started the on-campus interview (OCI) process at Brooklyn Law School. I submitted my résumé and high first-year grades to Cleary Gottlieb and I was *not* selected for an interview. (They picked twenty-five people to interview and I was not one of them.) Shortly after the process started at Brooklyn, I was accepted to Harvard and started their OCI process in September. Through the process at Harvard, I was granted interviews at all of the big name Wall Street firms (firms were not permitted to refuse interviews, and Harvard dictated who the firms interviewed) and received twelve job offers. Most notably, I received and accepted a job offer from Cleary Gottleib, which did not even select me to interview at Brooklyn Law School. In my case, the firm I worked at after law school is a direct result of going to a top-tier school, so for me it definitely made a difference.

To summarize, your job prospects if you graduate from a school like Harvard are fantastic and much better than if you graduate from a second-, third-, or fourth-tier school. This may seem obvious, but I was certainly surprised at just how much of a difference it made in both the public and private sector.

The same trend occurs for judicial clerkships. At a school like Harvard, virtually everyone who wants to clerk (provided they do not have geographical limitations) will be able to find a clerkship. At a school that is not ranked as highly, only students at the top of the class will easily find clerkships, and many will not be successful. Clerking is viewed very positively in the legal profession, so those who do it are at a significant advantage.

**TIP** *Law school rankings are very important, and there is a significant difference in job prospects between first- and second-tier schools. While rankings are important, you should not decide on a school just because of a very minor ranking difference. The real value of a top school comes when the school is internationally recognized or there is a significant difference (greater than 35 or 40 points) between two schools.*

## How Much Does Law School Cost?

Another important factor to consider when applying to different schools is the cost of attendance, and all law school bills are not created equal. Most private law schools charge just over or around $49,000 per year for tuition, and the estimated total cost per year (which includes room and board, books and tuition) is around $65,000 to $70,000 per year. Unfortunately, the cost does not decrease after your first year but rather stays constant over all three years. If you do not have rich parents or a trust fund, you can usually get loans from the government and graduate with a mere $200,000 in debt. That amount is, of course, is in addition to any undergraduate debt you carry. While a law degree can be quite lucrative, it is not always a money press. As such, a low-cost law school or one where you can get a scholarship are aspects that may impact a decision of where to go.

There are many ways you can reduce the cost of attending law school.

First, you can go to a state law school. Depending on the state, law school tuition could run from $10,000 to $20,000 per year instead of $45,000. This is a good way to save over $150,000 over three years, and some state schools are quite good. You should, however, check residency requirements in some states to see if you are eligible for the reduced tuition. That is, in some cases, the state will only provide reduced tuition if you live or have lived in that state.

Second, you can also save money if you select a private school based on the tuition amounts, as the tuition for each private law school may vary. When I started writing this book, tuition for Brooklyn Law School was at least $1,000 per year higher than Harvard, and the tuition at Harvard was approximately ten percent cheaper than Yale. The tuition amounts can change yearly, so you should check the latest tuition amounts by visiting the law schools' websites.

Third, you can pick a school where the cost of living in the city is low. As you may know, there is a stark contrast between living in New York City and living in Wisconsin. I have a friend who went to law school in the midwest and he paid $400 per month for a palatial two-bedroom apartment. I paid $3300 per month for a small one bedroom in Manhattan.

Fourth, you can also reduce the cost of tuition through scholarships and grants. In some cases you may be eligible for a school award simply by signing up for the benefit. For example, Harvard had (regrettably it only lasted for one year) a program where your third year of tuition was free if you made a commitment to practice public interest law for five years after graduation. All you had to do was sign something indicating that it was your intention to do that. If you did not end up practicing public interest law, you were required to pay back the tuition plus interest. It is important to know these things, as $45,000 gives you 45,000 reasons for selecting a particular school.

Believe it or not, there are many organizations out there that are willing to give you money. The first place that you should look is the school that you are applying to, as many schools have merit-based scholarships that are primarily based on the strength of your application. The primary driver of these scholarships is your grades, and they are offered to incentivize you to come to the school. Being a student is one of the few statuses in your life where there will be lots of opportunities for you to get free money. Take advantage of these opportunities, as you may not have this opportunity again.

You should also investigate other means of obtaining scholarships from different organizations. There are two primary ways to search for these. You can contact the financial aid and awards departments of the schools to which you are applying. They will often have lists of potential scholarships that are just waiting for your application. When I started my M.B.A. many years ago, I was surprised to find out that getting most of my tuition paid through a scholarship was as easy as filling out an application. In fact, if more people in my entering class had filled out the application, I may not have received the scholarship because the number of scholarships was limited and there were most likely several competitive applications. Lucky for me, most of them did not apply.

In many cases, these scholarships or grants will be available to anyone in the country or in the particular state rather than being school-specific and many people do not know about them. As such, you can contact any financial aid and awards department to which you have submitted an application to get information. I have many friends who, with combined scholarships, got a "free ride" (all of their tuition was paid) through law school while I paid over $41,000 per year.

The other way to search for a scholarship is the good old Internet. While you will have to focus your search, start with any aspect that is unique to you such as gender, race, sexuality, disability, or ethnicity. You may also look to your areas of interest, as some might offer money for a commitment to practice law in a particular area. For example, a generous sponsor might offer a scholarship for someone who wants to practice immigration asylum law. Others might offer money if you plan to engage in a career that is public service–related. Also, often people want to give you money just because you have something in common with them so you should also look for that. For example, someone might give money to law students who have a background in track and field. Keep in mind that many of these scholarships are set up by individuals who simply want to give away their money, so the parameters are endless.

High grades also often will get the checkbooks out. Moreover, some institutions will offer money just based on a showing of financial need or overcoming some significant obstacle. Suffice it to say that there is plenty of money out there and you just have to go out and find it. As I have stated above, the financial aid offices at the schools you are applying to can help you, but you have to ask them about it. There are some additional places to find scholarship money included in the Useful Resources section.

*http://www.finaid.org/scholarships*
(Information on different scholarships and how to find them)

*http://www.fastweb.com*
(A scholarship search website that allows you to compare your background with various types of scholarship awards)

*http://www.lsac.org/LSACResources/Grants/lsac-minority-program-grants.asp*
(Grants available from the LSAC for minority students)

---

 *Beware of scholarship scams, and avoid applying for scholarships that make you pay an application fee. Also, research the donor to ensure that they are legitimate prior to giving them any confidential information.*

---

Here are some real-life examples of people who received scholarship money from different sources. I have a friend who has parents who were born in Columbia, and he received scholarship money based on his Latin ethnicity, although I do not think he has spent even a day in Columbia. I have another friend who obtained money from a Jewish organization based on his adherence to the faith. I have another friend who was given almost a full ride based on financial need and hardship, as his parents were deceased. I have yet another friend who was awarded money from the state for excellent academic performance.

Do not be afraid to ask law students if they can point you in the right direction to get money, as you can rest assured that someone pointed them in the right direction. (I wish someone had pointed me in that direction.)

One thing to note for noncitizens. Unfortunately, many scholarships are limited to permanent residents or citizens. If you are not a U.S. citizen, you should inquire as to whether or not you are eligible.

---

**TIP** *There are several different sources of scholarship money out there, so you should look for them. Seek and you will probably find. First check with the financial aid and awards departments of the schools that you are applying to, as they will often be able to give you a list of scholarships to apply for that are not school-specific. You should also independently look for scholarship money by searching the Internet and asking other students. There are plenty of scholarships that are available to applicants based on good grades, race, gender, disability, and several other factors. Do not miss the free money that is just waiting for you to ask for it.*

---

So why do schools offer money? There are many reasons schools offer scholarships and they regularly offer money to compete for students. First, if you decide to attend the school, it will get at least partial tuition from you for the next three years, as scholarships are often not full rides. Moreover, in some cases, the scholarship money comes from foundations or sponsors, so the school is actually receiving the full amount of tuition. Also, your acceptance helps the school in the rankings because your high grades and LSAT are reported to the organization that maintains these rankings. Finally, the school gets an academically gifted person who will be able to contribute to class discussion and enhance the curriculum.

Private law schools are learning institutions but also businesses. As such, do not be afraid to negotiate and ask for more. This is especially the case if the school is not covering all of your tuition. I know many people who asked for more scholarship money prior to enrolling and who told the school that they would not enroll without it. This strategy worked for them, as the law schools often increased their scholarship awards.

In addition, you can often use offers that you get at other schools as a bargaining chip. A school is not offering you money because it likes you personally but rather because it wants you to enroll. Moreover, schools often have money from rich benefactors and sponsors, so at times the money that they offer you is coming from someone else. This money is given to the student, and the student in turn gives the money back to the school for tuition.

---

*If you get a merit-based scholarship that is not a full ride, ask for more. There are many reasons that the school wants you to enroll, and this strategy can be particularly effective if you have scholarship offers from other schools. Remember: Do not exaggerate offers from other schools and only provide the school with accurate information. Also, meeting with the Dean in charge of scholarships to ask for more money is much more effective than sending an e-mail. (It is much easier to say "no" in an e-mail.) Do not take the answers or the process personally; a law school is not only an educational institution but also a business.*

---

You should check directly with the school to see what is required in order for you to keep your scholarship going forward. A good scholarship award in your first year will not mean much if you are not going to be eligible for much in years two and three. Some schools make your future awards conditional upon your performance in the school. This can be problematic for some, as your award is often conditioned on maintaining a fairly high class rank.

In the true business fashion, and although a school would never admit it, schools often deal with limiting the amount they pay in future years by creating something called a "seminar" or "special" section. These special sections house all people who were admitted with strong academic credentials and who were offered the most generous scholarships. As such, maintaining a high class rank in these sections can be difficult because the competition is very stiff.

In addition, combining all of the scholarship students will have an impact on your ranking because of the curve system that is used in all law schools. The law school curve is discussed in more detail below, but for now, it is sufficient to say the class ranking and curve system, combined with the "seminar" section, can really skew your ranking and impact your future because the curve system limits the total number of high grades that can be distributed in any one class. As such, if all of the students who were awarded scholarships are in one class, only a limited number of them can get an A.

This is particularly problematic, as even one or two mediocre grades can drastically drop your ranking and knock you out of the top ten percent. (This is especially a problem if you are at a second-, third-, or fourth-tier school.) I have a friend who was placed in one of these sections, and it was very tough for him to keep a high class ranking and his scholarship in future years. Since he was in a class full of academically gifted students, it was also very tough for him to get the high grades that he saw some of the other first-year students receiving in other classes. As your first year is key in terms of grades, you should really investigate whether a school you are considering adopts this practice, and consider the potential impact on your grades. Your first year is not the year to have the deck stacked against you.

---

 *When deciding which law school to attend, be sure to fully understand what you will have to do in future years to keep your scholarship. Also, ask about seminar or special sections to assist with the determination of the likelihood of keeping advanced standing and high grades.*

---

### Common Question Regarding Scholarships—Should I Go to a Top School and Pay Full Tuition When I Have Scholarship Offers from Other Lower-Ranked Schools?

I have a friend at Harvard who wonders if she made the right decision because she now has $200,000 of law school debt, and when she was accepted to Harvard, she had scholarship offers for full rides at other law schools. Did she make the right decision? I think she did, but the correct answer really depends on what an individual is looking for in a law school.

There are a few things you should keep in mind when deciding which school to attend. In my opinion, you will get a similar legal education in most schools and this opinion is based on attending both a second- and first-tier law school. At the end of the day, the curriculums are similar, and there are good and bad professors in every school. I did not notice a significant difference in the instruction or the quality of education in the first- and second-tier schools that I attended, and the students were bright at both schools.

While the quality of education is similar in a first- and second-tier school, there will be a significant difference in the opportunities you will be afforded and this could impact your income potential and your decision on which school to attend. For some, though, income potential may not be important, and some people may just want to become lawyers. For example, when I started law school at Brooklyn Law School, I did not intend to practice law full-time since I had a lucrative banking job. As such, I was not as interested in a top school. In fact, when I first applied to law school, I could have attended a school ranked much higher than Brooklyn, but I selected that school because I liked its public interest program.

If you know beyond a shadow of a doubt that the thing that is important to you is the learning process and the idea of becoming a lawyer, you may not want to shell out over $150,000 when you could get scholarships and pay nothing. Also, if you are a top student in a second-tier school, you will be afforded opportunities. The problem really occurs when you are not in the top ten or fifteen percent, as your job prospects and opportunities will decrease.

Getting back to my main point, I cannot help but think that if this profession is going to be your future, it is better to have as many opportunities available to you as you can, even if this means incurring a bit of debt. You can always make more money to pay off the debt, and graduating from a top school will put you in a better position to make lots of money. In terms of deciding where to go to law school, I personally would not be guided by incurring debt, but it is a personal choice that is really up to you.

### What Is the Law School Known For?

Another important factor that should be considered when selecting a law school is the school's focus. It is important to research what the law school specializes in to see if its specialization or focus is consistent with your goals. For example, Columbia Law School successfully produces a large number of students who go on to work in corporate America. While they do have public interest programs, there are most likely other schools where public interest is more of a focus. Also, at Harvard there was a period when the school attracted students who were interested in environmental law.

The focus of a school will not only impact the culture and the students it attracts but also the course offerings. It would be a shame to start law school because you wanted to be an immigration asylum lawyer only to find that that course is not offered at the law school you selected.

You can get information that gives you a good idea of a law school's focus from its website and from the various legal blogs such as *abovethelaw.com*. In terms of the school websites, look at the statistics that show what type of jobs the graduating class holds.

---

**TIP** *If you have a particular interest or area of law you want to practice, make sure you check to see if the school to which you are going to apply focuses on that area. If a school is known to specialize in a particular area, it will attract professors—and offer many courses—in that field. If not, you should perhaps consider another school.*

---

## Where Is the Law School Located?

Geographic location is also important. While Harvard is a great school, you should not choose to enroll there if you feel you will be miserable during the cold Cambridge winters. Climate can often make the difference between happiness and misery.

Similarly, choosing a school in an area where you have a strong family or support network may be important to you. Law school is quite intense, and you are almost certain to have several very long nights in your first year. Do not underestimate the importance of good friends and family and the support role that they can play. While having them around is good, make sure you let them know that there will be times when you will not see them. If you forewarn them, it will not come as a surprise when you go into hibernation for a month during final exams. Again, law school is not like college—it is far more intense.

You should also consider whether you are a big or small city person and what the cost of living in that particular city is. While New York may be the perfect city for some, others hate it. Law school is three years, and that is a long time to live somewhere that you hate.

A school's location also often dictates the state law that is taught in the classroom, so if you know you want to practice in a particular state, this may influence your decision. For example, most law schools in New York will focus on New York law, while a law school in California would focus on that state's law. Remember that when you sit for the bar, you will sit for a different exam in each state that you want to practice in and a portion of the exam will focus on state-specific laws. Moreover, some courses—for example, a course like New York Civil Practice—would only be offered in law schools in New York State.

---

*In real estate they say that the key to buying property is location, location, location. While the location of a law school may not be as important for all, it is an important consideration if you have a strong aversion to cold or a preference to live in a small or big town. Also, the cost of living in each state is very different, and the location will impact the courses that are offered at the school.*

---

### *Perks or Incidental Factors to Consider*

You may also want to consider some other factors that I will call "incidental." I say incidental because they are incidental to me, but they will likely be important to some. Even though you will pay well over $40,000 for most private law schools, the services and amenities that you will be offered will vary drastically. For example, the library at Harvard is palatial. Not only is it large and exquisitely appointed, but the study areas are comfortable and spacious. This includes a lounge area with comfortable sofas and chairs as well as separate cubicles with comfortable leather desk chairs.

In addition, there are multiple stand-alone computers throughout the school for students to use, and each morning, coffee is provided at no cost at multiple stations throughout the school. In fact, on Mondays, bagels with assorted jams and cheeses are offered along with the coffee. The tuition at Harvard also includes use of state-of-the-art gym facilities, which would cost approximately $2,000 per year if you were to find comparable facilities in New York. Next, the cafeteria at Harvard is run like a mid-tier restaurant with a vast array of exotic and national cuisine, which is supplemented with a wide array of desserts. Moreover, the food is subsidized by the school, so the prices are low.

While the cafeteria is great, you often do not have to pay to eat at Harvard as there is free food everywhere on a regular basis. Along with the many events at which free food is offered, each professor at Harvard gets a budget for his or her class that is supposed to be spent on students. Also, every Thursday evening, the student government hosts a pub night where free drink tickets are distributed. This is not a comprehensive list, but you should get the basic point I am making here—that is, Harvard (and schools like it) have lots of money, and this often makes the life of a student easier.

As a transfer student, I was shocked at just how many "free" (or included in the tuition) things were available even though the cost of tuition at Brooklyn Law School was higher than the tuition at Harvard. Now do not get me wrong; the facilities at Brooklyn were fine, but they were not like Harvard's facilities. To compare and contrast, Brooklyn has a large library and also hosts events where free food is distributed, but the scale was nothing compared to Harvard. Also, if you wanted a gym membership at Brooklyn, you were on your own. Finally, the cafeteria at Brooklyn was not that great and the food was expensive. Moreover, the school did not serve free coffee, and if you wanted a bagel on Monday mornings, you would have to buy it at the local deli.

---

**TIP** *There is a big difference between the amenities and services that law schools offer. Find out what the school offers to its students on a day-to-day basis. The best way to do this is to read blogs and speak to students. To this end, a visit to the school can be very helpful. It will give you a chance to see the facilities for yourself as well as speak to the students. Added facilities and amenities may not seem like a big deal, but they can make your life more comfortable and enjoyable.*

---

## Are the Students and Faculty Different in Different Schools?

The student body and faculty are also very important and will influence your decision on which law school to attend. One key thing to note here is that schools generally fall into an international or national category—that is, the school attracts either primarily national or a mix of national and international students.

This is well illustrated by looking at Brooklyn Law School and Harvard Law School. I did not see many international students (except for Canadians) at Brooklyn Law School, but Harvard was full of them. This again will impact the course offerings and also the perspective and discussions in class. At Harvard, it was very common for students to start their statements in class with, "In my country." While this may be attractive for some, others may prefer a completely U.S. focus.

You should keep in mind that an international focus of some schools may attract different lecturers and speakers. I recall at Harvard a current justice from South Africa's Supreme Court who presented to our Comparative Constitutional Law class one day, and the presentation was impressive and inspirational. This type of international attraction was common at Harvard but may not be as prevalent at other schools.

In terms of the quality of the education, I do not think there is much difference between the schools. First, in terms of professors, all law schools will have good and bad professors. Some are more interested in research than teaching, and some just cannot teach. Others, however, love their profession and do an excellent job communicating knowledge to students. I did not notice any discernible difference between the instruction at Harvard Law School and Brooklyn Law School. In general, they both had excellent professors and a few bad ones.

Regarding the students, generally speaking, almost all students at Harvard are very bright and academically inclined. That being said, I found making connections or friendships with people there more difficult than at Brooklyn. Brooklyn students were generally more down-to-earth and friendly. Of course, my experience may have been a function of the fact that I entered Harvard in my second year after many relationships had already been forged there.

The students at Brooklyn were also bright, but it was a bit more evident that there was a bottom twenty percent of the class who did not really know what they were doing and who perhaps did not want to be there. For the most part, this did not impact the top eighty percent much, but at times the bottom percent's inane questions could be irritating. I remember one person in my small legal writing class who submitted a brief that was significantly over the page limit. While this itself did not impact the rest of the student body, this particular student harped on the incident (during class and outside of class), and his ranting became somewhat irritating and distracting.

## How Large Is the Law School and Will This Impact my Enjoyment?

You should also consider the student body in terms of its size. One of the reasons that Yale has been able to keep its top ranking is because of its small size. Based on Yale Law School's website, the class profile for the class of 2014 was as follows: 3,173 applicants, 252 accepted, 205 enrolled. Of the 205, forty-seven percent were women, thirty-eight percent were of color, and the median age was twenty-four.

In contrast, Harvard admits approximately 557 students for their J.D. (Juris Doctor) program. In addition, it admits over 100 LL.M. students who take their classes with the regular law students. The first-year J.D. students are broken out into seven sections of about eighty people each, and you are in the same section and have the same classes with everyone in that section for the first year. Eighty students is not a bad size (perhaps a bit large) for a class, but Yale's smaller class size is much more desirable for some. Brooklyn Law School is somewhere in between Yale and Harvard. According to Brooklyn Law School's website, one year's class profile is as follows:

### 2012

|          | Total | Full-Time | Part-Time |
|----------|-------|-----------|-----------|
| Applied  | 4,597 | 3,966     | 631       |
| Admitted | 1,711 | 1,589     | 122       |
| Enrolled | 365   | 319       | 46        |

So which is better, a large or small school? When considering which school to go to, it might be important to be in a school where you are not lost in the crowd. I noted a distinct difference when I transferred to Harvard. Not only were some of the upper-level classes crowded (over 150 students), but as a top student at Brooklyn Law School, I really stood out and received a large amount of personal attention, which I did not receive at Harvard.

I recall on one occasion at Brooklyn Law School the Dean of Students called me into her office to discuss my progress and offer me advice. In addition, professors sought me out to be their teaching assistants. A friend of mine who also had good grades received preferential treatment on his student housing, and that was based solely on his grades.

In contrast, I felt like one of many at Harvard. First, the new grading system makes it tough to stand out as a "high pass"; it does not mean the same as an A or A+. Also, the size of the school made personal attention and recognition very difficult, and some upper-level classes had over 150 people in them. I know a woman who was accepted to Harvard but went to a much smaller, lower-ranked school because she thought she would be "lost" at Harvard. For her it was the right decision.

As such, the choice of big or small really depends on your personality and how you feel about large and small environments.

### Other Factors to Consider—How You Will Be Evaluated and the Grading Curve

#### How Will Students Be Evaluated?

It is also important to ascertain how the law school evaluates students. First, at least two schools—Yale and Harvard—no longer use the traditional grading system and have moved to more of a pass/fail approach. At Harvard, and it is similar at Yale, the grading system is as follows: honors, pass, low pass, or fail. Low passes and fails are discretionary, but in 2009, the first year that the new grading system was implemented at Harvard, approximately eight percent of the class received a low pass grade. As this was immediately identified as the kiss of death for a student when he or she sought employment, Harvard sent out a "clarification" to professors regarding the grading policy and emphasized that low passes were discretionary. Now I understand that low passes are not that common.

Harvard Law School has published suggested distribution grades in the past but will not do this going forward. Under any system of distribution, though, a fail is very difficult to "obtain" unless you do not take the exam or truly do nothing all year.

This type of grading system definitely takes off some of the pressure, and may be very appealing to some. While I was at Harvard the system changed from real grades (A, B, C, etc.) to this pass/fail system, but the support from students was somewhat split. Many students liked the old grading system and fought to keep it. I guess it is just a matter of preference. If you like the pass/fail system, then one of these schools is for you.

Grades are only the first step to assess how a student is evaluated, however, and you should know how the school is going to evaluate you before you decide to go there. Almost all schools rank students to show their performance relative to other students in the class. Only a small number (around the top ten schools) do not provide students with information about their ranking.

For some schools, you will be ranked after your first year. In some cases, the rank will just be a class or section rank rather than a rank of all the students who enter the first-year class. For example, if your section has eighty students and the entering class is made up of four hundred students, you will be ranked from one to eighty even though there are four hundred people in the first-year class. Some schools will give you a ranking within your section and also a ranking out of the four hundred students. Other schools will simply give you a ranking out of four hundred. Some schools will not rank at all. You should understand these rankings as they will have a *significant* impact on your job search and activities going forward. For example, firms often post a "cutoff" ranking that will determine whether you are even eligible to apply for a job with them.

Some schools will not rank in the first year, and I believe this is a very positive thing because the rankings are somewhat artificial and at times are not properly used. For example, my ranking was number four out of approximately fifty-four people in the part-time program. I was lucky that I could say that I was in the top ten percent; if I wasn't, I may not have been able to apply for some jobs that were posted (only people in the top ten percent were permitted to apply). In fact, I was ineligible to apply for the jobs that said only the top five percent could apply.

Another problem with rankings is that they can give a distorted picture of your performance. I was ranked number four even though I had almost a 4.0 GPA. The person who was ranked number six likely had a very similar GPA but would not be able to claim that he/she was in the top ten percent. This is especially a problem, as one A– or B+ will *drastically* impact your ranking, and this effect is exacerbated when there are many students who are being ranked. As such, one mediocre grade will immediately knock you out of the top ten percent, even though you may have almost a straight A average.

*If you are not fond of rankings, try to find a school that does not rank. Rankings will significantly impact your future, and one or two average grades can drastically drop your ranking.*

## *How Does the Law School Grade Curve Work?*

While a small number of law schools have moved to a modified grading system, most still use the traditional A, B, and C grading system. One important thing to note about grading: law school is not like college, where several people fail. In fact, the lowest grade you will see (unless you do not sit for the exam or do nothing) is a C. What is different about the law school grading system is the use of a curve. A law school curve is quite simply a predetermination of what percentage of the class will receive a grade of A, B, and C and a cap on the number of each of these grades in each class. For example, a school may establish a curve as follows (the percentage corresponds to the percentage of people who can receive this grade in a particular class):

| | |
|---|---|
| 1% | A+ |
| 10% | A |
| 19% | A– |
| 20% | B+ |
| 20% | B |
| 10% | B– |
| 10% | C+ |
| 10% | C |
| 100% | Total |

Once the curve is established at a school, it simply means that if there are one hundred people in the class who sit for an exam, they are ranked and then the grades are allocated to them in accordance with the curve. For example, based on the above curve, one person could get an A+, ten people could get an A, nineteen people could get an A–, twenty people could get a B+, and so on. As such, your performance on any exam and your ultimate grade is always relative to the performance of the people in your class or section that sat for the exam with you.

This relative grading could mean that you are awarded a grade of a B even though you have written an excellent paper, and this would just mean that other students in the class wrote better papers. While this may all work itself out in a large class based on some mathematical distribution, some classes only have twenty or so people, so grades can be somewhat skewed. In terms of selecting a law school, though, all schools use curves so it is impossible to get around this.

*It is very unlikely that you will fail out of law school. Most schools use a curve system, and the lowest grade that you will often receive is a C. This is, of course, contingent upon you showing up for class, taking tests, and turning in assignments. Only around four percent of students nationally leave law school because of poor grades. The ABA maintains statistics on this topic by school so you can check to see where your school falls.*

I have one final comment regarding how a law school will evaluate you. You should spend some time reviewing the registrar's web page and your student handbook so that you fully understand how your grades are determined, how you will be ranked, and other options you may have. At Brooklyn, for example, you can choose to take one upper-level course on a pass/fail basis, but you may not find this out until your third year. This option allows you to take at least one course without having to spend the time and effort needed to get an A, and the grade is not included in your rank or GPA. Other schools may offer similar things, but you cannot take advantage of it if you do not know about it. Also, the registrar's page will describe exactly how you will be ranked and may also list some awards that will be available for you for stellar performance after graduation. While a financial award for, say, the highest grade in a course may or may not incentivize you to aspire toward obtaining it, the knowledge is always useful.

## The Year Before Law School

Most students now take a year off between college and law school, and this is a great idea. In fact, the majority of Harvard's entering class in 2011 took a year off. When thinking about what to do before law school, many prospective law students wonder whether or not there are advantages associated with taking a job as a paralegal. In fact, this question came up recently when I sat on a panel with two other lawyers and a law student at Harvard University, at which a college student asked about the benefits of spending a year after college working as a paralegal. The panel members had mixed responses, and I will now give you an overview of the discussion that ensued. First, this description only addresses the specific question of whether or not you should work as a paralegal in order to increase your chances of getting into law school. A job as a paralegal is a very respectable job, and this commentary does not address whether or not you should select that as a career.

### *Will a Job as a Paralegal Make Your Law School Application More Competitive?*

There was general consensus among the panel members that a job as a paralegal is not going to make your law school application any more competitive. In fact, some felt that you may be at a slight disadvantage, as many associate the role of a paralegal with administrative tasks. If you really want to make your law school application more competitive, you might be better off taking a year prior to law school pursuing something that you are interested in so that you can passionately describe an interesting chapter of your life to the admission's committee. If being a paralegal fits this description, then that is fine, too, but describing your year as a paralegal will at best show a general interest in law, and it is not certain that you will be able to talk about your experience in a way that will impress most lawyers or admission's committee members.

One college student at the panel discussion also wondered whether a paralegal job would provide him with valuable "legal" experience. Generally, the consensus was that it would not. This is especially the case if you are a paralegal in a large firm where the administrative tasks will far outweigh any substantive experience. Some panel members did note, however, that they had jobs in the not-for-profit sector, where paralegals gained valuable experience and performed tasks similar to those that lawyers perform. I have also seen this in smaller companies, where the paralegal was able to perform substantive tasks.

### Will Being a Paralegal Help You Get a Job as a Lawyer?

Generally, the consensus was that taking a job as a paralegal prior to law school would not help you find a legal-related job, but the results here could differ if you perform substantive tasks. In addition, one important thing to note is that many are under the mistaken impression that if you work as a paralegal in a large firm, they will hire you after law school. While this is possible, I know many people who worked as paralegals at large firms and were not picked up by that firm during the recruitment process. Even if you are hired, it will definitely be because you had great grades and were an attractive candidate. I personally do not feel that being a paralegal adds much to making you an attractive candidate, but opinions may differ here. Also, I know people who worked as paralegals for large firms and are now employed there. Again, though, these students had excellent grades and were probably offered positions at other top firms, and I doubt they got the job because they were a paralegal at the firm. Also, I know many more people who were not ever offered a job at the firm where they worked as a paralegal.

## What Are Some of the Advantages of Being a Paralegal?

The key advantage associated with being a paralegal is that you get a firsthand look at what being a lawyer is like. A preview of the life of a lawyer can be particularly helpful if you are a "big law" paralegal because it may give you insight as to whether you want to commit to that lifestyle (long hours, unpredictability, etc.). I am not sure that this is a good enough reason to work as a paralegal, though, as you could get good insight by speaking to lawyers or perhaps doing an internship during law school. Moreover, as a paralegal you may be exposed to one narrow area of law that may turn you off to law altogether. Lawyers often end up in numerous fields, and this one glimpse may not be enough to make an informed decision regarding a career.

## Advice on What to Do During Your Year Off

If you take time off after your undergraduate studies, focus on something that you have a passion for and something that you want to do. This will make you happy and will also make for excellent material for your application. With many good students applying to top law schools, the schools are often looking at that time off to determine what type of person you are and what makes you stand out. I am not sure that being a paralegal does a great deal to put you ahead of the person who, for example, went to a third-world country to feed the starving or build schools. Moreover, if you do want to work as a paralegal prior to going to law school, sit down and talk to some lawyers who worked as paralegals prior to going to law school. You should also speak to several current paralegals to see what they like and dislike about their jobs.

To conclude, I believe that being a paralegal is a very respectable job, but if you want to know if it will help you get into law school or get a legal job, my answer is no.

# 2. The First Year of Law School

The first thing you should know about your first year of law school is that it is challenging. When I started law school, I had already completed a bachelor's degree, a two-year master's degree in business administration, and I had successfully obtained two professional accounting designations. To obtain all of these degrees and designations, I had to study extensively and take intense, difficult exams. Even with all of that, I found the first year of law school tough.

In addition, in law school you are exposed to a very different way of thinking and writing, and this—combined with the enormous workload—can be daunting. Be prepared for a challenging first year, and plan your schedule and manage your relationships accordingly.

---

*Your first year of law school is extremely difficult, and you will be left with very little free time. Ensure that you prepare yourself for this, and also make sure that the important people in your life understand that they will not see much of you during your first year. Law school is not like college, so you should not expect the same schedule. This is especially the case if you want to do well.*

---

Law school life does get easier in the second and third years, though, and we will address those years in subsequent chapters.

## First-Year Courses

Most law schools have a similar curriculum for the first year, and your schedule (both the courses and their time slots) will usually be preselected for you. While there are some minor variations, you will usually take the following courses in your first year: Torts, Property, Contracts, Criminal Law, Civil Procedure, Constitutional Law, and Legal Writing. Prior to starting law school, it is helpful to have a basic understanding of what these courses are all about, but it is not really necessary to do much, if any, background reading to prepare for the courses.

---

*While it is always better to know more, it is not really necessary to study for any of the courses you will take in your first year prior to starting law school. The professors assume that you do not have any legal background, and they will teach you everything you need to know. You will have a million things to learn when you start law school, so the best advice is to relax and take it easy before classes start.*

---

The following pages give a brief summary of what these courses are all about.

## *Torts*

I have started with a course that has a name that is not that intuitive or self-explanatory. A tort sounds like a dessert, but it is a fancy way of saying a bad act that causes harm or injury to others. This is an area of law that you read and hear about every day, and the best example is someone who is suing someone else for injury that he or she sustained in a car accident. You may have also heard tort lawyers described as "ambulance chasers" because they are always at the scene of an accident asking if someone involved wants to sue. In fact, this reputation at one time was so prevalent that there are now ethical professional responsibility rules that restrict lawyers from approaching people immediately after an accident.

You may have also heard the term "negligence," and tort law is where this word comes from. While negligence is a tort that stems from an accident, there are also intentional torts that may stem from criminal activity. For example, if you punch someone in the face and that person has to go to the hospital, he or she may sue you based on the tort of battery or assault. In this example, the person that hit you may also be subject to criminal prosecution, but criminal prosecution is something that is done by the state. When an individual sues another individual for something like battery or assault under tort law, that person is suing for money damages to compensate for the injury that he or she sustained.

A tort does not have to relate to physical injury. For example, you may also be familiar with the tort of defamation. Here, one person has said something that has harmed another person's reputation, and the person who suffered harm to his or her reputation sues under the tort of defamation. You may have heard of movie stars who sued gossip magazines when the magazine printed or said something about an actor or actress that was factually incorrect and harmed his or her reputation. During this course, you will learn to define the various different torts and what you have to do to win a case in court.

### Criminal Law

This course does not require much explanation. If we look at the same tort example above where someone punches someone in the face, the state may prosecute the puncher, and this is dealt with in criminal law. While enrolled in this course, you will learn the details related to various crimes that are codified in statutes. You will also learn exactly what you have to do in order to convict someone of a crime. The course covers crimes such as murder, rape, theft, assault, kidnapping, drug crimes, and others. In addition, the course will present the defenses that people can put forward.

Depending on the law school, this course will also cover criminal procedure topics such as what the police can and cannot do during an investigation. For example, you will learn whether or not the police can search your house, your person, or your car without a warrant. In addition, you will learn what your rights are if you are arrested and whether or not you have a right to a lawyer. Almost everyone is familiar with the famous Miranda rights, and you will read the case that establishes the famous phrase that is so often quoted on television: "You have the right to remain silent… if you give up that right everything you say can and will be used against you in a court of law…."

After you have completed the course, you may view some of the legal and police television shows somewhat differently. I still often find myself commenting, "That would not happen" when I watch *Law and Order* or any other legal or police dramas. For example, Tom Cruise's famous line in *A Few Good Men*, "Did you order the code red?" and Jack Nicholson's spontaneous confession almost never happen in the real world. In fact, while cross-examining a witness, a lawyer will almost never ask a question that he or she does not know the answer to, and being "caught" on the stand does not often happen.

## Civil Procedure

This course walks you through the steps that you would have to take to sue someone and file a case in federal court. This generally means how one party sues another party to get money. The course is one of the more complicated courses because it is based on a detailed, voluminous, government-developed guide called the *Federal Rules of Civil Procedure.*

To illustrate what you will learn, let us look at part of an employment discrimination litigation case. Say that Mary was fired and sued her employer for employment discrimination, claiming that the employer discriminated against her because she is a woman. (You are not permitted to do discriminate based on gender in the United States based on the Civil Rights Act and the Constitution.) She would (and should) hire a lawyer, and the lawyer—among other things—would put together what is called a complaint. The complaint would specify who Mary is suing, the reason she is suing, and what she is suing for. After the complaint is filed with the court, her ex-employer would file an answer that denies the allegations. The ex-employer may also put together a document to try to get the case dismissed. Of course, Mary— through her lawyer—would be able to answer or oppose this attempt to dismiss (motion to dismiss) the case, and the judge would ultimately decide whether the case was dismissed or whether a trial was going to occur. For all of these documents—complaint, answer, the answer to the answer, motion to dismiss, etc.—the *Federal Rules of Civil Procedure* set out the content and format of the documents, the timing, and the court process.

Note that everything described above happens before the case even gets to a trial or the jury, and there is a significant amount of back-and-forth before a case ever sees a courtroom and the case often lasts for years. In addition to determining the content, format, and timing of the court documents, the *Federal Rules of Civil Procedure* also define the steps and policies that govern all of this back-and-forth, including which court a person can sue in, how to add different defendants to a case, how to file a counter- or cross-complaint, and more. When it comes to courtrooms and lawsuits, there are rules for everything, so this course ends up being quite comprehensive.

### Constitutional Law

Constitutional Law is a required course at most law schools. I say most because I was more than a bit surprised to discover that it is neither a first-year course nor a required course at Harvard Law School.

If you are American, you may think that you know all about the Constitution, but this course will prove you wrong. It will usually have three main components. First, you will study the three branches of government (judiciary, executive, and congress), and you will become intimately familiar with the roles of each branch. You will also look at specific parts of the Constitution that give these branches their powers, and you will also spend a fair amount of time talking about how and why the Constitution was formed.

Second, you will study and learn about different parts of the Constitution and the related amendments. Moreover, you will study the case law surrounding various aspects of the Constitution. Case law refers to how the Constitution has been interpreted over the years. As you may know, the Constitution is not a long document, and most laws that stem from it are based on interpretations over the years. For example, an area of law that is based on constitutional interpretation is abortion. While the Constitution does not ever mention the word "abortion," the current laws in America stem from a number of cases that were decided based on a few sentences in the Constitution. Similarly, cases have defined exactly what limits, if any, can be placed on the ownership of firearms based on language in the Constitution. You will also look at the 14th Amendment and learn how and why schools in the United States were desegregated and how the Constitution deals with discrimination based on factors such as race, gender, and sexuality.

Finally, like the important Supreme Court cases related to abortion and race discrimination, you will study and understand exactly what the Supreme Court does when it looks at an issue and the analytical standards that are applied. You will also assess other fundamental rights like the right to free speech. You will also learn about rights, such as housing and education, that are not guaranteed in the Constitution.

---

 *Constitutional Law is arguably one of the most fascinating courses in law school but also one of the most difficult, as the cases are long and complex. Moreover, it is a course that invokes strong divisions in opinions. Take the time to get the big picture, and the pieces should fall into place.*

---

## Legal Writing

Effective legal writing is a skill that you must master, and you will learn how to write like a lawyer in your Legal Writing course. The sooner you realize that legal writing follows a very specific set of rules, the better off you will be. Accordingly, the best way to approach this course is to go in with a blank slate and forget about the writing styles you have learned. While you may be a fantastic literary writer or an English major, legal writing is very different from anything you have encountered, and lawyers and judges expect to see memos and other documents written in a manner that adheres to the legal writing style.

You will find that people who have literature or other writing-intensive degrees sometimes have a tough time adjusting to law school writing. Some complain that it is dry and not flowery enough, while others say it is too direct. Although you will have your own opinion on legal writing, which may not be favorable, you are expected to write this way, and deviation from that will only result in poor grades. Again, if you master legal writing, you will do well in law school, and even if you are stuck on exams you will be able to revert to what you have learned in this course. Moreover, the essay questions on the bar examination expect you to follow the same format that you will learn in this course.

To this end, legal writing will teach you how to write a legal memo that clearly states what the issue is, what the rule of law is, the application of the facts in the case to the rule of law, and a conclusion. Those who understand the previous sentence often succeed in law school because they can revert back to it on any exam or in any legal situation. If you do not understand the previous sentence yet, do not worry; you have time to learn.

In your legal writing course, you will be taught a fundamental way that lawyers analyze issues. This is commonly called "IRAC," which stands for **I**ssue, **R**ule, **A**pplication, and **C**onclusion. What this means is that for every law problem, you first describe what the issue is, then you define what the rule of law is based on (either a statute or case law), then you apply the facts of your case to that rule, and then you conclude.

Legal writing is usually a two-credit course that you take in your fall and spring term (four credits total). In the fall, you are exposed to the basics regarding how to write a legal memo, and you are graded on several memos that you write. The first memo is typically graded on a check, check plus, or check minus basis and will not count toward your final grade. The purpose of this memo is to show you the process and let you practice. Your second legal memo, however, will usually be worth around 30 to 35 percent of your final grade. For all memos, you will receive a substantial amount of feedback, and you usually will have to meet with your professor to discuss the assignment. Moreover, you will soon realize that for memos, legal documents, and examinations, you will often be doing the same thing—that is, applying IRAC.

Let's take a look at a simple issue regarding whether or not a person who hides a chocolate bar in his or her pocket and is arrested before leaving the store is guilty of theft. To apply IRAC, we first define the issue. In a legal memo, the issue might be defined in the form of a question. For example, the issue might be: Is John guilty of theft, as defined by the theft statute, if he put a chocolate bar in his coat pocket in a store, but he was arrested before he left the store? This question makes it clear that the issue stems from the fact that John had not yet left the store before he was arrested. (Clearly, he would be guilty if he left the store.) The issue could also be worded as follows: Does an individual have to take something that belongs to someone else outside of the property of the owner in order to be guilty of theft?

The next step is to define the rule of law. For example, the law might say that theft is defined as knowingly (on purpose) *taking* property of another without their permission. While the definition might at first seem clear, in order to decide the case, we have to know what "taking" means. In order to determine what taking means, you will have to review several cases to see how the courts have defined taking in the past.

What will normally happen is that terms like "taking" will appear in a statute but will not be defined, so you must look to cases for the definition. Once you get this definition from cases, it becomes part of the law and is called "case law." In this case, "taking" could mean taking off the shelf and putting the item in your pocket, or it could mean walking outside of the store with the property.

Now let us say that, based on several cases, taking has been interpreted in the past as moving the property from the property of the owner to a location that is not property of the owner. For example, there may have been a case where taking was defined when a person took a wallet from the purse of another. Another similar case may relate to a person who took a shirt and left the store with it. Another case that would demonstrate that taking meant leaving the property of the owner might be an instance where a person did *not* meet the taking requirement when he or she attempted to steal a car from a lot but was stopped prior to getting the car off the lot. These past decisions or case laws are what are called precedent, and they are as much a part of the law as a statute.

Now that you have stated the issue and you know the law, the next step is the application. To apply the facts of this simple case to the law, you would note that John did have the intent (he knowingly, or purposefully, took the chocolate bar) to steal as evidenced by hiding the chocolate bar in his pocket, but he did not leave the store with it.

Finally, you must state the conclusion. For example; John is not guilty of theft because he did not take the chocolate bar out of the store.

Now this is a very simple example in which the law is clear, but it demonstrates the basic point of what you will be doing in law school—that is, looking at facts and using the law to determine who will prevail in a particular case. Often the facts and case law will not be clear, so both sides usually have arguments. In fact, as part of your legal writing course, your class will likely be divided into two groups and given the same fact pattern to work on. Although you will all be given the same facts and same cases, each group will be required to use cases to make arguments for their side.

So what does a legal writing memo look like? I have included one of my legal writing memos from my first year. The memo is far from perfect, but I received an A on it.

---

 *Legal writing is an extremely important course, and you should dedicate a sufficient amount of time to it. This course will provide you with a basis for how to perform legal analysis, and almost every document that you will create as a lawyer will follow the format that you learn in this class. Moreover, your law school exams and the bar exam will expect you to answer essay questions based on what you have learned in this course.*

---

## Legal Writing Memo—Grade Awarded: "A"

*To:        Honorable Mary Meade*
*From:      Ian E. Scott, Law Clerk*
*Subject:   People v. King Gudea., Cr. No. 07-234*
*Date:      November 20, 2007*

**Question Presented**

*Does King Gudea (Gudea) have the right to represent himself at trial, and if so, are there any limitations on that right?*

**Conclusion**

*Yes, Gudea's right to conduct his own defense is guaranteed by both the Federal and New York State Constitutions subject to the following limitations established through case law: a) he must make a clear and unconditional request before his trial starts, b) he must waive his right to counsel voluntarily both understanding what he is doing and the related implications, and c) he must act in a manner that will not disrupt the court.*

**Statement of Facts**

*In August, 2007, political protesters called the Sumerian Liberation Army entered the galleries at the Metropolitan Museum and spray painted some pieces of priceless art. The damages amounted to $500,000. The protestors also threatened to blow up the museum if its curators did not purchase and provide equal space for Sumerian art. The police apprehended the leader of the group, who identified himself as King Gudea and claimed to be a direct ancestor and incarnation of King Gudea of the Lagash dynasty, who ruled in the Mesopotamian kingdom of Sumer circa 2144–2124 BCE. King Gudea has been charged with criminal mischief in the Second degree (P.L. s 145.10).*

**Discussion**

*This memo addresses Gudea's right to self-representation and the limitations on that right. The New York State Constitution states, "In any trial in any court whatever the party accused shall be allowed to appear and defend in person and with counsel." NY Const, Art I, § 6. In addition, this right to self-representation is guaranteed by the Federal Constitution. US Const 6th Amend; Faretta v. California, 422 US 806 (1975). In order to promote the orderly administration of justice and to prevent subsequent attack on a verdict claiming a denial of fundamental fairness, the right to proceed pro se is not absolute and is subject to limitations. People v. McIntyre, 36 N.Y.2d 10, 17 (1974). A defendant may invoke the right to defend pro se provided: 1) the request is unequivocal and timely asserted, 2) there has been a knowing and intelligent waiver of the right to counsel, and 3) the defendant has not engaged in conduct that would prevent the fair and orderly exposition of the issues. Id. If Gudea wishes to proceed pro se, he should make a clear, nonconditional request that expresses his determination and intent to proceed pro se prior to the start of the trial. The court should then repeatedly describe the dangers of proceeding pro se and the advantages of having a lawyer to Gudea. In addition, the court will also conduct a "searching inquiry" to ensure Gudea is competent and understands what was explained to him, and Gudea will be required to reaffirm his request. The court's inquiry should be compassionate, and both prior to and during the trial, the court will assess Gudea's behavior to ensure he does not forfeit his right to defend himself by not acting in good faith or acting in a disruptive manner.*

*1) Unequivocal and Timely*

*Unequivocal*

*The pro se request must be clearly and unconditionally presented to the trial court. McIntyre, 36 N.Y.2d at 17. In People v. LaValle, 3 N.Y.3d 88 (2004), the defendant requested new attorneys because his counsel did not agree on a defense strategy. When the request was denied, the defendant said, inter alia, "The only thing I see, and that's my last option, is to represent myself, not that I want to...". Id. at 105. After additional discussion, the trial court explained at length why self-representation would be a "disaster" and urged the defendant "to think about what you have said." The defendant did not comment and simply smiled. Here, the appellate court concluded the defendant did not make an unequivocal request because the words were not clear and his true intent was to change one of his lawyers. This was evidenced by phrases like, "not that I want to" and "that's my last option," which demonstrate hesitation and convey a sense of obligation on the defendant's part. In contrast, in People v. Providence, 2 N.Y.3d 579 (2004), the court held the defendant's request was unequivocal when, after repeated and increasingly detailed warnings regarding the dangers of a pro se defense from the trial judge, the defendant repeatedly and unambiguously used phrases like, "Yes, I, Eric Providence, wish to proceed pro se...Yes I do." Id. at 582. Similarly, in* Williams v. Bartlett, *44 F.3d 95 (2d Cir. 1994), a case that started in NY State Court* People v. Williams, *181 A.D.2d 995 (1992 N.Y. App. Div.), the 2d Cir. reversed the decision of the District Court and State Court and remanded the case back to the State for retrial. Here, even though the defendant requested to proceed pro se and then changed his mind, the 2d. Cir. held the defendant's request was unequivocal when, after being warned of the dangers of self-representation, he said, "I will represent myself" and "It's . . . my intention...now to go pro se. Before I wanted to have an attorney, but I can't afford a private attorney. That's why I'm going pro se."* Williams, *44 F.3d at 97. In* People v. Jimenez, *253 A.D.2d 693 (N.Y. App. Div. 1998), the court held the request to proceed pro se was not unequivocal because it was overshadowed by his numerous requests for new counsel and repeated applications for adjournments and conditioned on his request for an adjournment.*

    *a) Unequivocal—Clarity*

    *The right to defend pro se lacks the force and urgency of the right to counsel and, as such, there is no obligation, constitutional or otherwise, to inform Gudea of his right to conduct his own defense.* McIntyre, *36 N.Y.2d at 17;* People v. Himko, *239 A.D.2d 661, 662 (N.Y. App. Div. 1997). If Gudea requests to proceed pro se, you should ensure he demonstrates a commitment to self-representation by making unambiguous, unconditional affirmative statements that describe his intent and desire is to proceed pro se. Like in* Providence *and* Williams, *the words used, like "I will represent myself," should concretely and affirmatively express his desire to proceed pro se, and the words should not reflect hesitation or obligation. Similarly, as in these two cases, you should explain the dangers inherent in self-representation repeatedly. After each warning, you should ask Gudea to repeat his request to proceed pro se and you should monitor any changes in his words, silence and/or hesitation that would suggest, like in* LaValle, *he is hesitant, not committed to self-representation, or has simply changed his mind. However, you should note vacillation does not necessarily mean his request is equivocal. In* Williams, *after much debate in the lower and state courts, the 2d Cir. held the request was unequivocal even though the defendant accepted counsel and then later decided he wanted to proceed pro se. Vacillation is simply one of the factors to consider when you determine the equivocal nature of his request, and the question here is one of degree. In Jimenez, the court held that repeated requests and complaints overshadowed the request to proceed pro se and denied the request.*

*b) Unequivocal—Unconditional*

*The request to proceed pro se should be unconditional, and like in Jimenez, should be denied if it is based on specific court performance (for example, an adjournment). However, you should note the "condition" of different counsel alone does not indicate the request is equivocal. For this condition, the courts have attempted to ascertain whether the defendant simply wanted a different attorney or whether he wanted to represent himself. If Gudea attaches a condition to his request, the best way to find out his desire or intent is to ask why he wants to proceed pro se. In Williams, the defendant's request explained why he wanted to proceed pro se: "I can't afford a private attorney," which is distinguishable from the situation in LaValle, where the request was made as a hypothetical and alternative as a ploy to remove an attorney.*

*Timely*

*A pro se application is timely when it is asserted before the trial commences, and once the trial has begun the right is severely constricted and granted based on the court's discretion in compelling circumstances. McIntyre, 36 N.Y.2d at 17. If the trial has started, the court has to balance the interests of the defendant in self-representation against the potential disruption of the proceeding already in progress by considering factors such as Gudea's reasons for the request, the quality of the assigned counsel, and the impact on the trial. Williams, 44 F.3d at 97.*

*Knowing and Intelligent*

*A defendant must make a **knowing**, voluntary, and **intelligent** waiver of the right to counsel. People v. Arroyo, 98 N.Y.2d 101, 102 (2002). In determining whether a waiver meets this requirement, the court should undertake a 'searching inquiry' of defendant. People v. Slaughter, 78 N.Y.2d 485, 491 (1991). The searching inquiry does not have to follow a rigid formula, and the courts have endorsed the use of a nonformalistic, flexible inquiry. People v. Kaltenbach, 60 N.Y.2d 797, 799, 469 (1983). However, the inquiry "must accomplish the* *goals of adequately warning a defendant of the risks inherent in proceeding pro se, and apprising a defendant of the singular importance of the lawyer in the adversarial system of adjudication." Id.*

*In Arroyo, the defendant informed the trial court of his desire to proceed pro se because he was not pleased with his attorney. The court noted: "A person has a right to represent himself, but it is usually not a good idea. ... I don't have to ask you any questions to know that you are sensible...". Here, the appellate court held the waiver to counsel was not effective because the trial court did not ask any questions to establish whether the defendant understood the disadvantages of choosing self-representation, and a reliable basis for appellate review did not exist. Kaltenbach, 60 N.Y.2d at 799. In addition, the court said appropriate record evidence is required, which "should affirmatively disclose that a trial court has delved into a defendant's age, education, occupation, previous exposure to legal procedures...". Arroyo, 98 N.Y.2d at 104. However, in Providence, the court held these factors are "best practices" rather than a firm requirement. Providence, 2 N.Y.3d at 579. In People v. Vivenzio, 62 N.Y.2d. 775 (1984), the court held the defendant waived his right to counsel knowingly and voluntarily when the court established, based on a review of the records, Vivenzio was an adult who had been involved in the criminal process before, and he had a lawyer advising him. In addition, the court provided the defendant with forceful warnings that he did not have the training or knowledge to defend himself, that others who had done so had been unsuccessful, and that if he insisted upon appearing pro se, he would be held to the same standards of procedure as would an attorney.*

*If Gudea requests a pro se defense, you are obligated to describe the dangers of self-representation and to describe the importance of a lawyer in the court system to him. Your goal here is to ensure that he understands what he is doing and the ramifications of his choice, so you should describe the perils of self-representation using the strong wording like, "Others who had done so had been unsuccessful," like in Vivienzo. In Arroyo, more general wording, like "usually not a good idea," was not sufficient. While there is some latitude on how the searching inquiry is conducted, you should record all questions, answers, and independent verification of the record in order to support appellate review. Also, while not required, as a matter of best practice, your inquiry should ask about age, education, occupation, and previous exposure to legal procedures. While prior legal exposure may support Gudea's knowledge and understanding, the courts have established a defendant need not have the professional skills and experience of an attorney to choose self-representation. McIntyre, 36 N.Y.2d at 17. You should also note Gudea's knowledge of what he is doing does, to some extent, depend on mental capacity. In People v. Reason, 37 N.Y.2d 351 (1975), the court held the standard for mental capacity to stand trial is the same as the mental capacity required to proceed pro se. As Gudea's claim that he is a direct ancestor and incarnation of King Gudea is not rational, as in Reason, you should consider assessing his mental competency to stand trial. At a minimum, given his statements, your inquiry should ask the defendant probing questions to assess competence. For example, you could ask about his understanding of the risks, whether he feels he has the tools for a defense, and whether his decision is voluntary. In order to better understand his competency, you should ask open-ended questions rather than questions that require a yes or no. You should be aware, while not a Constitutional right, the appointment of standby counsel to assist a pro se defendant has received judicial approval and is discretionary. People v. Mirenda, 57 N.Y.2d 261 (1982).*

*Forfeit*

*When a defendant's conduct is calculated to undermine, upset, or unreasonably delay the progress of the trial, he forfeits his right to self-representation. McIntyre, 36 N.Y.2d at 17. In McIntyre, when the trial court denied the defendant's pro se request, the defendant said "F\*\*\* the jury" and had to be restrained. There, the court did not find the defendant forfeited his right because the outburst occurred as a result of the denial rather than prior to it. In addition, based on the trial court's belief that the defendant's motion was disingenuous, the trial court conducted his inquiry in a mocking manner. For example, he said, "He [the defendant] thinks he's probably the greatest lawyer and God's gift to the legal profession. That comes after talking with three or four jailhouse lawyers." The appellate court concluded the trial court's inquiry goaded the defendant and that outbursts based on this provocation would not justify a forfeiture. The appellate court concluded the trial court should have* conducted a dispassionate inquiry into the pertinent factors and concluded on the defendant's motives based on that assessment. _McIntyre_, 36 N.Y.2d at 17. In _People v. Anderson_, 133 A.D.2d 120 (N.Y. App. Div. 1987), while proceeding pro se, the defendant attempted to flee the courtroom, feigned muteness after indicating that he wanted to make an opening statement, and was ultimately bound and removed from the courtroom. Here, the appellate court found the trial court should not have allowed the defendant to continue to proceed pro se once the defendant demonstrated his intent was not to pursue his self-representation in good faith.

While trial courts are afforded a wide latitude as to how to deal with disruption, permitting disruptive behavior could result in a reversed decision. _Id_. At the same time, a decision to forfeit based on disruption must be balanced with a defendant's constitutional right to represent himself. Here, Gudea may mount a political defense, and as such, the likelihood of disruption may be high. The appellate courts have not demonstrated much tolerance when the defendants, like _Anderson_, are clearly playing games with the court. In contrast, the appellate courts have displayed some level of tolerance toward the defendants where, like in _McIntyre_, the defendant legitimately was trying to conduct a defense or where the trial court had provoked or goaded the defendant. As such, you may want to exercise some tolerance for verbal disruptions provided you believe Gudea is acting in good faith. You could also consider warning Gudea at the beginning of the trial that disruptions will not be tolerated and any disruptions could result in a forfeiture of his right. Also, you should ensure that you conduct your searching inquiry in a compassionate manner and that it is not viewed as provocation. In _McIntyre_, the trial court was quite harsh with the defendant, and the appellate court felt this constituted goading. Finally, given Gudea's chance for disruption is high, you may want to appoint standby counsel so that they can take over in the event Gudea does forfeit his right. You should note that you are not required to obtain Gudea's approval to appoint standby counsel.

When you are assigned your first legal writing memo, take a look at this memo again to see how you can improve certain points of your memo.

## *Property*

Property is one of those courses that you will either love or hate. I am not sure why there is so much divergence in opinion, but some find it an utter bore while others realize that they have found their calling. I found that I was part of the latter group. The property course will deal with a few key topics. Generally speaking, the course will answer the question regarding to whom property belongs. For example, if someone catches a baseball in a baseball park and then immediately drops it and someone else grabs it, property law will sort out who the owner is. Similarly, property law will dictate what one can and cannot do with property. For example, you can only sell a car if you have the title, that is you have legal ownership of it.

Property law may also come in handy for everyday occurrences. For example, through a law topic called bailment, you will learn what your rights are if you leave your coat in a coat-check or your car in a parking lot and something happens to your property or something goes missing. You may be surprised to find out that often the signs that state "we are not responsible for lost items" may not have much legal effect.

Property law also deals with all aspects of land, including purchase, sale, mortgage, trespass (the right to keep people off your land), adverse possession (when people use land that they do not own for many years and get ownership because they have possessed the land for a long time), easements (the right to use other people's land, such as the right to use someone's driveway because you cannot get to your land otherwise), and many other land-related topics.

Somewhat related to land, property law also covers all aspects of lease agreements, including both residential and commercial leases. As such, you may pick up some useful bits of information that you will be able to use to ensure your landlord is treating you in accordance with the law.

Finally, the course will cover the Constitutional provision that permits the government to take some land away from private individuals for just compensation.

In addition to the basic law, you will learn the policy and social reasons that have shaped the laws over the years. While the course in law school is not that difficult, this is a very tough subject to prepare for when studying for the bar exam. The bar examiners note that, of the six subjects that are on the multistate exam, candidates score the lowest on the property section. I will refer to this and the other five subjects later in the book when I discuss preparation for the bar examination.

## Other Courses

Many law schools also include one or two additional courses in the first-year curriculum. For example, at Harvard Law School, first-year students are also required to take a legislation and regulation course, and this type of course is becoming more and more common in the first year. The course walks a student through how laws are developed and the steps that the Congress and Senate take to enact law. The course also gives an overview of the three branches of government and discusses how these three branches work together as well as how the federal government works with state and local governments. Finally, it may also cover the basics related to how a person goes about suing another person. While this is covered in more depth in civil procedure, you may not have civil procedure until your second term, so this foundational course may give you perspective that will be useful in other courses. The course is somewhat general but teaches lawyers some fundamental concepts that all lawyers should know. In this sense, it may be one of the more practical courses.

*I have already told you that grades are very important in your first year. In addition to getting good grades, you should keep in mind that first-year courses are foundational courses that will prepare you for all of the other courses that you will take* in law school. Moreover, these courses are all heavily tested on the bar exam regardless of which state you take the bar exam in. This is not the time to slack off. If you do, you will severely limit your future options.

## How Law School Courses Are Taught and the Socratic Method of Teaching

Now that you have seen what will be covered in the first year, it is important to explain how these courses will be taught. The style of teaching in law school is part of what makes the experience so daunting, and the reason is that law schools use something called the Socratic method of instruction. Let me explain by first talking about how some laws are developed.

Many of the laws that we follow are not laws that have been written by Congress or local government. The United States is a common law country, and this means that a large part of the law is made up when cases are decided and judges write opinions explaining the reason that one party won the case over the other party. For example, the basis for the laws related to abortion are based primarily on common case law rather than a statute. I discussed this briefly when I talked about your legal writing course and referred to this as case law and precedent. Case law and precedent are as much a part of the law as any statute written by Congress.

In order to learn what precedent or case law is, during your first year of law school you will read hundreds (perhaps thousands) of cases and the related decisions, and you will review and discuss these cases during class. The way you discuss these cases is where the Socratic method of teaching comes in, and most—if not all—law schools use it.

The Socratic method was named after the classical Greek philosopher Socrates and is really a form of inquiry and debate between people with different and opposing points of view. It is based on asking and answering questions to stimulate thinking and generate ideas, but it often just generates terror for law students. While this rather technical definition sounds like there is a back-and-forth or give-and-take, what it means in law school is that the professor is the one asking all the questions and you are the one answering in front of your classmates.

A less technical definition is as follows: Student is "called on" by professor and grilled on all of the intricate details of a case or cases. This questioning can go on for one minute or thirty minutes depending on the professor.

If you only had one case to read, perhaps this method would not create too much of a problem, but you will always have many cases to read. Moreover, you will never know which case you will be called on to speak about or which issue within a case the professor will want to discuss. While a professor may permit a student to "pass" on discussing a case every once in a blue moon, the embarrassment associated with this makes it uncomfortable, and passing is something that should be avoided. In addition to the embarrassment, passing may impact any participation grade that the professor may assign to a class. Also, it is not uncommon for professors to publicly humiliate you when you pass. Perhaps "humiliate" is a strong word, but you will leave class feeling very poorly about yourself.

I say that the Socratic method is part of what makes the experience so daunting for several reasons. First, there is an enormous amount of preparation that is required in order to be able to speak intelligently about a case when called on. Questions are often not basic, and you are often required to perform analysis on the spot. For example, a professor might ask about a particular case and then change a key fact in the case and ask you to explain how this would impact the outcome. Second, there is a significant amount of pressure to look good in front of your classmates. Remember, you are in the same classes (the entire first-year section usually takes all classes together) with all of these people for the entire first year. Third, your grade can be impacted by your performance in this area because some professors will base part of your grade on participation. Finally, many people are not used to loudly (some classes have microphones) communicating their ideas in front of eighty (or more) strangers. Surveys have shown that public speaking is the number-one fear for many people—higher on the list than death.

*Do not let the Socratic method of teaching stress you out. Everyone is in the same boat, and everyone will look unprepared at least once. As I was writing this book, I spoke to a first-year student who was so terrified of being called on that she skipped classes. One day she was so worried, she went to class and then left halfway through for fear of being called upon. This, of course, is a big mistake because attending class is key to doing well in law school.*

Luckily, the anxiety really lasts only for one term. You will be surprised at how relaxed people are after the first term when everyone realizes that being called on is not such a big deal.

There is another key thing to remember about being called on in class. The threat of being called on will actually help you because the preparation that you do every day for class will better prepare you for the final exam and the bar examination. I, for one, noticed a stark difference when I had to prepare for exams for classes that had a professor who did not use the Socratic method of teaching. (All of your first-year classes will generally be Socratic, but this changes in upper levels, where only some will be Socratic.) For classes that use the volunteer method, I would always read the cases, but did not spend the additional time to prepare for being called on. Also, it was easier to fall behind and say to myself that I could review and understand the material later. When exams came around, though, I had to work twice as hard to review and absorb the information. You will quickly learn that you cannot cram for law school the way that you may have done in college. Relax and have fun with the Socratic method!

So how do you ensure that you are prepared for this ordeal? The key to preparation is properly briefing cases.

## What Do I Have to Do Each Day to Prepare for Class?

### What Is a Brief and Why Do I Need to Brief Cases?

At the beginning of each class, the professor will usually distribute a syllabus for the course. This syllabus will contain all of the topic areas you will cover as well as the cases that you will be assigned to read. For each class, you will have several cases assigned to you, and these are the cases that the professor may ask you about in class. Unfortunately, reading and taking notes on a case usually is not sufficient to get you through being called on in class.

To prepare for this event, most students do what is called "briefing the case." A brief summarizes all of the key points of the case and does this in a manner that will likely address most of the types of questions you will be asked by your professors. The main purpose of a brief is to help you organize the material and prepare you for class, so the format is really up to you. It should, however, contain several key pieces of information. The sooner that you can master how to use and make an effective brief, the better off you will be.

## *How Do I Make a Good Brief?*

A good brief classifies the relevant parties, identifies the important issues, states what the court has decided, and explains the reason the court decided that way. While a brief can take on any format, it usually has the following headings: title, facts of the case, issues, decision of the court, court reasoning, opinions from other judges, and other analysis. Your law school will go over brief writing techniques when you start, but I will give you a very brief summary here.

The title simply states who is suing whom and is usually the case name. For example, the title might be "Smith v. Jonson." When you identify the parties, you should also state who is suing whom so that you can keep the roles straight. For example, Smith is the plaintiff (the one suing) and Jonson is the defendant (the one being sued).

The facts summarize the facts of the case, that is, they describe what the case is all about and could also include what happened in the lower courts. Often, when you are called on, a professor will first ask you to summarize the facts. Although a professor may accept you not being able to answer a question that involves application of the law, every professor expects you to be able to recite the relevant facts of a case. Remember that some cases are over forty pages long, so you have to sift through and only pick out the facts that are relevant to the decision. You will also be asked what happened in the lower courts, so you should clearly be able to state who won, who lost, and who is appealing. If these things are clearly marked in your brief, you will not have a problem reciting the information.

The next section deals with the issue or issues that were presented before the court. In the legal writing example used earlier in this chapter related to the theft of a chocolate bar, the issue was whether or not someone could be guilty of stealing if the person had put something in his or her jacket pocket but had not walked out of the store yet. You should be very familiar with what the issue or issues are, as they will drive almost everything about the case. Often, the facts that are included in the case are facts that are used to decide the issue at hand. When phrasing issues, it may help to phrase them in terms of a question that has a yes or no answer. This will often clarify how important the issue is and whether or not it is the main issue. Also, cases will often contain more than one main issue.

The decision of the court is the answer to the question or issue presented and is often called the "holding" of the case. Depending on how focused the question is, this can be as simple as a yes or no. Often, though, the holding can usually be summarized in one concise sentence. For example, the holding in our legal writing example discussed earlier is as follows: "The plaintiff is not guilty of stealing because he did not take the chocolate bar outside of the store and, as such, he did not meet the taking requirement in the statute." If you are called on, you will almost certainly be asked the holding, so this should be a prominent part of your outline. Again, given the length of some cases, you will often not have time to sort much out if you are not prepared.

The reasoning is the explanation that the court gives for its decision. For an easy case or issue, this reasoning can often be combined with the holding. For a complex case, however, judges will list several reasons why they have decided a particular way. Often these reasons are based on how other cases were decided, but sometimes the explanation is based on analogy, public policy, or the judge's own opinion. You should be familiar with the judge's reasoning and be able to communicate it to your professor when called on. A professor may also ask you whether or not you agree with the judge's reasoning and why you feel that way.

Your professor may also ask you about other opinions in the decision. For some cases, there are panels of judges, and the majority rules. For example, when cases are decided at the Supreme Court, all nine judges vote, and the group that has five votes wins. However, sometimes the four judges who lost will write what is called a dissenting opinion that states why they think the decision was flawed. While the dissenting opinion is not law, it often provides very interesting insight into the decision, and the dissenting opinions are often the subject of debate in class.

Finally, your brief may include an analysis section. This section could describe the impact of hypothetical changes, the relationship of the case to other cases, the effect that the decision may have on society, and the "correctness" of the decision. This is really a free-form section that is used to stimulate and promote thought.

*Do not use commercial briefs! Since many of the cases that you read in law school are commonly read cases, there are prepackaged briefs that you can purchase. This defeats the purpose of a brief, as a large part of the benefit associated with the document is its development. The purpose is NOT for you to just be able to answer the questions in class; you should be learning about the case as you put the brief together. Moreover, developing your own brief forces you to constantly go back to the case for details, and this will help you when it is exam time.*

An example of a good brief is included below.

### *An Outline for a Good Brief of a Case for Class*

***(Party 1) v. (Party 2)***
*(Court Name)*
*(Year)*

***Procedural Basis:***

*List the courts that the case has made its way through. You should know the procedural posture of the case including whether the case is at the trial, appeal, or other procedural level. Also, note who is the plaintiff and who is the defendant.*

**Facts:**

*Brief summary of the relevant facts. These are often summarized at the beginning of a case. A professor will often ask you to recite the key facts as the first part of his or her questioning. For example, D threw a firecracker into a crowded marketplace where it was thrown around by several people several times until it landed on plaintiff, where it exploded. Plaintiff was injured and is now suing the person who originally threw the firecracker. The person who threw the firecracker says it was not his fault, as others threw it after him.*

**Issue:**

*Use one sentence for each issue; this will usually be in the form of a question. For example, based on the above facts, did the defendant cause the injury to the plaintiff given that others touched and threw the firecracker before it injured the plaintiff?*

**Decision/Holding:**

*This should be a short answer to the question. For example, verdict for the plaintiff: defendant was liable for the natural and probable consequences of his act. Also, the injury was direct because the intermediate actors acted out of necessity, so defendant's actions had not come to rest.*

**Concurrences/Dissents:**

*At times the professor will be most interested in the dissents or explanations in the concurrences. Make sure you document them and understand them.*

**Analysis:**

*This could simply be anything interesting you wanted to note about the case, or other analysis pointed out by the judge in the case. For example, for the above case one might point out, "This case highlights the difficulty in basing liability purely on test of direct/indirect causation."*

---

*NOTE: Case briefs do not have to be long, but they should be able to jog your memory enough to be able to answer questions in class.*

---

# How to Get High Grades in Your First Year and Beyond

There is no easy fix or trick to getting good grades in law school. A silver bullet or magic pill does not exist, so do not waste your time looking for one. Instead, follow the various tips outlined in this book and you will be astonished at how well they pay off. If you buy a book that promises easy grades or a quick fix, you will waste your money; instead, there are several factors that, if combined, will help you obtain good grades.

As mentioned at the beginning of this book, the first and most important tip is to do everything in your power to get high grades in your first year. This is easier said than done, but there are several things you can do to improve your chances of success on examinations.

To make this accomplishment appear even more daunting, on your first day of class your professors will give you the surprising news that your entire grade for a course is usually made up of one final exam. This do-or-die scenario can be quite a shocker when you first hear it, but there are things that you can do to help you get an A even without formal feedback throughout the term.

A number of people have asked me how I did well in my first year. There are several reasons, which I have outlined below.

## *Go to Class, Go to Class, Go to Class*

The first—and most important—advice I can give you about doing well in your first year is to go to *each and every* class. Several people who were not doing well after the first term asked me for advice on how they could improve their grades, and invariably, they were people who did not feel that going to class was that important. I cannot tell you how many times I heard, "He just repeats what is in the textbook," or, "I go to most classes." Going to half of the classes will get you half the grade, and if you do not mind a B– or C, then do not bother going to class.

This advice is applicable for all years in law school, but it is especially true regarding the first year. Even in my third year of law school, I would read and brief a case and be surprised when I would attend class and find that I missed a significant point. In addition, often when I read cases and then subsequently went to a class, I found that I may not have paid as much attention to the part of the opinion that the professor found most interesting. If a professor finds a particular aspect of an opinion fascinating, you can bet that this aspect is what is going to show up on the exam.

For example, in some cases, the professor may find the dissent (when there is a panel of judges and the judge who loses writes about why he or she disagrees with the majority opinion) most interesting, and you may have just skimmed this to focus on what the winners said. This is just one example but rest assured that almost all professors gear their exams toward what was covered in class, which is what they found most important.

In addition, when you have decided that you will not go to class, you will not prepare. Remember those great briefs that you just read about and how much work goes into them. Even if you do prepare something, you will not be as thorough because you won't worry about getting called on to answer questions. While the Socratic method might be a bit of a pain, the good thing about it is that it keeps you up to date so that studying for the final exam is easier and will not take as much time. Time, of course, is something you will not have much of during the exam period.

When you attend class, ensure that you are there in body and in mind. What I mean by this is avoid surfing the Internet. This is further discussed later in the "Use Your Laptop Effectively" section.

*Unless you are a genius, you will do poorly in law school unless you go to class. Some people feel that they can learn everything they need to know from the textbook and do not learn anything in class. Whether or not this is true is irrelevant because the professor's exam is going to be based on what he or she teaches in class, and you will not do well if you are not there. Despite what you may think, you are learning things while in class; and going to class forces you to prepare more.*

Finally, there is one more important reason to attend class. In law school, in order to study for law school exams, almost all students make an outline. An outline integrates the key points from your class notes, your briefs, and the professor's syllabus. It is an invaluable tool, and if you do not have class notes, making an outline becomes difficult or nearly impossible. Outlines are covered in more detail in the next section and are the second key to doing well in law school.

## Make Your Own Outline

### What Is an Outline and How Do I Make One?

You should make your own outline—do not use commercial outlines. Because of the amount of material that is covered during a semester, law students develop outlines as study tools. An outline is really the class syllabus expanded to include relevant parts of your summarized notes and a summary of the relevant cases and holdings from your class briefs.

As mentioned, a key element of the outline is your class notes. In fact, most people make their outlines by starting with their notes and relating them to the syllabus. The next step is to go through the voluminous notes, eliminating any extra detail while summarizing the key rules and take-aways from each section.

Students continue to supplement the outline with information from their briefs, discussions and meetings with other students and professors, and reviews of problem sets and old exams. You will add to and review your outline right up until your exam. If you are not in class, it is virtually impossible to make your own outline, and notes from other students is a poor substitute for your own notes.

You should also note that most exams in law school are open book, so you are permitted to bring your outlines to the exam with you. That being said, there are usually time constraints in exams, so you have very limited time to use them. Also, bar examinations are not open book, so you are not allowed to use any study aids. As a result, more and more professors are banning outlines and other study aids during exams. Regardless of whether you can use them during an exam, though, they are an essential tool that has to be developed in order to study effectively for an exam.

Another key to an effective outline is the incorporation of points from past exams. Professors will often provide you with sample exams and solutions, and it is very helpful to go through these and add relevant parts of the solutions to your outline. You will find that professors only have so many ways to test certain topics, so common themes and tricks often appear year after year. Old exams are only useful if they were developed by your professor. Exams developed by other professors will not help you, and you will waste your limited time reviewing them.

An outline is usually a lengthy document and often can exceed thirty or even seventy pages. I have seen some that are one hundred pages. It is important to index and properly label the outline so that it can be an effective tool during an exam. You may also want to familiarize yourself with the various search tools on your computer because, for open-book exams, you are sometimes permitted access to your hard drive. A word search using the "find" tool in the computer application is obviously faster than flipping through fifty or more pages of a hard-copy outline.

An index to an outline that I used for one of my classes is included below.

## Index for Sample Outline

### INDEX

## *Should I Use a Commercial Outline or Make my Own?*

I started this section with the warning that you should not use commercial outlines and should instead make your own outline. You should know that for every course, there are many enterprising companies that will publish outlines. In fact, you can get most of them for free if you perform a Google search. For example, if you wanted an outline for property, you could just Google "property law outline" and several commercial outlines will pop up. There are two main problems with commercial outlines.

First, they usually just cite the black letter law, and they will not have any information specific to your class. As such, you could have a property outline that devotes a significant amount of detail to adverse possession (a topic you will learn in this course) when your professor just mentioned it in passing. If the topic was just mentioned in passing during class, it is unlikely that it will show up on an exam.

The second, and more significant problem with commercial outlines is that they stop you from making your own outline. There is a substantial benefit associated with developing your own outline, as it makes you sit down and think about what is important. There is a stark difference between developing something yourself and reading what someone else has done, and there are many studies that prove this. In my opinion, the only *very limited* use, if any, of a commercial outline is to supplement an outline that you have already completed yourself.

In my second year, I was lazy and used a commercial outline for my Corporations class, and that was my lowest grade in law school.

 *Because you will always face time constraints, you should know the material in your outline inside and out and should not use it as a crutch. This means that it should be used to jog your memory rather than be used as the sole basis of your knowledge. It is a big mistake to assume that because you have cases summarized, you can "learn" the rule of law while you are sitting for the test. While you are studying, you should treat every test as if it were closed book so that you fully understand the topics that you cover and you are not lulled into the false sense of security that you will have time to search for everything you need in your outline.*

### What if I Am Stuck and Do Not Have Time to Make my Own Outline?

There is one other type of outline that is somewhere between your own outline and a commercial outline—that is, an outline that someone else made, but for the same professor and course that you are taking. These outlines are usually available through school websites and can also be obtained by random Google searches. We have included the website for "outline depot" in the "Useful Resources" section. Believe it or not, there is a law school outline depot where you can upload your old outlines and, in return, you can select another outline from a professor you currently have that someone else has posted. I have looked at a few of these, and the quality of the outlines is generally quite good. (The submissions are reviewed by a person who works for outline depot before they are posted.) If you do not have any outlines to upload (or you do not want to give away the outline that you spent weeks working on), you can pay a small fee to download other people's outlines.

While these outlines are better than commercial outlines and may be satisfactory if you absolutely do not have time to make your own outline, I strongly suggest that you make your own outline and perhaps use these as a supplement. The outline website is quite easy to use and lets you search by both course and professor name.

Finally, your law school may have a spot on its website for uploading and downloading outlines. For example, there was a Harvard-affiliated website that stored outlines from both current and old Harvard professors. All you needed was the professor's name and course, and you were able to download the outline at no cost.

You can, of course, ask fellow classmates for their outlines but this is ill-advised. First, most people would simply say no. Second, by the time a friend in your class has completed the outline, it will likely be very close to the exam. Third, you will not get the benefit of completing your own outline. Moreover, asking someone for his or her outline borders on impertinence. It also demonstrates that you are lazy, and just asking for someone else's outline harms your reputation. The best advice I can give is to make your own outline.

### *When Should I Start Developing my Outline?*

You should start your outline approximately between one and two months, after classes start. Some people start it earlier, but it is hard to see where the class is going or to get the big picture prior to that date.

There are three primary reasons to start your outline early. First, an early start will highlight exactly which areas you do not fully understand, and this will give you ample time to get the help that you need. Second, law school information takes a fair amount of time to digest, and this early review will give you a significant advantage over other students since the outlining process forces you to systematically go though your notes and all of the cases that you have read, which reinforces and enhances your knowledge. In addition, this will help you prepare for your exams, and according to most exam schedules I have seen, you will have a couple of days at most between your classes and your first exam to study. As such, the more review and study you can do beforehand, the less you will have to do during the exam crunch. Finally, finishing the outline well ahead of your exam allows you to focus on old exams and problem sets rather than focusing on a first review of the material.

---

*You should avoid splitting up the development of an outline with other students, as this really defeats the purpose of developing your own outline. While they are time-consuming, you are studying while you are making them, and it is this process that is going to help you on exam day.*

---

### *Practice Makes Perfect, so Do Old Exams and Problem Sets*

Another key to doing well on exams is to complete as many old practice exams as you can. As I mentioned, you will only have one exam at the end of the term, and it will likely be open book. Although the exam occurs at the end of the term, you should practice much sooner. Most professors are happy to provide you with examples of their old exams, and if they do not, request that they provide them. In addition, professors will sometimes provide answer keys, which you should review after you do a practice exam.

It is important to do practice exams under exam conditions (timed and with no interruptions) as well as to solicit feedback on your answers from professors or other students. Law school exams can be tricky, and often you think that you have spotted all of the issues but students often miss several important issues.

---

**TIP** *When you are studying for final exams, do as many practice exams as you can. Ensure that you review your answers with the professor or other students, as exams can appear deceptively simple but often can be tricky. Practice exams will reinforce the material and show you if you need to spend more time in particular areas. If you do many practice exams and do well on them, you will not encounter any surprises on exam day.*

---

Also remember that you are graded on a curve, so the key is to get as many points as you can as fast as you can. Professors tend to repeat many of the same issues and tricks on exams, so old exams are a very valuable tool to help you bring those issues to the forefront. Only old exams from the professor you have are relevant, and you should not waste your time taking practice exams from other professors.

In my first year, I had a contracts class that was worth five credits (this is a very large number of credits for a course and the only five-credit course of the year). Since this professor had been teaching for years, he had many old exams available with solutions to the questions. I sat for seven of the exams under exam conditions, and it paid off—I received an A in the course. I noticed many similar types of issues coming up on the exams, and many were repeated in the final exam that I took. Members of my study group also completed all seven exams, and we all discussed possible answers afterwards. In addition, we reviewed the answer keys with the professor, and this was imperative to ensure that we covered everything. They, too, received an A in the course.

Another way to improve your score on exams through practice is by completing problem sets that you can get from your professors. Law can be a deceptively simple thing, and it is best learned through application. This is really the case for all courses, but in particular for some of the more technical or difficult courses like Civil Procedure, Constitutional Law, and Property. Problem sets are similar to old exams in that they give you that practical application that really shows you whether you understand the material. Also, if a professor takes the time to develop problem sets, you can rest assured that his or her exams will be patterned after those problem sets.

During my first year, many students were having trouble with Constitutional Law, as it was one of those courses in which the law seemed straightforward but the application was tough. My excellent Constitutional Law teacher asked the students for feedback on how he could improve the course, and many said that we needed to apply the concept more rather than just learn the theory. As a result, he developed a number of problem sets that helped us to better understand the law. I was pleasantly surprised at how similar some of those problem sets were to questions on the final exam. I was lucky because I did the problem sets beforehand and received feedback from the professor on my answers during office hours. Many students did not even look at the problem sets, and they saw the questions for the first time when they sat for the final exam.

## Find a Good Study Group

### Should I Look For a Study Group?

Another factor that contributes to success in your first year is a good study group. I was fortunate to have a great study group. The three of us studied together for each of our first-year exams, and the study group experience was extremely positive.

A study group is important because it is nearly impossible to absorb all of the possible angles of all of the cases by yourself. In addition, even if you are the best note taker in the world, you will probably miss some important points that your study partners will help you understand. I often sat for exams that covered the exact points of clarification that my study group informed me about just prior to taking the exam. The group definitely improved my grades, and I also helped them as well.

### How Do I Select a Good Study Group?

The selection of a good study group is tough. You obviously want to find smart people, but you also want to avoid the obnoxious people who will monopolize the entire session with their inane ideas. Also, you want people who are conscientious and will come to the sessions prepared and ready to contribute. Finally, you also want people you get along with to make the pain of intense studying a bit more pleasant.

So how do you pick? Here are a few pointers.

Regarding the selection of someone smart, remember that the people who are the most vocal in class are not necessarily the people who do the best on exams. More often than not, you will find that the person who receives the highest grade in your class is a person who has not said a word all semester. Perhaps this is because the quiet type is often paying attention and is not distracted by what he or she is going to say next. As such, do not discount someone because they do not speak in class, as they may be exactly the type of person you would like as a study partner. Both of the people in my study group were very smart and did not say a word in class unless they were called on.

Another thing to consider regarding finding a smart person is that some people who did very well in their undergraduate studies may not grasp law school very well. As such, it is tough to really know who is "smart" from who is not, and you will really have to go with your gut.

To sum up my opinion on finding the right people for a study group, I will say that you do not need the people in the class with the highest grades but rather the people who work hard and have assimilated all of the information throughout the year. These people will be excellent members of your study group.

Also, it is important to find someone you can coexist with for a long period of time. I remember many long nights in my first year, and it was nice to spend them with people who did not get on my nerves. I still regularly go out to dinner with my study group, and I am sure we will be lifelong friends who shared a very positive bonding experience.

### What Should You Look Out For When Selecting a Study Group? Beware of the Barnacle!

Beware of the barnacle. He or she is the person that latches on to your study group and you just cannot get rid of them. This person wants to join your study group so that he or she can benefit from all of the work you have done, but this person is a freeloader. The barnacle usually contributes nothing and will actually waste your time. Moreover, he or she will irritate you and stress you out. My excellent study group during my first year attracted a barnacle, and we finally got rid of him after the second exam.

Unfortunately, it is hard to identify a barnacle, as this person usually puts forth a very good sales job. A good first clue is when the barnacle repeatedly suggests exchanging outlines before any work is done. The barnacle at my school suggested exchanging outlines even before we had our first meeting, and we all thought that was a bit odd.

So how did the barnacle gain access? The barnacle seemed to know what he was talking about, so we let him in. Once in, the barnacle consistently missed scheduled appointments, showed up late, and came unprepared for every meeting. He also invited others to the meeting, and the invitees were not helpful. In fact, during the few meetings we had with him, the barnacle would frantically take notes as if we were in class and we were his professors.

The barnacle also had a different excuse each day to explain why he was either absent or did not complete an assigned task. The excuses ranged from things like the dog ate his homework to life-threatening surgery. I could write a book about the excuses, but it would quickly bore you like his excuses bored us.

In addition to being alert to the barnacle, you should also not select someone who always misses classes. If a person misses classes, he or she will miss study sessions. Moreover, a person who never attends class will not be able to fill you in on points that you may have missed during class because they will not have class notes.

Also, be careful of the "holdout." Holdouts will join your group to take what they can get but will be silent even when they have relevant things to share. Unfortunately, some are preoccupied with the curve and think that any information they share with anyone (even their study group) will mean a lower grade for them. Everyone in your study group can get an A, and it is very unlikely that any assistance you give to other members of your group is going to have any effect whatsoever on your grade.

## What Do People Do in a Study Group?

A study group meets to review and discuss the cases and material assigned in class. The group normally meets prior to the examination period, but at times meetings can occur if there is a particularly difficult topic that is covered in class. The meetings usually are not brainstorming sessions or traditional studying, and it is a good idea to meet after all members of the group have had a sufficient amount of time to review and digest the material. In some cases, meetings occur after each member in the group has completed the same practice exam so that the group can compare answers.

So what are the logistics for a study group? One model for a study group is to meet once all people in the study group have made significant progress on their outlines prior to the examination period. This ensures that everyone is prepared and provides a solid foundation to review the material. In addition, the development of the outlines may prompt discussion about many of the topics that may appear on the exam.

After the outlines have been substantially completed, the meeting should involve going through areas that members of the group found difficult. This is an excellent way to really see if you understand the material, and you can use the discussion to supplement your outline. Also, a good way for you to figure out how well you know the material is to see if you can explain a topic to another member of the study group.

Once the outlines are almost done and you have met a few times to discuss them (and if you trust your study group), exchange outlines. Trust is important here, as you do not want your outlines distributed to the entire class, so be clear with your study group that you do not want your outline given to others. It is a great idea to exchange them with your study group because the outlines will serve as a good review prior to the exam and you will always find things that you missed.

Two key things to remember here. First, only exchange outlines once you have completed a thorough outline, as making your own outline is the key to success. Second, do not give your outline to people outside of your study group. This advice may seem obvious, but you will be surprised at the sob stories you will hear when exams approach. Do not let people take advantage of you by getting the benefit of the hard work that you have done. Also, you are not really helping your classmates because they would be much better off making their own outlines. Do not reward their laziness.

## Get to Know Your Professor

Most grading in law school is done anonymously, but it is still important to get to know your professors for a few reasons. First, they are the people who will develop your exams, and unlike in college—where you get many opportunities to see what exams will be like—it is a one-shot deal at law school. As such, it is important to really understand their style and get a good understanding of what they are looking for. One way of doing this is to visit them and ask questions about topics that you do not understand.

In addition, when you go over old exams, you should meet with your professor and see what he or she thought of your response. Professors are often willing to go the extra mile for students and are really encouraged by a student's eagerness and drive. Also, most professors are fascinated by the material, and this is why they became law school professors. I remember that my Constitutional Law professor gave us problem sets and told students that he would read and grade their responses so that they knew which areas they had to improve on before the exam. He is one example of a fantastic professor.

It is also important to get to know your professors because you may need their recommendation at a later stage. For example, you require at least two letters from professors for all of the following: judicial clerkship applications, most fellowships, an application to transfer to a different law school, an LL.M. or JSD application, some teaching assistant positions, and any teaching position. You will find that it is very easy to cultivate a relationship with a professor, and meeting and interacting with that professor both in and out of the classroom will actually go as far as, and in some cases further than, getting a high grade in their class. Before I started at Harvard Law School, in terms of a reference I asked three of my professors to write me letters, and they were all happy to do so.

---

 *It is important that you get to know your professors. During my last year at Harvard, I spoke to a student who said she was interested in performing a judicial clerkship after she graduated but had not yet applied. I asked her why, and she said that she had not cultivated any relationships with any professors, so she would not be able to get the two required letters of recommendation. Do not let this happen to you.*

---

## Do Not Borrow Time from Subsequent Exam Questions

Another key to law school success is time management on exams. This is yet another area on which person after person will offer the same advice, but during the time crunch of an exam, many reject it. Here is the key piece of advice yet again. At the beginning of an exam, take note of how much each question is worth and divide your time accordingly. Once you have done this, DO NOT BORROW TIME FROM OTHER QUESTIONS. Although it is hard to do, you should get into the habit of noting the time, and once the time is up on a question, you should stop and move on to the next question; if you are mid-sentence, however, go ahead and finish that up before moving on to the next question.

There are a few good reasons for this strategy. First, you have likely picked up the majority of the points you will gain on the question you are laboring over, and the time you will spend will likely not yield many more points. Second, if you do not move on from a question you are stuck on, you may not finish the exam, and a blank exam question means a low grade. Third, the subsequent questions on the exam may be easy. When I sat for the New York Bar, the last question on the exam was a very simple corporations question. If I had borrowed time from the first few more difficult questions, though, I would have missed easy points on that last question. At the end of the day, a point is a point, and I will gladly take an easy question that takes me one minute rather than ten minutes. Finally, you can always go back to a question if you have time. This is a far better strategy, and the break from the question may even give you alternate ways to approach the question when you return to it.

This was one of the first pieces of advice that my first law school professor, Linda Feldman, gave the class for my first law school exam. Regrettably, many of my classmates did not listen to her. The exam was made up of two questions, and each of them was equally weighted. The first question was tough, and I could have spent the full exam period trying to nail it down, but instead I stopped writing after half of the time and moved on to the second question. The second question was almost identical to a question that the class had gone over during a review of an old exam, so it was easy to pick up easy points. I ended up with an A on the exam, but many of my fellow classmates left the exam barely touching the second question.

## Use Your Laptop Effectively

A laptop can both hurt and help you in law school. It can help you because laptops are an efficient way to take notes in class, thus enabling you to record more of what the professor says. This, of course, assumes that you know how to type. In addition to note taking, electronic copies of documents like your briefs and your notes make the outlining process much more streamlined.

If you use your laptop to sit for examinations, you will have a significant advantage over those who handwrite their exam. You may be able to use search tools when looking for things on your outline. Also, you will likely get a higher number of points because you are often awarded more points on law school exams if you write more. Given that most people can type faster than they can write, the advantages are clear. One of my professors performed an informal study and concluded that those who typed their exams scored significantly higher than those who handwrote them.

While a laptop can be an effective tool, it can also hurt you as it can serve as a distraction. Unfortunately, most law schools are fully equipped with full access to the Internet, and most students with laptops are connected during class. At any given point, while you are in class, you can survey the room and see people shopping, watching (and listening) to sports, planning vacations, and even watching xxx-rated broadcasts. (Believe it or not I have seen this.) Although some think that they are great at multitasking, it is scientifically proven that you will not retain much of what the professor is saying if you are surfing the Internet.

To get the most out of class, you should disconnect the wireless feature on your laptop and avoid connecting to the Internet. Even short stints on the Internet can make you miss important things that the professor is saying.

In addition, surfing the Web is distracting to other students and disrespectful to the professor. Do not think that your professor is fooled and thinks you are paying attention when you are on the Internet. It is obvious to him or her and obvious to your classmates. Moreover, why pay over $40,000 per year to play on the Internet? You could do that for free. In fact, the problem of surfing is becoming so bad that some professors are banning the use of laptops altogether. This was the case for my Criminal Procedure class and others. This is unfortunate given the efficiency advantages of using a laptop.

## Participation During Law School Classes

Should you participate in class discussions in law school? You will of course have to participate when you are called on, but the question is how much you should participate in class when your grade does not depend on it.

There are two schools of thought here. First, you could avoid participating in class. The big advantage here is that you will remain focused on what the professor is saying and will avoid distractions associated with anxiety and what you are going to say next. This could have the impact of improving your note-taking ability, which may suffer if you are "on stage." This may be beneficial, especially if you experience anxiety when speaking.

In addition, while not empirical, it has been my experience that the people who are at the top of a law school class are often the people who you do not hear a word from during classes. In fact, during my first year of law school, the people who received the Center for Computer-Assisted Legal Instruction (CALI) (an organization that awards for the highest grade in a course) awards for the highest grade in the class were all people who did not say a word all semester other than when they were called on by the professor. This is not to say that there is definitively a relationship between silence and high grades, but it is something to consider.

The final argument for remaining silent relates to the controversy surrounding some of the discussion. Although I was quiet during my first year, I must say that there were several people in my class who I avoided like the plague because I did not like what they said in class. While commentary in class is often not meant to be offensive, it can often come across as such. Remember that the law touches on very controversial issues such as abortion, human rights, sexuality, national security, gender, and many other topics. I guess it is human nature to stay away from people you disagree with, and giving your honest opinion (even when you may not feel that strongly about it) could engender negative feelings toward you.

The other school of thought, however, also has strong arguments for the benefits of participating in class. First, participation will improve your oral advocacy skills, which can be important for a lawyer. For some of the people who received top grades in my first-year class, it became apparent when we did moot court competitions that their oral advocacy skills needed work. Remember that, depending on your job, oral advocacy can ultimately be important in both the corporate and litigation arenas, so anything you can do to improve this skill will help you in the long run.

Second, participation is fun and will enhance your law school experience. During my first year, I was very quiet, although I was one of those people who received the highest grade in a course (Criminal Law) and did not say a word unless I was called on. In my second year, however, I was a bit more relaxed and regularly participated. I cannot stress enough how much fun participating was and how it enhanced my experience. Also, I learned more as I asked questions about things that confused me. Moreover, I engaged in constructive debate with classmates and professors, which improved my analytical skills.

Third, participation can help you develop a strong relationship with a professor. A word of warning, though: Professors are all academics, so irrelevant or poorly-thought-out participation will not help you much. If you do participate in a thoughtful manner, though, this will go far, and you may be able to use the professor as a reference. In many regards, good participation in a class will go further in terms of a very positive reference letter than a top grade in the class.

Another strong argument for participation is that it may impact your grade. Many professors will use participation to raise or lower your grade and this is very common. In terms of the process, exams are usually graded anonymously, and then the grades along with the student names are given to the professor to make any participation adjustments. Usually, a lack of participation will only negatively impact your grade if you fail to answer when you are called on. It is, however, very common for professors to increase grades based on good participation. Moreover, a few professors include participation as a regular component of the grade.

## Use the School Services

Your law school wants you to succeed, and it will provide you with resources to help you. While most people do not take full advantage of the services offered, others reap a significant amount of benefits from them. When looking for academic coaching, your first stop should be the professor and/or the teaching assistant. In addition to these individuals, your school will most likely have someone in charge of academic advising.

At Brooklyn Law School there is an excellent academic advisor, and several students who were not doing well in their courses used her as a resource to improve their grades. Her services range from general counseling and explanation of study aids to a detailed review of student exams. Your school may also have mentor programs where you can get similar advice and support from either other students or faculty. These services are included in your tuition, and you should take advantage of them. It is important to seek help immediately when you feel you are in trouble; at times even a pep talk can put you back on the right track.

Below is an example of some of the programs offered to help students at Brooklyn Law School, according to its website:

> *We offer a range of classes and programs to help you maximize your potential as you encounter the rigors of law school. Our goal is to promote an environment of learning through practicing the essential skills that are vital to your success as a lawyer.*
>
> *Our Academic Success Program includes:*
> - *Summer legal process class*
> - *Legal writing support program, English as a second language, and grammar workshops*

- *Seminar paper workshops*
- *Academic success workshops*
- *Case reading, briefing, and study skills*
- *Outlining*
- *Exam skills*
- *Scholarly journal*
- *One-on-one exam review workshops*

You should also check to see if your school offers any type of preparatory course during the summer before you start law school. Brooklyn Law School offers an excellent summer preparation course at no cost to certain students. The program targets certain groups such as minorities and people who have been out of school for many years and offers a firsthand look at what law school life will be like. The class reviews several cases that look at the development of case law as it relates to product liability, and students also learn how to write a legal memo and brief a case.

This type of course provides a solid foundation, shows what law school will be like, and really just lets students figure things out before they are inundated with work for four or five classes. This can be a good and more relaxed time to figure things out, as most people are quite stressed out by the time October arrives. As such, for those who are nervous about starting and want some extra help, check to see if your school offers something similar and try to get into one of these classes. Brooklyn Law School offers this course at no cost and gives students two academic credits.

### Dedicate Sufficient Time to Your Legal Writing Course

Let's not forget about the importance of legal writing and the legal writing course. As discussed in the section on first-year courses, legal writing is a foundational course that shows you how to write legal documents, analyze legal issues, and take law school exams. I have also included it in this section because your legal writing course is one of the keys to success in law school. If you can master the skills that are taught in this course, you will win most of the battle.

---

*Do not let the fact that the legal writing course is only worth one or two credits stop you from providing a sufficient amount of attention to this course.*

---

## Keep on Top of the Material and Be Strategic

A key to success is organization and planning. Moreover, it is essential to stay on top of the material and do the work as it is assigned. Given the amount of material you will cover in your classes, you *cannot* cram for law school; if you attempt to do what you did in college, you will not be successful.

A disorganized student will do very poorly in law school, and since the workload in your first year is heavy, you will need a good system for ensuring that you are keeping up with your classes. You should use a diary or calendar as well as a planning worksheet. The worksheet simply maps out your day and will ensure that you know when you have free time available and get done what you need to get done. The worksheet is great because it also identifies good times to get in extra studying. For example, you might realize that you have an extra half hour between two classes, and you can use this half hour to read or brief a case. It is essential to use these short breaks effectively, as the reading assignments are often long and you will retain more if you break it up.

*You should ensure that you are devoting the proper amount of time to each course. I cannot tell you how many times I have seen students spend all their time and effort on a two-credit course and ignore their five-credit course. This is a mistake. First, you should not ignore any course. Second, you should divide your time proportionately so that a five-credit course gets the attention it deserves.*

It is important that I reiterate one word of warning regarding the last tip. Legal writing is a one- or two-credit course, but you should treat it as if it were worth four or five credits for several reasons. First, it is a foundational course that will teach you how to write as a lawyer. Not only will you use this in the future, but you have to write the same way on most of your exams throughout law school. Second, although the course is only worth two credits, you have to do the second part in the spring term and that is worth another two credits. As the second course builds on the first, a poor grade in the first part may result in a poor grade in the second part, and you cannot afford to have four credits reflecting a poor or mediocre grade. Finally, the small class size makes it a perfect class to bond with your professor and try to secure a reference letter later on. As class sizes are often around fifteen students, you will not get lost in the crowd here. In other classes, there may be eighty students who all want the professor to write them a letter.

*Organization is something that you will struggle with in law school, as you will almost never have enough time to complete everything. Take comfort in the fact that EVERYONE in your class is in the same boat. You may encounter people who claim to have had time to read every case thoroughly and who claim to have briefed every case like a pro. They are not being honest and are likely trying to stress you.*

An example of a planning chart that you can use to manage your time is included below.

## *Planning Chart Sample for a Monday*

| Time (Week 1) | Mon. | Tues. | Wed. | Thur. | Fri. | Sat. | Sun. |
|---|---|---|---|---|---|---|---|
| 6:00 | Sleep | | | | | | |
| 6:30 | Sleep | | | | | | |
| 7:00 | Sleep | | | | | | |
| 7:30 | Sleep | | | | | | |
| 8:00 | Breakfast | | | | | | |
| 8:30 | Train to School | | | | | | |
| 9:00 | Crim. Law | | | | | | |
| 9:30 | Crim. Law | | | | | | |
| 10:00 | Brief Case | | | | | | |
| 10:30 | Contracts | | | | | | |
| 11:00 | Contracts | | | | | | |
| 11:30 | Contracts | | | | | | |
| 12:00 | Lunch | | | | | | |
| 12:30 | Lunch | | | | | | |
| 1:00 | Brief Case | | | | | | |
| 1:30 | Lexis Training | | | | | | |
| 2:00 | Reading Crim. | | | | | | |
| 2:30 | Reading Crim. | | | | | | |
| 3:00 | Reading Crim. | | | | | | |

| Time (Week 1) | Mon. | Tues. | Wed. | Thur. | Fri. | Sat. | Sun. |
|---|---|---|---|---|---|---|---|
| 3:30 | Civ. Pro. | | | | | | |
| 4:00 | Civ. Pro. | | | | | | |
| 4:30 | Civ. Pro. | | | | | | |
| 5:00 | Break | | | | | | |
| 5:30 | Break | | | | | | |
| 6:00 | Dinner | | | | | | |
| 6:30 | Dinner | | | | | | |
| 7:00 | Brief Cases for Tues. | | | | | | |
| 7:30 | Brief Cases for Tues. | | | | | | |
| 8:00 | Brief Cases for Tues. | | | | | | |
| 8:30 | Reading Crim. | | | | | | |
| 9:00 | Reading Crim. | | | | | | |
| 9:30 | Reading Contracts | | | | | | |
| 10:00 | TV | | | | | | |
| 10:30 | TV | | | | | | |
| 11:00 | Relax | | | | | | |
| 11:30 | Sleep | | | | | | |
| 12:00 | Sleep | | | | | | |

## *Application, Application, Application—Everyone Knows the Law, So You Have to Apply the Facts*

On every exam you will be given a fact pattern and then asked a very general question. In some cases, the question may simply be, "Discuss the liability of each party," "Discuss," or "Does John or Mary have a case?" For all of these scenarios, though, you will be required to use the good old IRAC (Issue, Rule, Application, and Conclusion), and you will usually have many issues on one exam. My Contracts exam had no less than fifty issues, and of course some were more significant than others. In the section on the first-year Legal Writing, we discussed the stolen chocolate bar example and went over the meaning of IRAC. What you should also know is the distribution of points in any given question. For each issue, points are generally distributed as follows:

| | |
|---|---|
| I (Issue) | 25% (for identifying or spotting the correct issue) |
| R (Rule) | 5% |
| **A (Application of Facts)** | **65%** |
| C (Conclusion) | 5% |

Yes, *almost all of the grades in a question are given for the application of the facts*. As such, if you jump to a conclusion and answer the question (e.g., "John Is Guilty of Theft"), then you may get five percent of the points. (Perhaps more, as the conclusion includes a bit of the issue.) The point, though, is that the key to doing well on law school exam questions is taking a look at ALL of the facts (often a fact would not be in the question if it was not relevant) and applying those facts. Remember that almost everyone in your class knows the rule or law, so the application of the facts is the only way to test whether a student truly understands the material. Once you read a question, take a few minutes to plan out your answer and jot down what the key issues are. After that, reread the question and look at EVERY fact and think about how that fact is going to be relevant for the application. You will quickly see how this will pay off.

## Do Not Stress Yourself Out! Have Confidence in Yourself and You Will Succeed

Many people who start law school quickly become overwhelmed. This stems from the volume of the material, the Socratic method of teaching, and the lack of familiarity with the subject matter. I know someone who started at Harvard and became so stressed that he had to leave after his first term. I know another person who, in her first term of law school, sent me a text message at 5 A.M. in November, convinced she was going to fail out of school. At most law schools, you will ultimately do fine, so do not let the law school experience get the better of you and do not let a few poor grades discourage you.

There are several reasons you should keep your head up. First, know that everyone is in the same boat and is stressed and adapting to the new way of doing things. Second, you will probably not fail. I am not just being nice when I say this but rather basing this on fact. Ladies and gentlemen, listen up!

You should realize that you will likely not fail out of law school unless you want to. According to the American Bar Association, the national academic attrition rate is four percent, and another nine percent leave law school for non-academic reasons. While the national average for attrition rates is four percent, the rates can vary significantly by school. As such, you should check the attrition rates by school by reviewing the website listed in the "Useful Resources" section. As I explained, the curve system makes a fail completely discretionary, and those who fail either did not sit for the exam or sat for the exam and wrote next to nothing. During my first year, there was one student who would sit for all of the three-hour exams and leave after one hour. Even he did not fail—he was awarded a solid C average.

The person who sent me a text at 5 A.M. was stressed about law school and had not even sat for an exam yet. The text that she sent had to do with a legal writing memo that she did not submit. It is ironic that her failing grade on that memo was a direct result of simply not handing it in, as the school penalized students one grade point every day the memo was late. I explained to her that if she had submitted the memo, the poorest grade she would have received was a C, and it was unlikely that she would have even received such a poor grade given that she was awarded a B on the first memo she submitted. Because she submitted the memo over two weeks late, her grade was really zero, since she lost every possible point due to the penalty. Regrettably, the day after her first exam (she did not even receive the grade), she ended up quitting law school even though she really wanted to be a lawyer.

The other student who dropped out of Harvard Law School after the first term returned in the second year when he was a bit calmer, and he successfully graduated and passed the bar exam on his first attempt.

The point of these examples is simple. You will succeed in law school, and the only way to fail is if you lose your self-confidence and stress yourself out so much that you are unable to perform.

## *Proper Use of Study Guides and Course Supplements*

Every law school course has several supplements you can purchase, and they are usually quite expensive. The guides that summarize the black letter law and provide further explanation of what is in your textbooks are called hornbooks and are useful for some courses. Often the hornbooks also point out the main points of the cases that you have read so that you can focus on what is important.

I purchased several supplements while in law school, but given the regular assigned reading and the workload, I often did not have time to read them. I am embarrassed to say how many I purchased that I did not even open. I believe I purchased them because I thought I would be at a disadvantage if I did not. Obviously I was wrong, as I did not read them and it did not impact my grades.

If you have time to read hornbooks, they can usually take complex topics and boil them down to understandable jargon. You will not need them for every course, so you should consider using them only when you are having trouble. However, there are two situations where a hornbook is essential. First, Constitutional Law is a tough course to take in your first year. There were often times when I read a very long case and did not understand a word. I found that the hornbook written by Erwin Chemerinsky was excellent, and many other students agree. It explained things in lay terms and it was often the difference between understanding or not. Another instance when a hornbook is important is when the professor is not that great. Unfortunately, it will take time for this to become evident, but if you are having trouble even figuring out what the legal rules are, it is time to get a hornbook. The professor of one of my courses during my first year was quite poor, and I found the hornbook extremely valuable because it permitted me to self-teach what I did not understand in class (which was most of what was taught). I still attended class, but I used the hornbook to explain what I was not understanding from class.

At the end of the day, if a hornbook helps you and you have money to buy them and time to read them, use them. Every little bit helps, and your first year is the year to master as much as you can. Also, I still use my Contracts hornbook when I am researching issues. Remember that your first-year courses are foundational courses covering topics that will show up in future courses. Moreover, the topics are tested on the bar, so you should do whatever it takes to master the subject matter.

Another problem with hornbooks is that they are expensive. As such, if you can borrow a hornbook rather than buying one, you should do that. You can always decide to purchase it later if you want to, and if you do not like it, you will have saved yourself between fifty and one hundred dollars.

---

 *Hornbooks are supplements to the textbook and often can be helpful. Unfortunately, they are expensive and you will often not have time to read them. Also, you should be careful and select hornbooks only when you need them. If you fully understand what is going on in a course, your hornbook will likely sit on your shelf collecting dust. If you can, borrow a hornbook or sign it out of the library. You will save money, and you can always buy the book later if it is helpful.*

---

I have included a list of some of the better supplements for first-year courses that you can buy if you are interested. These are just examples, and you should ask your professor which one he or she recommends. To be safe and ensure that the book will be relevant for your course, be sure to ask your professor before purchasing it.

### *List of Good Hornbooks**

1. Civil Procedure: Glannon (*Examples and Explanations*), Moore (*Moore's Federal Practice*)
2. Contracts: Farnsworth (*Contracts*), Blum (*Example and Explanations*), Corbin (*Corbin on Contracts*)
3. Property: Sprankling (*Understanding Property Law*), Powell (*The Law of Real Property*)

---

*Before buying, check to see if there are treatises that are available on Westlaw or Lexis. These may not cost you anything since you will get a student account for free.

4. Torts: Epstein (*Introduction to Torts*), Abraham (*The Forms and Functions of Tort Law*), Keeton (*Prosser and Keeton on Torts*)

5. Criminal Law: Dressler (*Understanding Criminal Law*), Robinson (*Criminal Law*)

6. Constitutional Law: Chemerinsky (*Constitutional Law Principles and Policies*) **HIGHLY RECOMMENDED**

## More Important Things About Your First Year

### Law Review, Journals, and Moot Court

Many students ask whether they should participate in other first-year activities like law review and moot court. The short answer is yes, and I will explain why below.

In addition to getting high grades, there are a number of other activities in your first year that are important. Some of them may seem like extracurricular or optional activities, but you may miss out if you do not participate. Although grades are important, you will quickly realize that a traditional curve allows for approximately thirty percent of the class to score an A– and above. What this means then is that in any given year where the entering class is, for example 500 people, you may have up to 150 of those people who only have some form of A on their transcript.

When I was ranked in my first year, I had a grade of A in almost every course. The only courses that I did not receive an A in were courses in which I received an A+ and B+. This gave me a GPA of 3.96, and even with this high GPA, I was ranked four out of fifty-four people.

The above discussion all boils down to the fact that, even with good grades, there is plenty of competition out there, so you will need other things to supplement your grades and make you stand out.

Since this is an extremely important point, I will reiterate the importance of doing well in your first year. It is essential that you keep in mind that your grades and other activities in first year will, in many cases, decide the job that you get when you graduate. For example, your first year will determine whether you get a judicial clerkship, whether you can transfer to a higher ranked school, whether you are eligible for law review, what type of summer employment you will get, what your scholarship opportunities will be, and your ultimate full-time job. As such, it is important to increase your chances of being noticed by participating in law review, moot court, research with professors, pro-bono work, or school organizations. Law review and moot court will both be explained in future sections, so do not worry if they are not clear now.

There are several reasons why participation in these activities during your first year is important. First, since most students do not have much work experience, participation in these activities demonstrates to an employer that a person can juggle more than just his or her classes. Also, most of these activities, like law review and moot court, are competition-based, so admission and participation is restricted to top students—and employers know this. As such, your participation can be used as a significant marketing tool and will greatly enhance your job prospects. In addition, participation shows initiative, and this is always a selling point for prospective employers.

Second, participation in these areas will enhance your legal skills and make you a better lawyer, as most of them involve practical tasks that lawyers do on a day-to-day basis. Like anything, practice makes perfect and these activities are a good way to apply some of the theory that you will learn in your first-year classes.

Third, for some activities, you will be paid and/or receive critical acclaim. For example, as a research assistant, in addition to obtaining legal expertise, you will be paid well above minimum wage. Also, if you participate in moot court and win, you will significantly enhance your oral advocacy skills and also receive national recognition and prizes. These prizes or critical acclaim can also be used as leverage and a marketing tool on a resume for employers, scholarship applications, transfer applications, or any other academic pursuit that you may choose.

Finally, these activities are fun. While you will be busy in your first year, some of these activities can break up the monotony of everyday law studies. In addition, you will meet and interact with more people who share common interests. Activities such as moot court are truly fascinating and fun.

## Journals and Law Review

Every law school has student-run journals or law reviews that publish law articles and notes. The journals focus on scholarly legal writing and can either be general or specific. A general journal is usually called the law review for the school. For example, Harvard and Brooklyn Law School both have a law review with articles that are written by students, professors, and practitioners. These articles are published in one of the two to four volumes that are issued each year. A journal can also be specific. For example, Harvard's *Human Rights Journal* publishes scholarly articles that are based on topics associated with human rights. Also, Brooklyn Law School's *International Journal* focuses on law topics that have an international focus.

The staff of these journals are usually made up of students, and there will often be a faculty member (or members) who act as advisors. The students then form a board, and various titles are allocated to the various board members. For example, at Harvard, I was a primary editor on the *Human Rights Journal*. The board usually jointly decides which articles or notes they are going to publish by reviewing the numerous submissions that they receive. Other titles may include president, managing editor, and executive editor. In addition, while some law schools permit students to join a journal in their first year, others reserve this "privilege" for the second year.

The submission process is centralized and automated, so any given school will usually receive a large number of submissions. Like everything else, the journals are ranked, and those who submit articles for publication often try to get their paper published with journals that are highly ranked. If you submit a note or article to a journal and the staff of that journal likes what you have done, it will extend an offer to you to publish your article and give you a certain amount of time to respond.

---

**TIP**

*The best time to publish a paper is when you are in law school. This saves you money (you have to pay to submit notes to journals when you are not in law school), and the staff of a journal will look at your work as a student. If you wait until you are out of law school, you will have to be an expert before a journal will look at your work.*

---

## Should I Participate in a Journal in my First Year?

Depending on the school you attend, you may have the opportunity to volunteer for a position on a journal during your first year. The available spots are usually "sub-cite" positions, which means your job is to check all of the references that are made in one of the articles that has been submitted to the journal. To summarize the process, an author submits his or her article to the journal, the journal accepts the submission, the author agrees that he or she wants to publish with that journal, the sub-citers and editors thoroughly edit and review the article, and the article gets published.

The cite checking process is done by the most junior members of the team and is intended to primarily verify the accuracy of the author's claims and ensure stylistic consistency. To this end, a sub-citer's role is to check the content of each footnote to ensure that the cited source says what the author claims it says and to ensure that the citation is technically accurate. This usually means going through a very long article and ensuring that there are no grammar or spelling mistakes, ensuring that quotes and references are accurate and also making sure that each footnote adheres to the proper *Bluebook* citation rules. My published article contained over 300 footnotes in the end, and the document was just over fifty pages.

Now I am not going to lie to you; I did not enjoy sub-citing and I did not love my job as an editor on the *Human Rights Journal*. That being said, though, there are some very good reasons to join a journal in your first year if this is an option.

First, you will become very technically proficient with footnotes, formatting, and citations. This is a very important skill as a lawyer because lawyers are extremely anal and there is a specified format for everything. The formatting "Bible" is called the *Bluebook*, and you are required to format and footnote in accordance with this book. The *Bluebook* is so common in legal circles that "bluebooking" can be used as a verb. You will be briefly introduced to the *Bluebook* when you take your legal writing course, and if you sub-cite you will become an expert. This skill will not only help you in your legal writing course but will also help you if you work at a firm or any other organization that engages in litigation.

Second, you will enhance your research ability while working on a journal. In addition to cite checking, you will also be asked to conduct research to ensure that the assertions made by the author are true and/or to assess whether the author is accurately summarizing the holding of cases. This can involve using search tools such as Lexis or Westlaw, and these tools will be used throughout your career as a lawyer. Legal research goes hand-in-hand with legal writing, so the sooner you become proficient at this, the better.

Third, when you work on a journal, you are afforded the opportunity to see hundreds of articles and notes that are submitted in hopes of being published. Out of the hundreds of works that are submitted, a committee will decide which ones get published. As part of this process, you may participate in the decision-making process and you may hear why some papers are selected and others rejected. This experience will give you valuable experience on how to put together effective papers, which may assist you if you choose to publish some day.

Finally, your membership on a journal is an extracurricular activity that prospective employers, other academic institutions, and judges look very favorably upon. Even though the tasks in your first year may not be that glamorous, everyone knows that the experience provides you with a skill set that will make you a better lawyer. Moreover, if you take board positions in your second and third year, you will gain valuable experience that will be marketable.

## How Do I Join Law Review or a Journal in my Second Year?

### What Is a Law Review Competition and Should I Participate?

In your first year, some schools afford you the opportunity to volunteer for a journal. In your second year, however, the stakes rise as you will typically have to compete for a spot on a journal. While there are some variations at different schools, most schools have a law review or journal competition immediately after the first year of law school ends.

So what is involved in the competition? Almost immediately after you sit for your final exams, the school will put together a multi-page package that consists of a number of cases. Over a period of several days, you will be required to write a comment or note on the package in a traditional law journal format, almost as if you were submitting a note for publication.

Make no mistake; the competition takes lots of time, and you will find that you spend all of the time you are given working on your assignment. After you submit the assignment, it is graded by current journal board members who decide whether to extend an offer to you to join the journal or law review. In some cases, you can "grade in." This means that the journal will accept you solely based on your first-year grades, and this is yet another reason to strive for high grades in your first year.

The comment or note that you will write is significantly different from any essay that you have written in the past, and you will have to learn the proper techniques before you start. Luckily, all law schools recognize this and hold comprehensive training programs to prepare students for the competition. It is very important to pay attention to the exact instructions that will be given to you at these sessions. They will tell you not only what they want to see in terms of content but also what the format should be. Divergence from the rules will likely mean that you are not accepted to the law review, and this would be a shame given the amount of work that will go into the competition and the benefits associated with being accepted.

**TIP** *A successful law review competition note is one that follows the instructions that are given by the school. While originality may make you feel better, this is not the time for it. Make sure that you follow both the content and format instructions. Although content is obviously important, things like going over the word limit, using incorrect font, or improper bluebooking will all be severely penalized.*

I participated in the law review competition in my first year and was fortunate enough to receive an offer to join the law review. I have included my successful submission, following. Keep in mind that the document is out of context without the case package that the school provided to us. As such, you should simply skim this document to get an idea of what a successful submission looks like.

## *Example of Successful Law Review Competition Submission*

### *Introduction*

    *In 2007, the nation along with the rest of the world became painfully aware of a national housing crisis that resulted primarily from poor lending practices. These practices included, inter alia, banks that gave mortgages to prospective home buyers that exceeded the purchase price of the home and loans that were extended without obtaining any verification of credit or employment information. The result is still being felt today with significant foreclosures as well as a general economic downturn. The public is now looking in every direction to find out what happened, how this happened, and who was responsible for regulating the banking industry.*

    *The primary form of banking regulation in the United States is the National Bank Act (NBA) which is a Congressional act that authorized the creation of national banks and allows them to engage in a broad range of business activities. The Office of the Comptroller of the Currency (OCC) is the federal agency Congress entrusted to implement the NBA and to oversee the exercise of the powers of the national banks, and this includes the regulation for lending for real estate mortgages. In 2005, based on New York State Executive Law, the New York State Attorney General began an investigation of the residential real estate lending practices of national banks that operated within the state, and the OCC and the Clearing House Association (an independent association of commercial banks) objected to this based on the "visitorial" provision in the NBA. This provision provides: "No national bank shall be subject to any visitorial powers except as authorized by federal law ..." OCC regulation interpreted this provision as precluding state officials from any prosecution enforcement actions to ensure national banks' compliance with state and federal laws. In the case* Clearing House Association, *the United States Court of Appeals, Second Circuit, held that the OCC interpretation, which significantly restricted state enforcement action, was within the OCC's delegated rulemaking authority and the regulation was a reasonable interpretation of the NBA visitorial provision.*

This comment argues that the Clearing House Association *decision erred because it narrowly and incorrectly applied the United States Supreme Court precedent; the decision inappropriately restricted the police power of the state, which raises significant federalism and preemption concerns, and the decision was contrary to proper public policy and economic well-being. This comment will also explore how this decision could erode the very fabric of our nation's banking system by reviewing the significant implications of this decision. Part I of the comment describes the facts and background of* Clearing House Association, *including some of the binding and persuasive precedent. Part II examines the United States Supreme Court decision in* Watters v. Wachovia Bank, N.A., *and how that decision should have been applied to* Clearing House Association. *Part III examines the significant flaws in the Clearing House decision by a) further examining whether or not a federal agency should be able to preempt state law and b) whether the* Clearing House Association *decision was consistent with public policy. Part IV examines the implications of the decision and possible future ramifications. Part V summarizes the main points and concludes.*

## I. Facts

*The National Bank Act authorizes national banks to engage in a broad range of business activities and also limits that ability for other agencies to exercise "visitorial powers" over the national banks. The OCC is responsible for the implementation and oversight of the NBA. In 2005, the OCC and the Clearing House Association filed separate suits that sought to bar New York Attorney General, Andrew Cuomo, from investigating possible violations of state and federal law related to discriminatory mortgage lending practices. The OCC argued that they had exclusive visitorial authority over national banks, and this barred enforcement actions or investigations of this kind. The Attorney General argued, inter alia, that his investigation was not a prohibited exercise of visitorial powers and that the OCC was not acting aggressively in this area. The United*

*States District Court for the Southern District of New York deferred to the OCC's interpretation of the statute and entered a declaratory judgment and issued the injunction sought by the OCC and the Clearing House Association. On appeal, the United States Court of Appeals, Second Circuit, affirmed the judgment of the District Court. The Court of Appeals applied a "Chevron" standard where the Court first looked at whether or not Congress had spoken on a particular subject. If, as here, the statute is silent or ambiguous with respect to the specific issue, the next step is to simply ask the question of "whether the agency's answer is based on a permissible construction of the statute." As this standard is quite deferential, the Court of Appeals supported the lower court decision. The* Clearing House Association *decision was consistent with two non-binding lower court rulings where the facts were similar. Specifically, in* Clearing House Ass'n v. Sptizer, *the Clearing House Association brought action to enjoin the New York Attorney General, Elliot Spitzer, from instituting enforcement action or investigation on national banks. There, the District Court held that the Association was entitled to an injunction preventing the Attorney General from bringing an enforcement action against its members. In addition, in a consolidated action, in* OCC v. Spitzer, *the lower court again supported the OCC and barred the Attorney General from enforcement and investigatory action. Finally, in early 2007, the relevant binding precedent was established in* Watters v. Wachovia Bank, N.A., *where the state of Michigan attempted to enforce two statutes related to mortgage lending against a national bank's operating subsidiary. The state statute imposed registration and disclosure requirements as well as granted inspection and enforcement authority over registrants. There, the court held that "states are permitted to regulate the activities of national banks where doing so does not prevent or significantly interfere with the national bank's or national bank regulator's exercise of its powers." There, the comprehensive nature of the statute was deemed to "significantly interfere" with the national bank and, as such, was not lawful.*

### II. Why Was the Clearing House Association Contrary to Existing Law

*The Court of Appeals did not properly follow the standard that was established in past United States Supreme Court Cases. Instead, the Court applied an incorrect deferential standard to assess the correctness of the OCC's interpretation that the visitorial provision of the NBA prohibited the Attorney General from investigation and enforcement action. The Court quickly defaulted to the deferential Chevron test that was utilized in the lower courts but should have used the "undue burden" test that was established in* Watters. *While the opinion of the Court of Appeals correctly concedes that* Watters *does not directly address the question at issue here,* Watters *does set forth a framework for how these types of cases should be analyzed and gives future courts room to shape public policy when required. Specifically,* Watters *sets out a standard that "states are permitted to regulation of the activities of national banks where doing so does not prevent or significantly interfere with the national bank's or the national bank regulator's exercise of its powers." The Court goes on to say that "we have repeatedly made clear that federal control shields national banking from unduly burdensome and duplicative state regulations." Key to the holding was the idea that the NBA itself, independent of the OCC's regulation, preempts the application of the pertinent Michigan laws because the Michigan laws sought not only enforcement ability but general monitoring and compliance functions that were already part of the OCC's mandate. Despite the fact that this standard was available to the Court of Appeals, the Court incorrectly applied the deferential Chevron standard where the assessment focused on the OCC's interpretation of the NBA.*

*If the Court applied the standard established in* Watters, *the decision would likely have been different. In* Watters, *the court asserted that the visitorial provision was in place "to prevent inconsistent or intrusive state regulation from impairing the national system and ... to shield national banks from unduly burdensome and duplicative state regulation in the exercise of their federally authorized powers." The Court of Appeals has not demonstrated how the Attorney General's review would cause inconsistent or intrusive state regulation or how the Attorney General's actions would be duplicative or burdensome. In fact, Cuomo's claim was that the OCC was not doing enough, so it is unlikely that there would have been overlap or duplication but rather his actions would have supplemented those of the OCC. In* Watters, *there was a strong argument that the nature and extent of the Michigan state statute duplicated the functions already established by the federal government, and that monitoring and some compliance aspects such as registration and licensing were truly preempted by the NBA. There, to allow the same additional state requirements would have been duplicative and would have constituted an undue burden, especially when compared to the relative value of the duplicate information. Here, the situation is quite different in that the Attorney General's actions are a reaction to probable reported violations, the information requested is not duplicative, and the Attorney General's actions are focused only on enforcement. Unlike the Michigan statute, Cuomo's concerns stem from events that were occurring rather than from a general sense of a desire to regulate banking. The banking crisis did not occur overnight, and by 2005 there were surely already some reports of discriminatory banking practices. Despite these differences, the Court of Appeals did not give the Attorney General the benefit of the doubt and quickly concluded that the United States Supreme Court "implied that investigation and enforcement by state officials are just as much aspects of visitorial authority as registration and other forms of administrative supervision." Given the facts in* Watters *are quite different from this case, this is not a logical conclusion and is not an accurate reading of the current binding legal precedent of* Watters *or past precedent.*

*This* Clearing House Association *decision is also inconsistent with other past precedent. As noted in the dissent, the Supreme Court addressed this precise issue over eighty years ago. In* St. Louis, *the attorney general of Missouri brought a proceeding against a national bank that had violated state law by establishing a branch. While the national bank asserted that the state did not have the power to enforce the law, the Supreme Court rejected this argument.*

*In addition to not following existing binding case law, the Court of Appeals decision fails for two additional reasons. First, there are significant federalism concerns related to preemption. Second, the decision is contrary to good public policy and will undermine the Court's legitimacy.*

### III. More Reasons the Decision Is Inappropriate

#### a) Federalism and the Dangers of Preemption

*The Court has developed a dangerous precedent whereby administrative agencies can preempt fundamental aspects of state law with little or no explanation. These agencies are not elected, are not designed to directly protect the interest of the state, and do not have to directly answer to the local constituents. This is especially a problem here, as the impact related to the federal agency will be strongly felt in the local community. In addition, the power that the agency is taking over is the police power of the state to investigate banking practices that are occurring in their state. In some cases, these practices amount to criminal activity like misrepresentation and fraud, and enforcement of criminal activity is a power that is for the most part reserved for the states. In this case the Attorney General has the responsibility to investigate civil rights violations being committed in New York, and he should be able to assert his right as part of his duty to enforce state law. He is not seeking a general monitoring and compliance function but rather the power to protect the people of the state. This idea is also supported by case law precedent cited above* (St. Louis) *as well as noted in the Cardomone dissent, "Considerable authority supports the proposition that states have the authority to enforce such laws against national banks." The idea of localized enforcement is important given the local impacts. As we now see, the effects of the real estate crisis are often localized and impact some states more than others. These communities often will not even know that the OCC exists, but they do know their local Congressman, Senator and other local government official. The local government is the one that is in the best position to quickly react to the local situations and is the one that is going to be accountable for any problems that result. As noted in the dissent in* Watters, *"For this reason, when an agency purports to decide the scope of federal preemption, a healthy respect for state sovereignty calls for something less than Chevron deference."*

*In addition, preemption is inappropriate because an explicit authorization from Congress to preempt state law does not exist. As noted in the* Clearing House Association *dissent, "the Supremacy Clause . . . grants the power to preempt state law to Congress, not to appointed officials . . ." The dissent also indicates, "Even when there is preemption by a federal agency, it may only occur within the scope of authority unmistakably delegated to it by Congress." This has clearly not occurred here, and given the deferential nature of the Chevron test, virtually any OCC rule would eliminate the state's ability to enforce its own laws. The concept of a state law without the power to enforce that law grossly adjusts that balance of power between the states and the federal government, and the courts should not allow this. As commented in* Lopez, *"It is so vital in preserving our freedom that a court should not refuse to intervene when the federal government has 'tipped the scales too far.' " This is where local citizens expect the court to really look beyond the words of a statute and assess what is really occurring and the implications of their decision. For example, the Court here finds that for something as important as banking regulation and the state sovereignty issues, the Agency's interpretation should be accepted unless it is "arbitrary, capricious, or manifestly contrary to the statute." The "letter of the law" approach ignores the important federalism and economic and personal impact issues and treats the case as a run-of-the-mill decision that has little or no importance. This does little to positively impact public policy or the perception of the court.*

### b) Role of the Court and Public Policy

*Public policy is harmed whenever the interests of big business are put before the interest of the consumer and the general welfare of the economy and nation. Here, the ruling for the Clearing House Association does not further any public policy and is especially disappointing as the Attorney General had the goal of investigation in an attempt to help consumers. While the idea of avoiding duplicative efforts and conflict is desirable, the banking industry has, on more than one occasion, demonstrated that there is a need for regulation. Both the savings and loan crisis and the current events surrounding the government bailout of Bear Sterns demonstrate this point. While regulation that is in direct conflict or that is duplicative should be avoided, there is a difference between that and the idea of real demonstrable signs that prompt local governments into action. The undue burden test in* Watters *should implicitly include a cost-benefit analysis as an important aspect that should be considered to see if the proposed state legislation or action is truly burdensome. For example, current knowledge regarding the poor lending practices would fully support the idea that a review of banking practices by a local government in 2005 would not have been burdensome and would have only helped the situation. A test where the undue burden as measured by the overlap in regulation and increased burden to the national bank, as compared to the potential benefit of the enforcement action, would certainly meet the objective of strong public policy in support of consumers. This approach is consistent with* Watters, *which lays out a general standard that gives the Court room to influence public policy where necessary.*

*This policy would also strengthen people's perception of the Court, as it is possible that some may perceive the Court's deferential treatment as giving in to a powerful lobby group. The Clearing House Association describes itself as dedicated to protecting the rights and interests of its member banks as well as advancing the broader interest of the domestic commercial banking industry and states that it is "interested in ensuring stability and certainty in the regulatory environment in which its member banks operate. While on the surface, these goals appear to be altruistic, a deeper assessment reveals that they are somewhat self-serving and look to benefit the corporate interests rather than the individual consumer. This association was created by commercial banks that organized to more effectively lobby to protect their own interests. One common interest is a decrease in regulation so that they are free to do what they want so that the big banks can earn more big profits. Now that the nature and extent of the discriminatory housing practices have been exposed, their interest of "ensuring stability and certainty in the regulatory environment" does not appear consistent with their actions.*

### IV. Implications of Decision

*The Court's decision will have far-reaching ramifications for lenders and consumers and will erode the public's confidence in both the government and the judiciary. While the idea of federal agencies and regulation is not objectionable, it has to be balanced with the practical implications of the decentralized aspects of our system. States have to react quickly to counter improper practices and, as such, their ability to enforce state statutes cannot be impaired. Here, an association that clearly is self-serving (Clearing House Association) and another unelected body (OCC) that is not in the best position to observe and remedy local housing and lending issues should not be able to stop an elected official from investigating and acting against improper activity that is occurring in the state. This is particularly the case when the agency that is charged with protecting the citizens has failed. While it is apparent now that the OCC did not protect the millions of people who have and will lose their homes, the* Clearing House Association *decision adds insult to injury by telling these people that this could happen again.*

### *V. Conclusion*

*It is evident that, as a result of the recent near Bear Sterns collapse and the discovery of the nature and extent of the poor lending practices, additional regulation will be implemented in the banking sector. Perhaps now, it is evident that the current system of "checks and balances" is not working and that the complete delegation of the power of enforcement to the OCC is not a good idea. While the OCC should have authority where the function is general monitoring and charter compliance, its authority cannot be absolute. Where a state attempts to enforce an improper banking practice that could have a significant impact on the state, the deferential review that was applied in* Clearing House Association *is not sufficient. An undue burden analysis should be conducted, where the burden to the bank and federal regulatory body is reviewed and weighed against the potential negative results of noncompliance. In addition, any decision should take into account significant factors such as federalism and public policy. This will achieve the goal of avoiding duplicative efforts but also restores the state's police power.*

Again this submission is really out of context as you have not seen the instruction package so you should only skim it for reference. Also, footnotes have been omitted.

## *Should I Participate in the Law Review Competition?*

Many ask the question whether or not they should participate in the law review competition, especially since the law review competition occurs immediately after the first-year exams and many students are burnt out. As such, many decide not to compete, and others start the competition and do not finish.

There are several reasons for participating. First, all of the reasons described earlier for joining a journal in your first year are still valid. Also, if you are selected (rather than volunteering) for law review or a journal, this is a significant accomplishment that will help you secure employment, obtain a judicial clerkship, obtain good summer employment, and more. Moreover, the more senior positions you hold on the staff of a journal, the more impressive a board position sounds. You could even be the managing editor or president. Barack Obama was president of Harvard's Law Review. Do not forget that a board position could mean that you are involved in some of the strategic aspects of the journal, such as article selection and direction of the journal.

While most, if not all, law schools will have a law review competition after the first year, some only have the competition for certain journals and allow students to freely join other journals based on interest. For example, Harvard Law School conducts a writing competition, but the competition is only for the very prestigious Harvard Law Review. For all other journals, students can join by sending a simple email to the editor. As such, at some schools you do not have to go through the grueling competition in order to join a journal, and you can get similar benefits.

*There are many good reasons to compete in a law review or journal competition. These stem from experience to resume building. While a journal job may not be that glamorous, it will help you secure full-time employment and/or other accolades.*

## Moot Court (Trial or Appellate Advocacy)

Another important law school activity is Moot Court. Moot Court is a make-believe courtroom where students act as lawyers and argue cases in front of make-believe judges and/or juries. It can take the form of either Trial Advocacy Moot Court or Appellate Advocacy Moot Court. Both are excellent ways to gain experience, improve your lawyer skills, and have fun.

### Trial Advocacy Moot Court (Mock Trial)

For Trial Advocacy Moot Court, students are given a package that describes a series of facts and events that result in the need for a trial with a jury. The package is developed to mimic a real-life situation where two sides have a dispute and come to court to resolve it. The cases can be civil, where two people are fighting against or suing each other, or criminal, where the state attempts to prosecute someone for a crime.

The package you will get for whichever case you are assigned will contain a description of what happened using made-up interviews, police reports, newspaper articles, and other evidence. The package will also describe a number of witnesses and will contain documents regarding the interviews of the witnesses and statements that they made in either an official or unofficial capacity.

The "game" requires several people because each side usually has two or three participants who act as lawyers, and it also requires several pretend witnesses and a judge. Once each team is assembled, the teams take on the roles of the lawyers who are representing either the person suing (or prosecutor) or the person being sued. Of course, in a criminal case, the lawyers' roles would be the prosecution and defense.

The Moot Court exercise is conducted in the same way that a real court is conducted. For example, both sides give an opening and closing argument, and witnesses are examined and cross-examined. Moreover, each side is free to object, and the judge will rule as to whether or not the objection is overruled or sustained. This is any television courtroom drama at its best, and the exercise is quite fun.

During the whole process, there are judges (not judges who are deciding on the case but rather judges who are reviewing and grading your performance) that will give you a score based on your performance as a pretend lawyer. At the end of the trial, a winning team is announced based on an accumulation of the scores.

While this sounds like all fun and games, there is a significant amount of preparation that is required in order to compete and do well in these competitions. Moreover, most schools require a tryout where the best students are selected to join the Moot Court organization. Before we move on to appellate advocacy, take away this tip regarding the trial advocacy tryout.

One key to success in trial advocacy competition is to know the details of the package that you are given. While you will not be able to memorize all the details, you should know who said what and you should be prepared to find what any given person said at any moment during your tryout. This is important in the real competition, but you will learn this if selected. It is especially important in the tryout because, at this point, you have not learned this important aspect yet and the testers will try to trick you in order to weed you out. So how does this all work?

Let us say that the case is about the murder of a man who was found in his home, and the man who was murdered was having an affair with a married woman. Now let us say that the record or package that is distributed tells you that one of the key suspects is the woman's husband, and his motive was jealousy. Let us also suppose that the record states that the husband stated in one of his witness statements at a preliminary hearing a year ago that he knew about the affair and it made him very angry.

For your test for the competition, your job is to cross-examine the witness (the husband), and you attempt to confront him with the statements that he made regarding his knowledge of the affair and his jealousy. Your job here is clear, and it is to get him to confess in front of the jury that he knew about the affair and that he was angry. Given the record, it may at first appear like an easy task.

Keep in mind that this tryout is just that, and the testers do not expect you to be an expert. They do, however, want to see how you will react to odd situations. So let us say that you ask the husband the following question: "Mr Jones, is it not true that you knew about your wife's affair with the deceased?" Of course you are expecting a "Yes, I knew," because that is what the record says. The trick here is that the witness will say "No." He will then go on to say that he had no idea about the affair and that he was good friends with the deceased. Most people get stumped and either just move on to another question or freeze. Unfortunately, this reaction will not get you selected.

So how do you handle this? In order to handle this well, you will have to confront the witness and quickly refer back to the record indicating he said that he knew about the affair. As such, the following might be a good response:

| | |
|---|---|
| *Lawyer:* | *Mr. Jones, are you saying you did not know that the deceased was having an affair with your wife?* |
| *Mr. Jones:* | *Yes, that is what I am saying.* |
| *Lawyer:* | *Mr. Jones, do you think it is important to tell the truth?* |
| *Mr. Jones:* | *Yes.* |
| *Lawyer:* | *Do you tell the truth when you are asked questions in a court of law?* |
| *Mr. Jones:* | *Yes.* |
| *Lawyer:* | *Do you remember testifying at the preliminary hearing on January 25?* |

| | |
|---|---|
| *Mr. Jones:* | Yes. *(If he says no, you simply show him the document from your package.)* |
| *Lawyer:* | *And when you testified at that hearing, were you telling the truth?* |
| *Mr. Jones:* | Yes. |
| *Lawyer:* | *Like you are telling the truth today?* |
| *Mr. Jones:* | Yes. |
| *Lawyer:* | *And when you testified on January 25, it was in court?* |
| *Mr. Jones:* | Yes. |
| *Lawyer:* | *And there was a judge there, a court reporter documenting everything you said, and someone was asking you questions?* |
| *Mr. Jones:* | Yes. |
| *Lawyer:* | *And you knew you had to tell the truth?* |
| *Mr. Jones:* | Yes. |
| *Lawyer:* | *Mr. Jones, could you read the two highlighted lines?* |
| *Mr. Jones:* | *(reading) I knew that my wife was having an affair with Jerry. It made my blood boil and I wanted to take him outside and settle this like a man.* |
| *Lawyer:* | *Mr. Jones, does that refresh your recollection regarding whether or not you knew your wife was having an affair?* |

| | |
|---|---|
| *Mr. Jones:* | *Yes.* |
| *Lawyer:* | *So it would be fair to say testimony that you gave earlier today was not the truth.* |
| *Mr. Jones:* | *No, it was not the truth.* |
| *Lawyer:* | *So Mr. Jones, I ask you again, did you know about your wife's affair with the deceased?* |
| *Mr. Jones:* | *Yes, I knew.* |

The key here is to be quick on your feet and to be able to point to specific things in the record that can make the witness look like he is lying. Now if you are like me, you will simply be shocked by the "no" response and not really know where to go from there.

When I auditioned for Trial Advocacy Moot Court, the record was quite long and I knew in the back of my mind that the witness had said something different, but I would not have known where to start looking for this. Instead, I just got flustered and moved to another area. Based on my poor performance, they did not pick me for Trial Advocacy Moot Court, but I did learn a very important lesson, which I have just conveyed to you. Luckily, I did much better when I tried out for the Appellate Division. Preparation is the key to success in Moot Court.

---

**TIP** *For Moot Court tryouts as well as actual competitions, know the details of the package that you will be given inside and out. When you try out, you will find that the witnesses will say different things from what is in the package, and if you are not prepared it will throw you off. In order to test you, the examiners are looking to see how you would handle different situations. Do not be caught off-guard.*

---

### Appellate Advocacy Moot Court

Appellate Advocacy Moot Court is similar to Moot Court in that it is a make-believe courtroom, but that is really where the similarities end. The big difference is that this type of Moot Court deals with appeals rather than a trial. As such, you are still acting as a pretend lawyer, but you are arguing something in front of a judge or a panel of judges rather than a jury.

The best example of this is the Supreme Court. In order for a case to reach the Supreme Court, it starts at the trial level and, as in every case, one party loses. The loser then appeals and a judge or judges will listen to the loser's explanation of why he/she thought they should have won. After listening, the court will either rule that what the lower court did was fine or they will overturn the decision. The winner or loser can appeal again, and the same process occurs at a higher court. The highest court that someone can appeal to is the Supreme Court.

Like in trial advocacy, the two sides are given a package that describes what went on at trial. For this mock trial, though, both sides have to write a lengthy document called a brief to support why their side should win. The briefs really use legal arguments rather than the witness back-and-forth, and the Moot Court exercise is the pretend lawyers making their arguments to the panel of judges. Usually you are given ten to fifteen minutes to make your argument, but while you are doing this, the judges will interrupt you and ask you questions. In order to be successful, you must be a good public speaker, be respectful to the judges, and know the law as it relates to the situation.

In order to get selected to compete for the school, you usually have to go through a tryout. Here you will not have crazy witnesses, but the panel of judges will ask tough questions. In addition, standing at a podium with three or four people firing away questions at you is not the easiest thing in the world. It is great practice, though, and you will learn a great deal from the exercise.

*During your second term, most law schools assign you to a legal writing section where you will write a first draft and a rewrite of an appellate brief. At some schools, your grade on the first draft of this document will determine whether you are eligible to participate in Appellate Moot Court. Many students do not realize this until after the first draft is submitted and think that they will have time to improve the document later. This, unfortunately, is not the case.*

*If you do not make Moot Court, you still may be able to take an appellate advocacy course in which you will get more practice writing briefs and performing an oral argument. You may also be able to take a trial advocacy course rather than participate in the Moot Court competition. Check with your school to see exactly how you can ensure you are on Moot Court or can take a course. You will be glad you did!*

### Should I Join Moot Court?

Both of these types of Moot Courts are excellent extracurricular activities for various reasons. First, the packages that you get are very similar to real-life trials and appeals, so you are getting a firsthand look at what lawyers do in court. Second, Moot Court looks great on your resume, so it will help you find a job and give you an edge for scholarships or other competitive endeavors. Also, most people know that for many schools, the people who participate in Moot Court were selected based on a competition or grades, so being a member of the group is viewed as impressive.

Finally, Moot Court is fun! I signed up for a three-week-long intensive trial advocacy workshop seminar, and it was the best three weeks that I had in law school. Also, I loved arguing appellate advocacy briefs and was thrilled when I was selected to join the team. While I was somewhat anxious when I had to examine and cross-examine witnesses or appear before pretend judges, I really got a kick out of the theatrics of a courtroom. Now as a lawyer, I have watched many actual trials, and the competitions are very close to the real thing. If you like being in a courtroom, you will love Moot Court.

## Student Organizations

If you have any interests, you will almost certainly find a student organization that is dedicated to your area of interest. At Harvard there are approximately ninety student organizations that cover everything—gender, sexual orientation, sports, hobbies, politics, racial groups, and much more. For the most part, the advantage of these groups is social interaction, but they may also enhance your job prospects if you take a board position. Even if you decide to just be a member of the group, though, the social networking is something that you will benefit from during and after law school. Moreover, because law school is quite intense, the distraction of a non-law-focused activity is often appealing.

# 3. The Second and Third Years of Law School

To get a law degree in the United States, you have to study either three years full-time or four years part-time. The standards, such as mandatory courses and credit hours, that you need to obtain a recognized law degree in the United States are set out by a governing body called the American Bar Association (ABA), and all law schools follow their rules. The ABA sets minimum standards, and each law school imposes additional requirements prior to awarding a degree from that school.

For example, at Harvard you must complete the standard first-year courses as well as a legislative regulation and international law course in your first year. In your second and third years, you are required to complete a professional responsibility course, a written work assignment greater than fifty pages, forty hours of pro-bono work, and fifty-two upper-class credits. The requirements at other schools are similar, but differences do exist. For example, at Brooklyn Law School, the upper-class credit requirements were different and the school did not have a pro-bono requirement. Moreover, the mandatory first-year courses at Brooklyn Law School and Harvard were different. Most notably, at Harvard, Constitutional Law was not a required course. The range of requirements do not differ much, though, so you can get a good sense of what the requirements for a law degree are by looking at the requirements in any one school. If you have any doubt regarding the rules at the school you attend or are thinking of attending, you should consult the local registrar's office.

One rule that you should be aware of is the residency requirements that schools impose. These requirements specify how many courses you must take during each semester and during a calendar year. For example, based on the ABA standards, schools impose a minimum number of credits that you can take in any given term. As such, you could not, for example, take only five credits in one term and nineteen credits in another term even though you may complete all of a school's credit requirements of twenty-four credits for a particular year. The biggest problem here is that the residency requirements would impose a minimum number of credits per term and would not permit you to take only five credits in your first term. While the requirements may differ slightly at different law schools, each must comply with the minimum number of credits per term that are set by the governing body. At Harvard, we had to take at least ten credits per term and twenty-five credits within a calendar year. In addition, some schools require that you attend classes a minimum number of days. For example, at some schools, you may not be able to schedule classes only two days a week.

If you do not meet the residency requirements, you will not graduate. Most registrar offices are quite good at keeping track of what you need to graduate, but it is your responsibility to ensure that you meet the requirements in order to obtain your degree.

## Common Second- and Third-Year Courses

Compared to your first year of law school, your second and third years will be a relative breeze. The first year of law school is designed to be the hardest, and the fact that your courses are preselected for you makes it tough. In addition, at most law schools, your workload in the first year is far heavier than your workload in subsequent years. In my final year and semester at Harvard, I only had ten credits, with classes only three days a week, and this compares to sixteen to eighteen credits for most during each term of the first year.

In addition to a reduced course load, during your second year of law school you may start to specialize a bit and select courses that interest you. Hopefully, the taste of many subject areas in the first year will give you some idea regarding areas of interest. For example, if you hated torts, it is unlikely that you will take an advanced course in, say, class action litigation. (This deals with torts in which many people sue based on similar injuries—for example, a group of people suing for injury because of contaminated water.)

You are truly free to take any course that you desire, but there are some foundational courses that almost everyone takes in either the second or third year. Also, because many people often want to take similar courses, the course selection is typically done using a lottery system, so you will not necessarily get into every course of your choice. Regarding the core courses that I will outline on subsequent pages, people usually take these courses either because they are heavily tested on the bar exam or they are subjects that every lawyer should know. These core second- and third-year courses include the following.

## *Corporations*

Given the large number of corporations in our society, most lawyers will have to deal with a corporation at one time or another. As such, it is a good idea to know what a corporation is and how they operate. This course will go over the basics of the different ways to form a business as well as the advantages and disadvantages of different organizational structures. In addition, the course will cover topics such as how to form a corporation; mergers and acquisitions; sale of entities; and the responsibilities of shareholders, officers, and board members.

Corporations is a fairly dry course, but many people take it because of the significance of corporations in our world. Also, most state bar exams have corporations as one of the topics on the local portion of the exam, so the course could help you prepare for that exam. That being said, I do not recommend that you take this course simply because it may be tested on the bar. Like most courses in your second and third year, you should take corporations if you have an interest or if you feel that the topic is something that you should know.

When considering this course, you should keep in mind that it is essential if you plan to work in a large law firm, as almost all of the firm's clients will be corporations. Moreover, the course may also be relevant for many government jobs. Even a criminal prosecutor may prosecute corporate board members and officers, so knowledge of how a corporation works is useful.

### Federal Income Taxation

This course is an introduction to the federal income tax system, with a focus on taxes for the individual. Some of the concepts, like the definition of income, are quite broad and will also prepare you for the more in-depth second part of this course that deals with corporate income tax. The course really follows the income tax statutes and teaches you everything you need to know about income, expenses, deductions, credits, penalties, and more. It is a good general interest course as well since you should know how to do your own tax return. In addition, many issues in the corporate world have tax implications, so a basic knowledge of tax law is very helpful.

I know several lawyers who did not take this course and regret it. If you work in a large law firm that has corporate clients, you should have at least a basic understanding of tax, as most corporate transactions have tax implications.

While it is an important course, it is a technically difficult course. You will get through it, but it is a bit different from other law school courses, as there are often calculations and the tax statutes are quite complex. You may even have to buy a calculator for this course. You should also note that tax is never tested on bar exams.

## Federal Courts

This course takes a more in-depth look at the Civil Procedure course from the first year. After you complete this course, you should be an expert on how the federal court system works and how to sue in federal court. In particular, the course will focus on which cases end up in federal court and the various steps a lawsuit goes through in federal court. In addition, the course explores the power of Congress to regulate the Supreme Court and the federal court's right to review state decisions. If you did not like Civil Procedure in your first year, you will not like this course. The course is particularly helpful if you want to be a litigator or if you want to clerk for a federal judge.

## Evidence

This course will look at the Federal Rules of Evidence, which govern what can and cannot be admitted as evidence in a courtroom. On television, you may have heard a lawyer object and say "hearsay." The hearsay rules are all spelled out in the Federal Rules of Evidence, and the voluminous rulebook contains several other rules on topics such as impeachment, cross-examination, authentification of documents, and confrontation. Some of these words may not mean much now, but you will be very familiar with them before you leave law school.

All bar examinations heavily test evidence. Evidence is one of the six subjects tested on the multi-state exam (the multiple-choice part of the bar exam), so it will make up almost eighteen percent of that exam. In fact, for the most part, evidence is the only topic of the six subjects that are tested on the multi-state day of the bar exam that is not a mandatory course in law school in your first year. We will talk about the multi-state exam later, but this portion of the bar exam is the portion that is written by everyone in the country. Also, evidence can appear on the local or state days of the bar exam, so it could account for a significant amount of your total exam.

I would not advise this for many courses, but Evidence is a course you should take so that you are prepared for the bar exam—you will be at a significant disadvantage without it. I offer this advice given the large coverage on the exam and because the concepts are not straightforward and take time to sink in and to comprehend.

Moreover, another strong reason to take Evidence is that it is one of those courses that will teach you things that every lawyer should know. If someone asked you to define hearsay and you did not know, I imagine that they would wonder if you really went to law school. While not everyone wants to be a trial lawyer, as a lawyer you should at least have a basic understanding of the rules of a courtroom before you leave law school.

Finally, you will have to take Evidence prior to participating in a trial advocacy course. Trial advocacy is a highly recommended activity, as I have described earlier.

---

 **TIP**

*Evidence is a course that every law student should take, as any good lawyer should have at least a working knowledge of what happens at trials. Also, Evidence is very heavily tested on the bar examination. In fact, for the most part, Evidence is the only subject of the six that are tested on the multi-state day of the bar exam that is not a mandatory course in law school. Because Evidence takes some time to sink in, you will have an advantage over other students if you take the course prior to the bar exam.*

---

### Constitutional Law: Fourteenth Amendment or First Amendment

Most students take Constitutional Law in their first year, but this course is not always a first-year requirement. For example, at

Harvard Law School, Constitutional Law is an optional course, and students may elect to take it in their second or third year or may elect not to take it at all. In some other schools, Constitutional Law is a requirement, but the focus is on the three branches of government rather than any of the Constitutional Amendments.

If you do not take a comprehensive Constitutional Law course in your first year, you should definitely take it in your second or third year of law school. A comprehensive Constitutional Law course would include the following: separation of powers between the three levels of government (executive, judiciary and legislature); the Equal Protection Clause; federalism, including some of the powers of Congress; and judicial review. The First Amendment is usually a separate course, and it is not that important to take this unless you have a strong interest in the subject matter. While the First Amendment is tested on the bar exam, you can easily learn what you have to know during your bar exam studies.

A comprehensive Constitutional Law course is a must for several reasons. First, it would be an embarrassment to leave law school without knowledge of what is in the Constitution. Moreover, most Supreme Court decisions are based on Constitutional interpretation, and it would be unbecoming of a lawyer to not have at least a basic understanding of how decisions are rendered.

Second, there is a heavy focus on Constitutional Law on the Bar Exam on the multi-state section. Like Evidence, Constitutional Law will be worth approximately eighteen of the multi-state bar exam, and a course in law school will greatly help prepare you for that part of the exam.

Third, many courses and cases in law school have Constitutional law components, and a basic understanding of Constitutional law will help you immensely in these courses. For example, I took an immigration law course in my third year, and one of the big issues had to do with the state's power to implement immigration laws. (You may have heard of the Arizona immigration law among others.) A court's analysis of these laws is almost exclusively based on the federal preemption doctrine of the Constitution. This is only one example, and there are many other courses, such as Property and Criminal Law, that heavily rely on Constitutional interpretation. For example, the ability of the police to search and/or detain you is built around the doctrine in the Fourth Amendment of the Constitution. Also, eminent domain (a topic you will deal with in your Property class that covers the circumstances in which the government can take your property for a fee) is based on specific language in the Constitution.

---

 *Constitutional Law is another course you should take and is, in fact, mandatory at most schools. If your school does not require it, make sure that you take a version of the course that is comprehensive. A comprehensive course will include the three levels of government, the Fourteenth Amendment, federalism, and other fundamental rights. This is another subject that is tested on the multistate bar examination, so it will also help you prepare for the exam.*

---

### Trusts and Estates

Many students also take Trusts and Estates. In this course, you will learn how to make your own will and how to structure a trust. The cases that you will study are rather interesting, as they often have to do with very sticky family situations in which one family member is contesting a will and attempting to get money from a deceased family member. I had a fantastic professor for this course and I loved it.

For the most part, this is another general interest course, like Tax, that may be useful for a person who is working on a will. In addition, some state bar examinations (for example, New York) test Trusts and Estates, so taking this course may give you an advantage there.

You can learn everything that you need to know for the bar exam very quickly; however, I would not take this course just to have a better standing when you sit for the bar. In fact, on the first day of my Trusts and Estates class, my professor told us not to take this course to prepare for the bar and that we could learn everything we would need to know for the bar exam in three days. Although this was an excellent course, his advice was valid—it is not necessary to take this course to do better on the bar exam.

## Clinical Courses

In your second and third year, you also have the opportunity to take clinical courses. These courses combine traditional classroom lectures with practical work experience. They are an excellent way to get experience before you leave law school, and you get academic credit for your work. While in law school, I did an immigration asylum clinic and an employment law clinic. During the classroom sessions, I learned the law that was in the statutes and also became familiar with the leading immigration and employment law cases. During the practical part of the course, I met with and represented real clients who had immigration and employment needs.

Although you are supervised by an attorney, you are given a significant amount of autonomy. For example, with proper supervision I interviewed my clients and was responsible for writing documents that were submitted to the court. Moreover, many students are afforded the opportunity to present cases in front of judges and/or other court officers. You will also enhance your writing skills and learn how to write the way both a law firm and a court would like you to.

These courses are great for experience but also help to boost your GPA because they typically do not have an exam, so you are graded based on how well you do your work. Since you are not an attorney, I found that the expectation was quite low, and it was easy to get an A if you put in the required amount of time and effort.

Moreover, these classes are usually very small and are not subject to the curve that I have discussed earlier. As such, it is completely within the professor's control to give all students a high grade. In fact, because you are often working for different lawyers, it would be unfair to rank students; therefore you are often judged based on your independent contribution.

These clinical courses also look great on your resume, and in many cases where a post-graduate job has an experience requirement, you can often count the time that you spent on the clinical toward this requirement. Moreover, many hiring managers are very familiar with clinical placements and realize that the experience is exceptional.

Finally, the clinical courses give you experience that will help you on the bar exam. Many states, such as New York, include a section in their bar exam called the Multi-state Performance Test (MPT). This section is part of the bar examination and is made up of a package of information that the exam candidate must sift through. After reading all of the information in the package, the candidate must write a memo recommending a course of action. The memo is very similar to the memos and legal documents you would put together in a clinical, so you will be at an advantage if you have seen them before. The MPT is discussed in more detail in the "Bar Examination" section of this book (Chapter 10) and is worth ten percent of the total grade for the New York bar exam.

---

 *It would be a shame to leave law school without taking at least one clinical course. You will gain excellent experience, and the combination of the class time and practical work experience is something you will not find anywhere else. Moreover, these classes are typically not subject to a curve, so getting a high grade is easier than it is in some other classes.*

---

## Professional Responsibility Courses

You are also required to take a professional responsibility course in either your second or third year. This is typically the only mandatory course that you will take after your first year, and it will teach you the rules of professional conduct and ethics. In essence, this course deals with what a lawyer should and should not do. You are also required to take a professional responsibility examination either before or after the bar exam in order to practice law in the United States. The examination is called the Multi-State Professional Responsibility Exam (MPRE) and is discussed later in this chapter.

*Try to take your professional responsibility course in your second year rather than your third. In addition to getting this mandatory course out of the way, it will prepare you for the Multi-State Professional Responsibility Exam (MPRE) that you will sit for at the start of your third year. If you complete this course in your second year, you will be able to reduce your study time for that exam the following year.*

## How to Register for the Courses You Want

The registration process for your first year is simple because you will be assigned to a section for which all of your classes and times are preselected. In your second and third year, though, you may get to enroll in the courses that you want, provided they are available. Normally, the law school schedules a period of time for students to go online and select and rank the courses they wish to take.

For example, if you wanted to take Tax, Corporations, and Trusts and Estates in one term, you would have to rank them from one to three based on your preferences. Since you may not get into all or any of these classes, you must also typically specify additional classes as substitutes. For example, you may rank Evidence, Family Law, and a clinic as four to six. Some popular classes—for example, Corporations—will have several sections, so you must specify which professor and section you want when you are ranking. While the registration process sounds simple, it can often be confusing and complicated. The best way to ensure that you get to take the classes you want to take is to be organized, plan, and make a registration schedule.

*Registration will typically occur in phases or stages in which the registration for a particular type of course will occur first for a two-week period and then registration for the next type will occur after that. For example, very popular courses that are usually foundational courses with many sections, like Corporations, usually register first. Next, clinical courses are registered. Finally, electives are registered. Because your choices in the different phases will impact later phases, it is important to be prepared, and you must be strategic. This usually involves making a registration schedule that lays out your choices, the times things are available, desired professors, and backups. The format does not matter as long as it clearly illustrates what you want to take and what you will take if your first choice is not available. You are paying quite a bit for tuition, so you should take this process seriously so that you can get the courses you want.*

The actual lottery or allocation and selection system can vary at schools, but here is an example of how the system works at many schools. After students submit their choices, the school system is closed and the computer randomly assigns students based on their preferences and selections. Some schools have a formula that assigns more preference to students in their third year given this is their last chance to take these courses. Once a class is full, the program will move to your next selection to see if you can be accommodated. This process sounds simple, but unfortunately, the registration process can be confusing and frustrating. Here are some tips to try to make it a bit easier:

1. Pay attention to the registration deadlines and review your emails, as most notifications will occur through email. I have met many students who either did not read their emails or simply ignored registration deadlines. If you miss the deadlines, you will only have the ability to register for courses that have space. If a course has spaces after the registration period, it typically means that the course and/or the professors are not that popular.

2. Plan for your two remaining years. Some courses have prerequisites, so make sure you are taking those early. For example, if you want to take Mergers and Acquisitions, you have to take Corporations first. Also, many courses are only offered once a year in one semester. As such, it is important to plan accordingly, since you will have at most two time slots during your law school experience to take particular courses (in some cases, you only have one slot). If you miss the option in your second year, you may have a time conflict in your third year, which would make taking that course impossible.

3. Take a specific course you want while you can. Do not assume that a course you see in a listing in your second year will be available in your third year. While registering in my second year, I almost signed up for a course but then decided to take it in my third year. As fate would have it, I did not take it because it was not offered in the third year.

4. Monitor Waitlists. If you are not registered for the course of your choice, you will be placed on a waitlist. Do not give up because you are far down on the waitlist; students add and drop courses frequently once the semester begins. In fact, many students register for sixteen credits when they only plan to take twelve and use the first week as a test to see which class they will drop. I know people who were number ninety-five on a waitlist and were admitted to the class. Keep your eye on the waitlist, as you usually will be given very little time to register for the course once a spot opens up. If you miss your chance, they will simply move to the next name on the list.

5. Register for a reasonable number of credits in each term. This means not taking too many or too few. A manageable course load is thirteen or fourteen credits. Taking too many credits will stress you out and may impact your grades in the courses. If you take too few, you are really cheating yourself of the law school experience and paying a great deal of money for nothing.

6. Speak to your professor or the registrar's office if you need special accomodation. If you have a strong interest in taking a particular course or you have some issue (personal, family, or other important issue) that makes a particular time slot for a course desirable, speak to the professor or the registrar's office. This will not work for every course, but they will often accommodate you if you have a good reason. For example, I know a student who was able to change the time slot of his Contracts class to accommodate child-care issues. Also, if you are in your third year and you want to be an immigration lawyer and you are number 120 on the waitlist for the immigration course, speak to the professor and the registrar's office to see if there is something they can do. The worst thing they can say is that they cannot help you.

Most of these recommendations address proper planning. You will spend over $40,000 a year in tuition, so you should take the selection of your courses seriously and not miss opportunities simply because you were late or disorganized.

## Publishing a Paper While in Law School

At a meeting at Harvard Law School, Dean Martha Minow told the students that they should try to publish two or three scholarly papers during their law school experience. She was correct—law school is an excellent time to publish a note or article for many reasons.

You will definitely have to write at least one comprehensive paper during your three years at law school, so you may as well try to publish it. Moreover, there are many journals that will look at a student's work and publish your work as a student but will only publish a non-student's work if the person is an expert in the field. Finally, there is a cost savings associated with publishing as a student. As you will see below, students have the benefit of submitting their papers to as many journals as they like for free. If you are not a student, you must pay over two dollars per journal, and since there are hundreds of journals, this can really add up.

There are several benefits associated with publishing a paper. First, it looks excellent on a resume. If you publish, you will gain instant credibility, and employers, scholarship committees, and other parties will immediately conclude that you are able to write well. Also, a publication will help you find a job and will make you eligible for other accolades such as scholarship money, clerkship positions, and praise from faculty and peers. A published work will also assist you if you desire a law professor position some day.

Second, the development of a scholarly piece of work will enhance your research and writing skills. As with any lengthy paper, you will have to devote a significant amount of time to research, but this will not only enhance your knowledge in a particular subject area but will also force you to access various database libraries to search for relevant material. You may have to perform similar research when you are a lawyer as well. Moreover, a significant amount of time will have to be spent formatting the paper and the related citations, and this detail-oriented focus will help you immensely. When I worked on the paper that I published, I spent over three days after the paper was done with the *Bluebook* fixing citation formats, and this task afforded me the opportunity to memorize many aspects of citations.

Finally, if you publish, you will put your name in print, which is a good feeling. You should be proud if you publish something, and there is no better feeling than receipt of the finished product with your name boldly splashed across the cover.

## How to Publish

### How Do I Start the Publishing Process?

The first step in the process involves selecting a topic. This sounds easy, but unfortunately there is an additional step that must be done. Once you have settled on a topic, you have to conduct something called a preemption search to ensure that your topic has not been written about in the past. This does not mean that you cannot write about the same topic, but if you do, you must make it different in some way. The preemption search process involves searching databases for similar topics and reviewing the articles to see what they have covered. One good thing about this process is that it may arm you with more information about the topic and different ways to look at what you are thinking of writing about.

The next step in the process is to write a paper. The words term paper, note, and article can all be used interchangeably, but you should pick one term and use that consistently in your cover letter and other references to the document. The paper should be complete before you submit it. This means that it should be finalized (not a draft), error-free, and with correct citations and formatting. If your paper is not a final product, it will most likely be rejected.

The completed product should also contain an abstract. An abstract is a summary, usually one page or less, that summarizes what the paper sets out to do, how it does that, and how the paper is organized. As an example, I have included a copy of the abstract for the note I published with a Law School Journal here.

### *Abstract from a Published Note*

**FAIR VALUE ACCOUNTING: FRIEND OR FOE?**

*ABSTRACT*

*In 2008, financial institutions faced unprecedented financial, economic, and social challenges. What began as a financial institution and mortgage issue has had devastating effects on all sectors of the economy, both in the United States and abroad. Scholars, investors, analysts, and the general public are all asking the same question: How did this happen to one of the most sophisticated financial systems in the world?*

*Some put the blame on the Securities and Exchange Commission (SEC) or the Financial Accounting Standards Board (FASB), and say that the requirement to account for securities on a mark-to-market or fair value basis played a key role in the financial crisis and banking failures. These proponents argue that in an economic downturn, fair value accounting causes excessive volatility that does not reflect the true underlying value of assets, forcing companies to impair their regulatory capital position by recognizing losses too quickly and all at once. Those who believe that fair value accounting is the best accounting measure argue that it better reflects the risks associated with the assets. These proponents believe that any other measure would mask real losses that should be taken into account by investors when making their decisions.*

*This note examines the fair value accounting standards in the United States and discusses whether accounting regulation played a substantial role in the financial crisis and bank failures. In order to make this assessment, the note reviews the fair value accounting literature for the measurement and disclosure of financial instruments as well as the history associated with the reasons these standards were put in place. This includes a discussion and analysis of the recently finalized accounting regulation on fair value accounting that was put in place to address the financial crisis. In addition, the note explores the arguments for and against fair value accounting and assesses these arguments using examples from the history of the United States and Japan, as well as some banks and investment banks that failed in 2008.*

*While there is some legitimate debate regarding which accounting measure should be used in certain situations, this note concludes that the arguments supporting fair value accounting for financial instruments are much stronger. In addition, this note concludes that fair value accounting did not cause or contribute to the financial crisis. This note also concludes that while the FASB's attempt to improve disclosures is a positive step, the "relaxation" of the current accounting regulation will only serve to degrade investor confidence in financial information and independent regulatory standard setters. Finally, this note advances the theory that accounting forms the basis for important regulatory and control functions in which capital regulators and auditors rely, and, given the complexity of our market place, that this is an appropriate role for accountants.*

---

 *The abstract and cover letter are the first things that a journal will read, so you should ensure that it grabs their attention. Make sure that you let several friends read this and give you feedback.*

---

> **TIP** *Make sure your paper is a final product that is free from errors. The journals are not looking for hints at what your paper will look like but rather want to see a finished product.*
> *Do not be fooled into thinking that since your paper will undergo significant revisions in the editing process, it does not have to be final when you submit it.*

## To Which Journals Should I Submit my Paper?

After you have completed your paper, you should decide to which journals you would like to submit it. For obvious reasons, you should try to get your paper published by a journal that is very highly ranked.

A list of the top five journals in recent years is given below.

1. *Harvard Law Review*
2. *The Yale Law Journal*
3. *Columbia Law Review*
4. *Stanford Law Review*
5. *New York University Law Review*

If you are submitting to a top journal like *Harvard Law Review*, you should consider submitting your paper exclusively to them for a period of time before submitting to other journals. The reason for this is that Harvard and other similar journals will not rush to review your paper if you have competing offers. As such, you would not want to accept another offer while your paper is still being reviewed by a top journal.

You should note that when you submit your paper to a journal and they decide to publish it, they only give you a very limited amount of time to respond. If you do not respond quickly, they will simply move to the next paper. When I published my paper, the journal gave me three days to decide. You can always ask for a few more days, but it is up to the journal whether or not they grant this. Keep in mind that if you are publishing in a top journal, they may give you as little as an hour to decide.

*When you submit your work to a journal and they make you an offer to publish, be prepared to make your mind up quickly, as journals will often only give you a few days at most to decide. For more popular journals, you may only get a few hours.*

When deciding who to submit to, you should also consider the content of your paper and perhaps submit to specialized journals. For example, my paper dealt with a business topic, so I primarily submitted to business law journals. Similarly, if your paper deals with human rights, you may want to consider submitting the paper to various human rights journals rather than more general law review journals. While a particular law review journal might be highly ranked, a specific journal may publish you because your paper is on a topic that rounds out the publication for a particular journal.

### What Is the Submission Process?

Thankfully, the submission process for notes is electronic, so you can easily submit your note to several journals simultaneously. The best way to make a simultaneous electronic submission is through a website called "Expresso." The website can be found in the "Useful Resources" section.

Expresso makes the submission process fast and easy, and best of all, it is free for students. With the help of this website, you may upload your note and cover letter and send it to over 550 journals.

Make sure that your cover letter is clear and concise and sells your paper. Often the staff of a journal will only read the cover letter and abstract and will make a decision on whether or not to keep reading. You may also submit your note via mail, but this is an inefficient and expensive way of submitting. Finally, you may go to the websites of law reviews or journals and submit your paper following their instructions. This process is similar to Expresso, except that you will have to visit each law school's website to do this.

Once you have submitted your paper through Expresso, the journals will send you a confirmation email indicating that they have received your submission and are reviewing it. After a few weeks, you will start to receive a number of rejections, and this is normal. Even people who ultimately have their papers published in the *Harvard Law Review* will receive rejections from numerous other journals, so do not be discouraged.

When a journal likes your paper, they will send you an email indicating that they want to publish it and will give you a deadline to answer them. The time frame really depends on the journal, but as indicated above, a top journal will give you a few days at most to decide. It can take some journals several weeks to review a paper and make a decision. Do not get discouraged, the journals get hundreds (or thousands) of requests and the papers often undergo several rounds of review before a decision is made.

Once you accept, you are required to sign a contract with the journal and the editing process starts. Your paper is then placed into the subcite stream, and various subciters will start to check your citations and edit your paper. Even for a good paper, the editing process is extensive. When I submitted my paper for editing, it contained fifty citations. When the editors were done with the paper it contained over 300.

Another phenomenon in the publication process is something called expedited review. This occurs when you have an offer from one journal but you really want to publish with another journal. In this case, you may contact the journal or journals you wish to publish with and tell them that you have an offer. If they have an interest in your paper, they will review it and give you a decision right away. However, a top school will not perform an expedited review, and this is why you should consider submitting to them exclusively prior to submitting to other journals. It would be a shame if you accepted another journal and one week later *Harvard Law Review* indicated they were interested.

---

 *While expedited review can get a journal to review your note quickly, some top journals will not perform one. As such, if you are submitting a note to a top school or journal, submit your note to that journal prior to submitting to others—that way, you can see if the top journal has an interest in your note and you will not miss an opportunity.*

---

Expedited review can also be used strategically and can be an excellent tool to get your paper selected by a higher ranked journal. First, the request highlights your paper by forcing the journal to look at it. Second, top journals often feel that your paper is only worthy of their consideration if a lower journal has accepted you. Note that it is unethical to state that you have an offer from a journal when you do not. A lie like this could cost you admission to the bar, so you should not ever consider it.

### When Should I Submit my Article to Journals?

You may theoretically submit your paper at anytime, but the best time to submit papers is either in the spring or fall. Spring season starts in March and lasts through April; fall season starts in August and goes until the end of September. If you submit in the spring, your submission would be considered for the fall issue of the journal. If you submit in the fall, it will be considered for the following spring. You should avoid submitting your paper at other times of the year, as you will be at a substantial disadvantage.

## *What Makes a Good Journal Submission?*

There are a number of tips related to writing a good law review paper and getting published:

1. Write about something you know. This could include something closely aligned to an old profession or something that you studied in college. If you are already an expert in a topic, you can mix this with legal concepts and your paper will stand out. For example, I was an investment banker prior to law school and wrote and published a paper on fair value accounting and the financial crisis. Another friend who was a doctor wrote a paper on health law. Another friend who worked as an auctioneer wrote a paper on art law. This combination of your experience and the law will be very appealing to journals and makes for interesting papers.

2. Make sure that the paper you submit is final and free from errors. In order to accomplish this, you should get as many people as possible to read and edit your paper. This will not only significantly reduce the amount of errors but will also alert you to areas of your paper that need work. Listen to their feedback!

3. Follow the journal's instructions! This includes font size, spacing, article length, submission timing, cover letters, and more. Several good papers are not considered because they do not adhere to simple guidelines.

4. A cover letter and good abstract are essential! When you submit your paper to a journal, these two documents may be the only thing that they read, and for ninety percent of the papers received, this alone is the basis for rejection. As such, you must use the cover letter and the abstract to market yourself and capture the reader's attention. When you make your cover letter, ensure that you tell the reader why he or she should pick your paper over the thousands of others. If you are writing about something you are an expert in, this can often be an easy sell. The key though is to succinctly explain your experience and why your paper is exceptional.

5. Do not plagiarize! Plagiarism involves stating or summarizing the work of others without citing them. All papers have a significant amount of citations, and this is normal. If you use someone else's ideas, cite them; if you do not, you could be subject to discipline and civil liability. It could even stop you from becoming a lawyer. Plagiarism equals cheating.

6. Keep it simple! I was an editor on the *Human Rights Journal* at Harvard, and many papers that the journal received were complicated and confusing. You are not writing a literary masterpiece, so use simple, plain language, and there is no need to use symbolism or complex metaphors. Also, if your paper deals with a complex topic like finance, for example, make sure that you either explain the terms you are using or simplify the language. The people deciding whether or not to publish your paper are law students and are not quantitative experts or economists.

# The Multi-State Professional Responsibility Exam (MPRE)

The Multi-State Professional Responsibility Exam (MPRE) is a sixty-question two-hour multiple-choice exam that you are required to sit for either before or after you take the bar examination. Ten of the questions are test questions and are not graded, but you will not know which ten questions are practice questions. Most people sit for the examination before taking the bar, and in some states it is a prerequisite to sit for the bar exam. In other states— for example, New York—you may complete the MPRE up to three years after sitting for the bar examination.

The MPRE is required to practice law in all but four jurisdictions, and a passing scaled score ranges from 76 to 86. A passing score in New York is 85, which equates to approximately thirty-three to thirty-five questions correct out of the fifty graded questions. You will not experience any time pressure on the examination (you are given two hours), and most finish with plenty of time to spare. Also, most people sit for the MPRE in November during their third year of law school. While most sit for the exam in November, it is also offered at other times of the year, such as in August.

---

 *You should sit for the MPRE in August prior to starting your third year of law school if you can. While most people sit for the exam in November during their third year of law school, it is only because they hear of the exam for the first time when they start their third year. August is a much better time to sit for the exam because it will not distract you from your course work. Moreover, you will have a gigantic smile on your face when most of your classmates are sitting for the exam in November. I made the mistake of sitting for the exam on November 7, which happened to be in the middle of a busy semester. If I knew about the August sitting, I definitely would have taken it then.*

---

The MPRE is based on the law governing how lawyers should conduct themselves when dealing with the public, in courtrooms, and with other lawyers. The examination deals with rules of professional conduct set out by the states, including disciplinary conduct for bad conduct. For example, you will learn that it is a breach of your conduct to comingle client funds with your own.

The MPRE is not an easy exam, but it is fair. If you study for approximately thirty-five hours, you will do fine. You may also listen to a four-hour lecture that is hosted by an organization like Barbri, which is very helpful. Barbri will also give you sample exams and outlines to practice. This organization has been around for decades and offers bar exam preparation courses for students. The bar exam preparation courses are discussed in more detail in the "Bar Examination" section of this book.

Although most people pass the MPRE, do not be fooled and think that you can take the exam without studying or that everything on the exam will be common sense. I know at least two people from Harvard who failed on their first attempt. I know another from Brooklyn Law School who achieved a score of 84, so he had to take the exam again since a passing score in New York is 85.

---

 *Dedicate at least forty hours to studying for the MPRE. Do not be fooled into thinking that it is a common sense exam or that you can wing it; some people do fail it and have to rewrite it. While retaking it is not a big deal, it is a bit embarrassing and may impact your confidence for the bar examination.*

---

# 4. The Summer Experience at a Large Corporate Law Firm

During the summer after the first and second years of law school, most students work in a law-related field. There are several options for summer employment, such as working for a judge, a public service organization, a large corporation, a large corporate law firm, or others. While some jobs are on a voluntary basis (unpaid), others pay from $5,000 to $32,000 for the summer. The big law firm jobs are the ones that pay the big bucks—$32,000 for just over ten weeks of work.

## Taking a Summer Position at a Large Law Firm

A full-time job at a large law firm may not be for everyone, but a summer job at one is a great experience and is highly recommended. This is the case even if you do not have any interest in practicing at a large firm after the summer. You should be careful, though, because many who have worked during the summer at large corporate firms and swore that it was just for the summer drank the Kool-Aid and went back to full-time positions after graduation. Whether or not you plan to accept a job at a large firm, there are several reasons why the summer experience at a large firm is a good idea.

First of all, it pays well. Secondly, your pay is for the most part tax-free because you are in school for the rest of the year and are therefore not subject to much tax. Given the work that you will do, the experience you will gain, and the fun you will have, it is the easiest money that you will ever earn.

---

 *If you can get a job in a large firm over the summer, you should take it even if you do not intend to practice at a large law firm after you graduate. Remember that you have two working summers, so you can easily split them between public interest and corporate law firm work.*

---

 *Whenever looking at a paid summer position, you should always look at the impact the job will have on your financial aid. Every school will have an elaborate calculation that will impact your ability to have some of your loans forgiven. In addition, these calculations may impact the amount of a loan or grant you are eligible for in future years. Make sure you understand how the salary can impact you prior to accepting the position.*

---

Although getting paid is nice, it is only one of many reasons to work at a large law firm for the summer. Another reason is that the summer will allow you to narrow down exactly what you want or do not want to do. Most people who are in law school may have a vague idea of which area of law they want to practice, but this may change when you see what working in that area is really like. As such, getting an up-close look at what the day-to-day activities are may reinforce or change your desire to work in that area.

For example, I was quite keen to work in the area related to mergers and acquisitions until my summer revealed exactly what lawyers who specialize in this do. I no longer have the slightest interest in that area. In fact, I was positioned to take a mergers and acquisitions course in my third year, and after an assignment in this area at a law firm during the summer, I decided that this course was not for me.

Another advantage of working at a large law firm in the summer is the experience that you will get. Even though the summer will be fun, you will actually do "real" work, and it will be similar to the work you will do if you accept full-time employment with the law firm. This experience will look great on your résumé, and you will quickly see how all the information you learned in law school works in practice. Moreover, there are also some perks of working at a law firm. While this at first may seem like the most superficial reason to work somewhere, you may feel differently after you see the over-the-top lavish treatment you receive. I guarantee that you will regret it if you decide not to work at a firm for the summer and you have to listen to your friends talking about being wined and dined for ten weeks straight.

The perks take on many forms, and they are all designed to get you to decide to stay with the firm after graduation. First, you are given lunch every day, usually from a very nice restaurant. You will be fed like a king or queen, but you should also remember to act like one by following proper etiquette. While the lunches are more or less a bonanza, you should try to order respectfully, and you should almost never order alcohol. There may be limited exceptions to the alcohol rule, but you are better off having a drink with your friends after work rather than with your coworkers during lunch. You should also not order food or drinks just for the sake of ordering, and you should avoid looking like you are being wasteful. A good rule of thumb is to order as if you were paying. I remember one lunch I was at where the full-time associates were complaining about a summer associate who ordered seven sodas when they took him to lunch. You do not want to be the person with that type of reputation. Just use common sense and you will be fine.

---

 *When you go to lunch or a firm event, the "interview" continues during the lunch. Do not be fooled and think that the lunch is a formality or a casual event. When I took interview candidates to lunch, I was required to complete an evaluation and give my opinion on whether or not they should be hired.*

---

Yet another good reason to join a firm for the summer is the social aspect. If you are a social person, you will feel like you have died and gone to heaven. In addition to the great lunches, the firm organizes a number of social events and dinners, and this of course is paid for completely. During the summer, I participated in the following events that were sponsored by and paid for by my firm.

- Theater night—Choice of seeing one of three Broadway plays/musicals with a pre-theater dinner

- Night at the Apollo—A guided tour of the Apollo Theater in New York, a live show, and a dinner buffet

- Private dinner at a partner's house—four or five students are invited to a partner's house for dinner and drinks. This is the "this is what you could have if you become a partner" dinner. Needless to say, the partner's house I went to was palatial and located in one of the best areas of the city.

- Private party – A party held at a chic hotel where all lawyers of the firm and a guest are invited; includes drinks and dinner

- Boat tour—A private boat tour with the other summer and full-time associates with dinner, dancing, and drinks

- Scavenger hunt—A very professional scavenger hunt in New York City with dinner and drinks after the hunt

- Scotch tasting—Premium scotch tasting at a cigar lounge (I could have done without the smoke, but this is great if you are a scotch fan)

- Shakespeare in the Park—Ticket to a live performance in the park with pre-theater dinner and drinks

Other perks may include the following:

- Transportation to and from the city for your summer employment and your interviews

- Lodging in five-star hotels during your interviews

- Gym membership during the summer

- Private banking access from major banks

- Discounts with many vendors

In addition to all of these perks and the other aspects discussed, a large firm gives you the added advantage of seeing how a large organization works. Most law students have never worked for a large company, so this opportunity could give you a sneak peak at what it would be like. Large companies are not for everyone, and it would be a shame to figure this out after you have given up another opportunity.

## Turning Your Summer Employment Into a Permanent Job Offer

If you have decided to work for a firm during the summer, here are a few things to consider.

1. You may get a job offer, but do not take it for granted. Most large firms have in the past extended offers to all of the summer associates, but the poor economy has changed this. While you will likely get an offer, you should not assume that you will get one and should act accordingly. This does not mean that you should stress out and worry; just do a good job and you should be fine.

2. Do not get drunk at firm events. This sounds obvious, but many students drink and act silly at firm functions. There is a summer associate story about an individual who worked at a firm one summer and jumped into the Hudson River while on a boat cruise. Even though this happened years ago, people still talk about it. Do not let this be you.

3. Bring a pen and paper to every meeting. You would be shocked at how many people do not do this, and it simply looks bad.

4. Do a bit of research about an assignment before you meet with the lawyer. Generally, the staffing person will at least tell you the company name, so you can Google the company and perhaps bring a printout of some documents to your first meeting to show you took initiative. During my summer, I printed out one Internet article about a company prior to meeting with the lawyer, and she noted this as a very positive element on my review.

5. Communicate with lawyers and tell them when you have too much on your plate. While the law firm wants you to enjoy yourself, they also want you to do work. You are ALWAYS better served though communicating that you have too much on your plate rather than just accepting work and either not finishing it or not doing a good job. If you communicate that you are too busy and explain why, the worst thing that will happen is they will find someone else for the task. Remember that every lawyer you work with thinks that you are only doing work for them, so do not assume they know about your other assignments.

6. Check in regularly with lawyers regarding the status of the assignments you are given. The lawyers you are working with will greatly appreciate if you regularly update them with the status of the assignments they have given you. Do not let them think that the work they have given you has fallen into an abyss—a simple call or email will go a long way. Also, let the lawyer make the decision about whether or not you stay late. I would often ask lawyers when they needed the work product and offered to stay late if they needed it. Nine times out of ten they would indicate that sometime in the future was fine and that staying late was not necessary.

7. Let your secretary know where you are at all times. There is nothing worse than having people looking for you and not being able to tell a partner or senior lawyer where you are.

8. Treat your secretary with respect. Some have lots of power in firms and can make your life miserable if you treat them badly. Moreover, a good working relationship with someone you will see every day just makes sense.

9. Enjoy your summer! The summer perks are amazing and you should make sure that you are enjoying the lunches, the theater, the scavenger hunts, the bowling, the concerts, the parties, and more.

# 5. Working at a Large Law Firm

N ow that you have heard about the perks of working at a large law firm, we will discuss a bit about the work. Most large firms have two primary areas of focus, and the experience you will get will fall into either corporate or litigation practice areas. These two terms will often be used while you are going through the interview process, and you should have a basic understanding of them before you go on any interviews. I cannot tell you how many times I was asked which area I was interested in, a question to which I always responded, "I do not know." The truth was that I did not really have a good idea of what the person was talking about. The next section summarizes exactly what corporate and litigation mean.

## Corporate Work in a Large Law Firm

If you plan to do corporate work, you will find that the work you are doing has little to do with much of what you learned in law school. I guess that this can be a good or bad thing, depending on your experience in law school. However you feel about law school, though, it is a fact that most corporate lawyers have never seen a courtroom and would not even know how to sign on to Lexis or Westlaw (legal research tools) to perform legal research. For those of you who did not like the law school experience or think that if you never had to read another law school case it would be too soon, there is still hope.

Corporate work in a large firm can best be described as legal consulting or advising, and there are many different types of corporate work. Examples of corporate work include mergers and acquisitions, initial public offerings, and bond issuance. For example, one transaction that I worked on during my summer at a large firm can be described as follows: Company A (a manufacturing company) wanted to issue some bonds to raise money. A bond is really a loan or "IOU"—the company gets money from people who invest in the bond, and the company has to pay back the person who gave it to them with interest later. Let us also say that the interest rate on the bonds is not fixed but rather changes when interest rates change. This means that if interest rates go up, the manufacturing company will have to pay out a higher amount of interest to the people who bought their bonds. If the rate goes down, the company will pay less.

Since some companies do not like to take the risk of interest rates changing, they can go to a bank and purchase a product called a derivative in order to limit the amount of downside risk related to the transaction. This really means that they pay the bank to assume the risk of interest rates rising so that the company can have a secure fixed rate of interest payments without worrying about rates rising—that is, the bank will pay any "extra" interest to the investor if interest rates go up. So what do the lawyers do when confronted with a complex set of transactions like this?

As you can imagine, the details related to the transaction may be quite complicated and would require the drafting of various contracts and legal documents. For example, the people who buy the bonds want to make sure that they get their money back in a timely fashion. Also, the manufacturing company and the bank will both have strong opinions regarding the details of the contract for the derivative.

Because the manufacturing company specializes in making goods, they typically would not have people working for them that could structure a deal like this. Also, the bank may not have this type of expertise in-house. Accordingly, they hire lawyers from large law firms to draft their legal documents. As the transactions relate more to consulting and advising rather than two people trying to sue each other, the bank and manufacturing company will seek assistance from the corporate side of the law firm.

Almost all large law firms have a corporate group that deals with the issuance of bonds and stocks along with several other corporate areas related to business transactions. In the above example, a corporate law firm could represent the manufacturing company that wants to issue the bonds, and the lawyers would help draft or word the documents related to the issuance so that it meets the company's objectives. While it may sound a bit mundane on the surface, the issuances are often quite complex and, as such, require the expertise of a lawyer or advisor to make sure the company is protected. This is particularly the case when the bonds have special features. For example, some bonds can be converted to stock if certain triggers are met. When drafting the contract documents, lawyers try to anticipate any potential conflicts that the two sides may have and work those into the agreement.

The example above also had a transaction in which the manufacturing company wanted to purchase a product called a derivative from the bank. In this transaction, both the bank and the manufacturing company may hire lawyers to assist them. They would each have their own lawyers, and the lawyers would be from different firms. In essence, the manufacturing company would tell the lawyers what they are looking for and the lawyers will draft the documents that specify exactly what the arrangement is between the two parties. After the initial document has been drafted, it is presented to the other company and their lawyers for comment and changes. Both sets of lawyers spend a great deal of time going through each provision in the document to suggest changes. This back-and-forth can go on for days and is a significant part of the process.

Assistance with documents related to stock and bond issuances as well as documents that explain the terms of derivatives are very common in these practice areas, and a large part of the process is drafting contracts that set out terms and rights of the parties. If you do not like drafting these types of documents and negotiating changes, you will not like most corporate work.

---

*If you do not like drafting and negotiating contract documents, you will most likely not like some corporate work. A summer experience in a large firm will illustrate exactly what corporate law groups do, and you can get a sense of whether or not this type of work is for you.*

---

If you decide to work in the corporate law area, you will see that there are some provisions in many of these documents that you will draft that are complex and you can become an expert in certain areas. You will also enhance your negotiation skills, as a large part of the job is negotiating wording changes and provisions with the other side. As such, a very helpful course to take if you are interested in corporate work is a negotiation workshop.

---

*If you are interested in corporate work, take a negotiation course in law school or read a book called* Getting to Yes. *You will find that a large part of your job relates to negotiating provisions of contracts and agreements, so a course or the book* Getting to Yes *will help you immensely.*

---

You should keep in mind that in your first few years at a corporate law firm, you will have to get used to being the person who prepares the initial draft, and you will have to become accustomed to an almost unrecognizable document when it is completed. This is normal, as there are various people commenting on the first draft and changes are part of the process. In this simple example, there can often be a few banks involved, and each will have staff that will have comments. Members on your team will also have many comments and suggestions. Moreover, some lawyers are quite anal and will bicker over unimportant words and phrases.

Another common corporate area is mergers and acquisitions (M&A). This corporate area sounds kind of interesting, and there is no question that it attracts type A personalities. This practice area really involves acting as a consultant to the various parties that want to buy or merge a company. In a typical merger, Company A wants to buy Company B, and they can accomplish this in a number of ways that are far too complicated to describe in this book. However, let us just say that the transaction and both sides are governed by a lengthy document called the merger agreement. The job of a lawyer is to negotiate the various provisions of this contract document. For example, the buyer might want a provision that gives him or her the opportunity to get out of the deal if there is a significant or material change to the business he or she is buying. The seller, on the other hand, would want to limit the possible reasons a buyer could get out of the transaction. The work can be fun, but a successful merger and acquisition lawyer is someone who is good at and likes negotiating, and also someone who likes working with contract documents. You will see that, time and time again, these two skills pop up when talking about corporate work.

M&A is not for me, but some people like it. In your first couple of years working in this area, you will perform a not-so-fun task called due diligence, which is a time-consuming task in which the lawyer reviews the seller's information (financial and other) to make sure the company that is being purchased is as good as the seller says and is worth the purchase price. In some ways, due diligence is similar to document review, which I will talk about when I discuss litigation. Both are necessary but fairly mundane tasks.

There are many other corporate areas, including project finance, financial institutions, structured finance, leveraged finance, and private equity. The key thing to remember is that these areas are better described as consulting, contract design, or advising, and you will not find any courtroom drama here. Moreover, negotiation is a key element of most corporate work. To get a description of the types of activities covered in these areas, you can review the website of any large corporate law firm.

## Litigation Work in a Large Law Firm

Litigation is a practice area that more closely resembles what you do in law school. While you will not see a courtroom for years if you work in a large firm, you will almost immediately start to perform all of the tasks that you performed in law school. For example, you will research legal issues, write legal memos, write briefs, and formulate legal arguments. Most firms have several subsets of litigation, so you can often specialize in areas such as white-collar crimes, securities litigation, pro-bono litigation, and more.

If you like the doctrinal first-year courses outlined earlier, you will most likely love litigation, as many litigation issues stem from torts, contracts, and property law. In terms of the work, it is more like what you see on television, except the work is behind the scenes rather than in a courtroom.

Here is an example to give you an idea of the process flow. Say Company A wants to sue Company B because Company B failed to deliver goods that it promised to deliver by a certain date. In this example, a separate law firm would represent each of the parties. In terms of process and what the law firm will do for the client, the lawyer of Company A—the party that wants to sue— files a complaint, and the lawyer of Company B—the person being sued—gets to file a written response or answer.

In almost every case, the party being sued moves for a motion to dismiss. This is a written motion that states that there is not enough evidence for the matter to go to trial or that the person suing has not done something that they had promised to do. It is usually a lengthy document that summarizes various legal arguments from both sides.

After the judge decides whether the case is dismissed, and assuming that the case is not dismissed, one party will take the next step, which is to move for a motion for summary judgment. This is similar to a motion to dismiss but has some technical differences that are too complicated to go over here. It is a long document that requires significant legal research and writing, and both sides submit their legal arguments.

You can start to see that there is quite a bit of behind-the-scenes work that goes on before a trail even starts. In fact, the behind-the-scenes work usually goes on for years while the trial (if it happens at all) may only last for a week. During my recent summer at a law firm, I worked on a case that related the World Trade Center terrorist attack in 2001, and the case had not gotten past the summary judgment stage yet. Ultimately, most cases either get dismissed or are settled, and this is why you will not see much of a courtroom.

As such, as an associate, a big part of your job will be assisting with the preparation of the briefs and arguments that are associated with these motions prior to trial. As I mentioned, you will not see a courtroom for years, and even when you do, it will be to watch. Most firms (and clients) will only allow partners to argue cases, and many cases do not even have oral argument.

---

 *Do not shy away from litigation just because you do not like public speaking. You can be an excellent litigator if you can write well, and there will be few instances where you actually have to get in front of someone to argue cases. The key to success in a litigation group during your first few years will be your writing ability and your attention to detail.*

---

When you are a partner and a case goes to trial, this is when you will see a courtroom and some of the TV courtroom drama might play out. Even with this, though, you will likely just argue in front of a judge rather than a jury. This is when good oral advocacy skills will be more important for a litigator, but for the first few years the key to success will be your writing.

The above description of writing briefs and arguing cases is the interesting side of litigation work, but not all of the work for a first- or second-year associate is that glamorous. Unfortunately, during your first couple of years one area that drives most associates to drink is something called document review. (This is similar to due diligence described earlier.) When Company B gets sued by Company A, Company A can ask to review Company B's internal documents through a process called discovery. When this happens, Company B can send Company A literally thousands of documents, and someone has to perform a document review—that is, that person must go through those documents to ascertain whether or not they contain something important. So who is the person who does all this work? You guessed it—the new associate. Some firms have contractors who do this, but usually, even when they do have contractors, they are only assigned to a portion of the documentation review. Also, some clients insist that firm employees (who bill over $300 per hour) rather than contractors (who bill around $50 per hour or much less) review their documents—clients who have money to burn of course.

---

 *If you loved the first-year law school courses, evidence, or reading cases, you will most likely like litigation work. Keep in mind that in a large firm you will not see a courtroom for years. Also, while some of your tasks in the first couple of years will be interesting, you will almost certainly be assigned to the boring task of document review.*

---

# Corporate Law and Litigation Compared

In some ways corporate and litigation work are extensions of each other. The corporate folks work on the agreement and contract to address possible things that could go wrong and the litigation folks resolve any conflicts that result when things actually do go wrong, and people sue each other. There are some important differences, which I've outlined below.

| Topic | Litigation | Corporate |
|---|---|---|
| **Length of Assignments** | Long—normally years. | Long—usually a couple of weeks |
| **Predictability and ability to plan your life** | Fairly stable, but remember, it is a law firm so you can have long hours | Very client-driven, so you could be leaving the office at 5 P.M. on a Friday and get a call from a client who wants to do a deal. This area can be extremely unpredictable, and it is very tough to make plans. Also, when a deal comes in, you could be working fifteen-hour days for a few days in a row |
| **Most Negative Aspect** | Due Diligence | Documentation Review |
| **Amount of Legal Research** | Significant | Minimal |
| **Court Time** | Very little, but some when you are more senior | None—most corporate lawyers have never gone to court |
| **Pro Bono Work** | Litigation lends itself very well to pro bono work as most people need litigators when they cannot afford to pay for an attorney | The nature of the work does not lend itself much to pro bono work, although there is a limited amount (for example, the set up of a not-for-profit organization) |
| **Hours** | Long | Long |

The firms also have specialty areas like tax and employee benefits. If you are interested in these or other specialty areas, you should check the ranking of the firms as they relate to the particular areas. This information can be easily obtained from *abovethelaw.com* and from the various vault surveys that are discussed later in "Selecting a Law Firm," Chapter 6.

Now that you have an overview of corporate and litigation law, we will talk about whether or not a full-time job at a large law firm is right for you after you graduate.

## Deciding if a Full-Time Job with a Large Law Firm Is for You

A large law firm is not for everyone; like anything else, there are advantages and disadvantages associated with joining one after you graduate.

### *Advantages of Accepting a Full-Time Job with a Large Law Firm*

The biggest advantage of working at a large firm is the pay. In several major markets, the starting salary for an associate with absolutely no work experience is $160,000 per year, plus a small bonus of around $15,000. This salary immediately puts a graduate who may have been on this planet for a mere twenty-five years among the top five percent of income earners in the country.

Also, this salary is compared to an average of approximately $45,000 per year for a public service job. Because many students leave law school with over $150,000 in debt, the idea of going to a large firm can be very appealing. In fact, I suspect that many people select big law firm jobs for this reason alone.

In addition to the high salary, large firms offer a comprehensive set of benefits including health care, gym memberships, and retirement contributions, among many other things. Moreover, a large firm will pay for your bar preparation course (almost $3,000), moving expenses, brokerage fees, and several other expenses if you decide to work for them. These expenses can add up to well over $15,000. Finally, most firms will give you either a stipend or a cash advance while you are studying for the bar exam. Cleary Gottlieb offers a $10,000 interest-free cash advance that is paid to you within a few months of joining the firm. As you can imagine, the money comes in handy after law school and while studying for the bar exam.

---

**TIP** *If you take a job at a big firm, be prepared to commit to the job for at least one year. If you do not, most firms will require that you repay all or some of the expenses that they paid on your behalf. Although you would have incurred bar preparation course fees anyway, moving expenses from a professional mover can run in excess of $10,000, and it would be a shame to have to pay those back.*

---

Another advantage of a large firm, and in particular a highly ranked firm, is the firm's reputation and the effect that reputation will have on your resume. Corporate America places a high premium on law firm experience, and if you have worked for a top firm for a few years, you can demand a significant premium when looking for another job. Like most things, the more highly the firm is ranked, the better. As you may know, there are hundreds of thousands of lawyers in the U.S., so companies often look at indicators of success—such as firm rankings—when making hiring decisions. As such, a job at a small law firm of four or five lawyers will not be as highly regarded as a law firm like Cleary Gottlieb or Sullivan & Cromwell, which fall within the top ten firms. You can find a list of the firm rankings in many different sources, and this is discussed at greater length in "Selecting a Law Firm," Chapter 6.

A large firm will also give you decent experience. While this is an advantage, most post-graduate law jobs will give you good experience. If you have an interest in the corporate areas described earlier, however, a large corporate law firm is the place to go, as many large companies and banks go to the law firms for assistance with their complex transactions. Moreover, it is tough to get this type of experience elsewhere. Also, you will not learn how to do corporate work in law school, and this type of work would not exist in a not-for-profit organization.

Large law firms also provide a very professional and non-bureaucratic work environment. The associates and partners at a law firm are all lawyers, and the organization is profit-driven. As such, you will usually be working with business professionals, and the focus is typically on the client and making money rather than politics and bureaucracy. Depending on your personality, this is either a good or a bad thing. During my first summer, I worked at the United Nations, and although I enjoyed the job, I knew that I could not work there permanently because the organization was far too bureaucratic for me. In contrast, I found the firm I worked at for the summer in my second year very efficient and much more aligned with my personality. You know yourself best, so you will have to make the call here.

### Disadvantages of Accepting a Full-Time Job with a Large Law Firm

The biggest disadvantage of working in a large corporate law firm is the long and unpredictable hours. It is not uncommon to work over sixty hours a week, and you will often work more. I just went to dinner with a friend who told me he worked ninety hours a week for two weeks in a row. He may have exaggerated a bit, but you get the point.

You should know that it is not acceptable to say "I have plans" unless the plans are something significant like your own wedding or a funeral. I have spoken to several full-time associates who told me their friends and family were accustomed to the fact that they would often have to cancel plans at the last minute.

This brings us to the next related big disadvantage of working in a large law firm—that is, your schedule, and at times your life, belong to the firm. This goes far beyond the number of hours that you will work and includes the unpredictability of the work requirements at a firm and the "on call" expectation. While working at a law firm, I was in Central Park on a beautiful summer day one weekend and received a call from a lawyer I work with who requested I return to the office to take care of an "urgent" matter.

Here are a few things to consider regarding being on call and the unpredictable nature of the job. First, you will often work on projects for several people, and every person feels that his or her project should take priority. This is especially the case if you are working directly for a partner, and as such, it is important to manage expectations. Second, the clients of a large law firm often decide on a transaction one day and then expect the law firm to execute what is needed in a very short time frame. For example, in the above example related to the manufacturing company, you can rest assured that the company will decide to issue bonds on a Friday at 3 P.M. for example, and when you are ready to leave the office at 5 P.M., your partner will call you and tell you that you have to work all weekend. This is normal and is something you will have to learn to live with while you are at the firm.

Moreover, you are always expected to have your Blackberry with you, and it is not acceptable to say that you did not see a message or that you did not check your Blackberry. Even if it is 9 P.M. on a Friday night, it would not be acceptable to ignore a call or message from the office. and you are expected to check your Blackberry regularly throughout the night and on the weekend. You are even expected to check your Blackberry while you are on vacation.

You should also note that while the experience is good at a large firm, if you are interested in litigation, you can get good experience wherever you go. In fact, if you decide to go to a small firm, a not-for-profit, or the government, you will likely see a courtroom faster and you may get more responsibility and control over your cases significantly faster. In a litigation group in a large firm, you will get good experience, but you will often work on pieces of the case rather than control the entire case. Moreover, you may spend many hours performing mundane tasks such as document review. You should also keep in mind that your work and written documents will be subject to far more layers of review in a large firm than at a smaller firm or not-for-profit.

## A Few Things That Will Help You Succeed if You Work at a Large Firm

1. When you start as a first-year associate, it is almost certain that you will feel like you do not know what you are doing for six months. Regrettably, most people you work with will not do much to rectify that feeling, as they themselves will be second- and third-year associates who do not really know how to manage others and either have an Attila the Hun management style or are passive aggressive. Do not let this feeling of not knowing what you are doing get you down. If you work at a large firm, it means that your grades are probably high. Know that EVERYONE is going through what you are going through. All you can do is ask lots of questions and know that you are not alone.

2. While the salary and future job prospects of large law firms are great, be prepared to give a large part of your life to the firm. The hours you will work in a firm are long and unpredictable, and in some instances you may have to cancel vacations and plans with family and

friends. Before I started at a firm, I used to think that paying twenty-year-old students with zero work experience $160,000 per year was crazy. Now I think that a first-year associate deserves every penny. A friend at the firm recently told me that a senior associate told her she should be checking her Blackberry every fifteen minutes between 8 and 10:30 P.M. (The senior associate thought that the junior associate was not "responsive" enough.) Knowing and understanding the commitment and expectation before you join a firm can go a long way toward getting you through a tough time. I was often surprised at how many people thought that the full-time job would be just like their summer experience.

3. If you decide to work in a large law firm, know when to say no! Keep in mind that it is always better to perform a limited number of tasks well rather than to perform a bunch of tasks poorly. Your best tool to deal with multiple requests is communication. Explain to whomever is asking you to do work that you have something that will keep you occupied, and give them a realistic time frame of when you can complete it. I have met many people who fall into the trap of taking on more than they can handle, and they are miserable. Moreover, their bosses are not happy because they have done a mediocre job.

4. All legal assignments and work that you receive in a large firm (or other legal job) will take you longer than you anticipated. Lawyers have to be thorough, and even a task that seems simple takes time. Make sure you give your boss realistic estimates of how long something will take. It is better to take your time and do things right.

# 6. Selecting a Law Firm

So how do you decide which law firms to apply to for a job? If you do decide to join a large law firm, the choice can be daunting at both the application and offer stages. You may, of course, apply to as many firms as you like, but the number of offers that you will receive will be governed by how attractive a candidate you are. For the most part this will mean your grades, but there are other factors that play a role in hiring decisions. Before we start looking at specific things you should look for when deciding which firm to apply to, I will give you a tip to try and lock in a few offers early.

In addition to activities like law review, moot court, and student organizations, one very important distinguishing factor that influences employers is what you have done prior to law school. This can include both your previous jobs and your previous extracurricular activities. For example, law firms love accountants. If you have a CPA designation, you should apply to some corporate law firms, since lawyers and accountants work very closely and the firm will know that you already understand business transactions. Conversely, an immigration firm may not be so quick to hire you if you are a CPA. If you apply to a few corporate law firms, with these special skills, you will likely get a few early offers even with mediocre grades.

In addition, a law firm that specializes in a particular area will find you very attractive if you have a degree or experience in that area. For example, a firm that handles malpractice suits against doctors would hire you in a minute if you were a medical doctor, since you would have interesting insight. I know a student who was an architect, and he received two job offers before the regular interview process started from firms that specialized in some type of applied design law.

This approach of applying to firms early when they will likely love your background may seem obvious, but it is often overlooked when people are looking for jobs. The on-campus recruitment process is one that could involve over 500 students, so it is easy to get lost in the crowd. Applying to key firms in advance of this process is an excellent way to lock in a few offers early! So how does one go about sifting through the many firms out there? The next section deals with the job search process and how to find a law firm for you.

## Finding a Law Firm That Is a Good Fit for You

### *What Are the Steps in the Recruitment Process When I Am Still in Law School?*

The search for a job for your second summer starts early. In fact, during the summer after your first year of law school, you will go through process called the "on-campus interview" (OCI), and this is usually conducted in August. The name may differ slightly depending on the school, but they all relate to finding a job for your second summer.

The process is usually an electronic and fairly streamlined process. First, employers contact the law school and express an interest to recruit from the school. These employers can be governmental organizations, not-for-profit organizations, corporations, and, of course, law firms. Once the school has a list of all of the prospective employers, the employers are electronically posted to a web page and the students pick prospective employers that interest them.

After this selection, students upload their résumé, transcripts, and a cover letter if requested. At this point, the students usually simply express an interest to interview with the employer and the employer then sifts through the information to decide who they want to see. This is one way that the selection occurs, but it varies depending on the school.

At some law schools, the employers go through the résumés and transcripts and select twenty to twenty-five people (out of over 400) they want to interview. In addition, the job descriptions often indicate what they are looking for in a candidate. For example, the job description may say that the law firm is only looking at the top five or ten percent of the class. If a law school is in the top tier, the law firm typically will not designate such a high cutoff. For example, at a school like Fordham Law School, which is ranked around 30, employers may look at students in the top thirty percent. The more prestigious the firm, the more selective they will be, and all firms want students with top grades from top schools. After the selection, the firm comes to the school and interviews the twenty or so students they have selected. Again, you can see the importance of grades in your first year since grades are all the employers see at this point, and it is almost the sole basis of their selection of the twenty to twenty-five people to interview.

At some schools, like Harvard, the employer does not have a say in who it interviews. Instead, Harvard uses a lottery system in which students rank employers and are matched up based on this lottery without any employer input. Hundreds of interviews are conducted at or close to law schools, and the interviews are very short and last only around twenty minutes. Because there are many employers, the interviews are often conducted in hotels or conference rooms close to the school. As such, do not be too surprised if you go to the interview and you are in a room talking about your first year of law school with a hotel bed right beside you.

After the interview process, if the employer likes you, they will give you a "call back," which you will usually get the next day. If you are not called back within one week, the process for that firm is over. Occasionally the firm will send you a thank you for applying, but most just assume that you know they are not interested if you do not hear from them.

---

 *If you get a call back, let the caller leave a message rather than answering the phone. The callers often have to call several people, and they typically would prefer just to leave a message. The message will contain information and contact information for the recruitment office, and it is NOT necessary to call the person who called you back unless you are calling to decline or they specifically request a call back.*

---

If you are called back and you wish to learn more about the firm, the firm pays to fly you to their office, and you go through four to six more interviews. It is usually a half-day event where they take you to lunch and tell you all the great things about the firm. After this, the firm will either make you an offer or send you a kind letter that explains that they have far more qualified applicants than available positions.

### How Should I Act at my Interviews?

The best advice is to be professional and courteous and, most of all, yourself. For most interviews the interviewer is just trying to assess your personality, and you would not be called back if they were not already at least satisfied with your grades (employers will always have a copy of your transcript prior to your interview).

If you have not interviewed before, you should go to the career counseling center at your law school and ask them about seminars or courses. These seminars will teach you the basics regarding how to dress and how to sell yourself, and most schools also conduct mock interview sessions. Also, many schools assign career counseling officers to students, and you should definitely take advantage of this service. During my first year I saw a career counselor, and she significantly improved the format of my résumé. This was the case even though I had been updating my résumé myself for over ten years.

Finally, although many organizations have adopted a business casual approach, you should always wear business attire to an interview. This is the case even if the interview is conducted on a Saturday or the organization indicates that business casual is acceptable. You can never be overdressed for an interview.

---

*Each law school has to publish statistics related to how many of their graduates find jobs. As such, in order to increase job placements, the schools all hire career counselors who offer excellent advice. Seek them out and get them to review your résumé and give you tips on interviewing. They are an excellent resource, and their services are included in your tuition.*

---

## What Does an Offer for Summer Employment Really Mean?

An "offer" means that the law firm is inviting you to "summer" with them, giving you a paid position with the firm for your second summer. If you have great grades and good experience and go to a top school, you may have many offers. An offer is great for two reasons: the pay is not chump change, and an offer often means that the firm may offer you full-time employment when you are done with law school. This means that your future could be decided right when you start your second year. Keep in mind that the whole interview process is usually wrapped up by November of your second year, and after your summer with a firm, most firms tell you about the full-time offers in August or September, either before or when you start your third year. I was offered a full-time job at Cleary in August before I even started my third year.

I cannot say this enough: *your fate or path as a lawyer can be and is often decided when you go through that on-campus interview process right after your first year of law school.* As such, employers are going to make their decisions based on your grades in the first year and the extracurricular activities, such as Law Review, that you engage in. While your second and third years are important in the sense that all years are important, the key year of law school is the first.

When the economy is good (and even at times when it is not), large firms typically offer full-time jobs to almost all of the people who summer with them. At my firm, they made offers to all ninety-five summer students, and this has been their practice for years. That being said, if you do something very stupid, you may not get an offer and the recent economy has forced firms to drop below the 100% offer rate they have had in the past.

### What Is a Cold Offer and Should I Accept It?

Organizations track and publish statistics regarding how many summer associates are hired and how many are offered full-time jobs. Because large top firms want to maintain their statistic of offering 100% of their summer students jobs in order to attract the best students, they will at times give students a "cold offer." A cold offer goes something like this:

*"John, your performance during the summer has not really been that great and we do not see that you have much of a future with the firm. That being said, we are going to make you an offer. You should really consider whether this place is the place for you and we strongly encourage you to do some soul searching before you accept the offer. Perhaps a large firm is not for you."*

A cold offer is not a good thing, and I would recommend turning it down unless you are desperate. If you do accept the offer, the firm is under no obligation to keep you after you start, and you will be "marked" the person who will be the first to be let go if there is ever downsizing. Moreover, as your performance is already in question, you could be terminated with cause shortly after you start. Also, in the United States, employment is "at will," which means an employer can terminate you even without cause.

## Can I Apply for Jobs in My Third Year?

If you examine the time line for a big law firm job, you can see that your destiny is often decided shortly after your first year of law school. Unfortunately, it is virtually impossible to find a job in a large firm during your third year of law school, so you should take the on-campus recruitment process after your first year seriously. I know many people who had excellent grades at Harvard but were not happy with their second summer firm experience and looked for different law firm jobs in their third year. They are all back at the firms that they originally summered with, as none of them found employment with another large firm in their third year.

---

 *It is virtually impossible to find a job in a large firm after the on-campus interview process has been completed at the start of your second year. Agencies publish statistics on how many third-year students are hired, and each firm may hire one or two people at most.*

---

### *What Should I Do if I Am Not Sure Which Employer to Select After my First Round of Interviews?*

If you are not sure about a firm, go back for a second round of interviews after your call-back interviews when you have received formal offers for summer employment. This is a great idea because if you are a strong candidate, most firms know that you will have several offers, and as such, they will encourage you to come back for a second interview to try to convince you to pick them. Second interviews are very helpful, and you should take advantage of them if you are not sure.

Typically, you should be deciding between two firms at this point, and it is not appropriate to go back to five second interviews. The great thing about the second round is that you already have the offer and you get to go back to the firm to meet with lawyers and ask them the questions that you want. This is the best way to find a firm for you, as you can be yourself and the focus is all on your questions. During the call-back process, this is a bit more difficult, as you are hoping the employer will offer you the job. I was deciding between two firms, and the second round of interviews really helped me pick the firm I ultimately chose.

### *Are my Chances of Getting a Job Impacted by a Poor Economy?*

One thing to note is that the above discussion relates to the process when the economy is good. Over the last couple of years, however, some of the things that students took for granted changed. For example, in the past, Harvard students really did not have to worry about a job. Many had multiple offers, but this has definitely started changing in recent years. Also, while most large firms still offer the entire summer class jobs, the one hundred percent job offer rate for summers is no longer a sure thing and is not the case for smaller firms.

In addition, cold offers are more common now, and most law firms have significantly decreased the number of summer associates that they select for any given summer. In recent years, many firms also deferred start dates for years.

All of these things illustrate the significant effect that the economy has had on the profession, and cost cutting and efficiency are likely to continue. This effect has also made firms more selective and has put additional pressure on students to stand out. It is now more important than ever to make sure that you do not commit errors and that you are as prepared as you can be. Moreover, given the economy, you should heed the advice that more offers are better than few. Remember that an offer here today may be gone tomorrow, so play your cards carefully.

### Does It Really Matter Where I Work for the Summer if I Only Plan to Summer There?

If you choose to work for a large firm for the summer, make sure that you select wisely, even if your current plan is to reject their full-time offer. I say this because I cannot tell you how many people I know who said that they were only going to summer at a big law firm, and they were sure they were going to reject the offer when they received it. Many of these people currently work in large law firms, so I hope they picked one that made them happy.

---

 *Ensure you pick your big law firm second-year summer employer caefully, as you will almost certainly accept a full-time offer from them. Even if you do not accept right away, you may decide to go to the firm after a clerkship or in the future. Moving to another firm in your third year is next to impossible, so pick wisely.*

---

## Narrowing the Choices of Where to Work

Picking the proper law firm involves finding a right fit from a practice perspective, a culture perspective and a location perspective. Here are some things to consider when making your decision.

### *Corporate, Litigation, or Specialty Area*

Firms specialize in different areas, but two broad categories that were discussed earlier are corporate and litigation. If you know after your first year of law school that you are interested in one of these areas, that is great; if you do not, do not worry—you can decide later. If you have decided between these two broad areas, ensure that you pick a firm that is known for that area.

You may also be interested in a specialty area, either within corporate or litigation, or in another specialty area such as tax. Whatever your interest, you should match up what you are interested in with the particular specialty practice areas of the firm. For example, if you want to be a corporate tax attorney, you do not want to go to a firm that only has an ancillary tax practice. You should look for either a firm that only does tax work or one that is ranked very highly in the tax area. Similarly, if you are interested in large institutional clients or financial institutions, you would want to consider a big-name firm in the field. The large corporations and banks almost always use these firms, and as such, you are certain to get interesting corporate and litigation work.

In addition to getting to do the type of work you want to do, going to a firm that has a good reputation in a particular practice area will assist you when you are looking for a job in that area later. The legal industry puts a large amount of emphasis on reputation, so even though you will do very similar work at every firm, a firm's reputation in a particular area is a great marketing tool.

You may also have an interest in other types of clients or areas like project finance, immigration, bankruptcy, trusts, divorce, or white collar, and it is easy to see how involved a firm is in these areas. To obtain information on what a firm is known for or specializes in, firm ranking publications such as *Vault* are good sources. "Above the Law" (*abovethelaw.com*) is also a good secondary source. Firm rankings and specializations are discussed further in the next section.

## Rankings and Prestige

Some people base their decision on which firm to go to almost exclusively on law firm rankings. Since law firms are ranked based on many different criteria, you should be able to find one ranking that appeals to you. For example, law firms are ranked based on prestige, diversity, work/life balance, best practice area, and many other factors. A website to the most famous ranking is the Vault Ranking found in the "Useful Resources" section.

If you examine the Vault rankings, you will find several different rankings with the most "important" being the infamous "prestige" ranking. Based on the 2013 survey, the most prestigious firms were as follows:

1. Wachtell, Lipton, Rosen, & Katz
2. Cravath, Swaine & Moore
3. Skadden
4. Sullivan & Cromwell
5. Davis Polk

There are also similar rankings for practice areas. For example, if you search the Vault site for best practice area for tax, you will find that Skadden, Cleary Gottlieb, Sullivan, and Davis Polk have often topped the list. You can search by any practice area, and this will give you a good indication of how firms are ranked. The rankings of practice areas can be helpful not only to find firms that specialize in your area of interest but also to see how much emphasis the market will put on your experience there. For example, even though a firm like Simpson Thatcher does not top the tax list, you will get good tax experience if you work there. That being said, if you wanted to specialize in tax, the market will place more value on the experience (even though it will be very similar) from one of the top tax firms such as Cleary Gottlieb or Sullivan & Cromwell.

I started out by saying that some people almost exclusively base their decision on a firm based on these rankings, and in particular on the prestige ranking. Be careful with this approach. While it may make sense to use the rankings as a guide, you should not select one firm over another just because it is ranked slightly higher. For example, if you are selecting between a firm that is ranked third and another that is ranked sixth, you should only select the firm ranked third if the reasons are separate and distinct from the rankings.

Clearly, there is a difference between how the industry views a firm that is ranked third and one that is ranked seventieth, so the decision process might be different. The advice here is to take the rankings with a grain of salt. The reason for this is simple—the rankings are not that reliable, and the process for accumulating the information is not very good.

Most people only learn this once they start at a firm, but you will be armed with the knowledge beforehand. The prestige (as well as other surveys) are based on a form that is mailed to lawyers who work in law firms, and the forms ask them to give their personal (and often uninformed) opinion on which firm is most prestigious. You will get the form in your first year when you join a law firm, and I had the form sitting in my inbox as I wrote this chapter. The questions will ask you to rank the firms from 1 to 10 based on your opinion on how "prestigious" the firm is, and this information is accumulated to form the *only* basis for the rankings.

As you can imagine, this survey is something that a new, young associate would very quickly fill out, and the survey does not contain any external input from clients or anyone in the industry. In fact, I have never heard of most firms in the country, and I suspect that people will just list big names even though they do not have a clue what type of business that big name specializes in or why they ranked them highly. Is this what you want to use as the only basis to decide which firm will be best for you?

---

**TIP** *Do not select a firm solely based on the prestige ranking. Rankings should only be used as a guide. Many law students fall into the trap of not understanding how informally the information is collected and focus on small ranking differences between firms. Rankings should be used as one of many factors, and small differences in rankings should not guide you.*

---

When I was going through the interview process, I very clearly preferred a firm that was ranked sixth over one that was ranked third but I was caught up in the whole ranking game. After I found out how the rankings were made, I made the decision to go with number six as that firm was a much better fit for me. I thank my lucky stars to this day that I made that choice, as I now realize I would have been miserable at the other firm.

## Location

The next thing to consider when selecting a firm is location. Do not pick a firm during your first summer just so you can spend your second summer in that location. While you may enjoy the summer, if you do not accept a job with the employer, it is very difficult to get a job at another firm.

Searching for a job as a 3L is a difficult and unpleasant experience. There are statistics published on how many 3L hires firms make, and the number is always low. I know a few students who did not like their summer 2L firm jobs and were looking in their 3L year. They are all back at the same firms that they did not like.

As such, pick your location based on where you feel you may want to live and practice. If you are unsure, select a firm that has multiple locations. While firms typically make offers based on location, you can sometimes get them to consider sending you to another place.

Many firms will also let you work part of the summer in one of their foreign locations. Usually, you have to speak the language, but there are many instances where people go to foreign locations and do not speak the language. The year I summered at Cleary, at least two people from the firm went to Paris and they did not speak a word of French. If you want to split your summer with one of the firm's other locations, just ask and make it known to the firm that you would like to do that. Firms really try to accommodate people, and most truly hope that all summer employees accept their full-time offers. At Cleary, everyone who wanted to go abroad for part of their summer was able to do that. Only large firms that have an international presence will offer an out of country option.

Firms sometimes also permit you to split your summer with another firm, but most insist that you spend the first part of the summer with them because this is when the orientation occurs. Splitting a summer is a good idea if you can get the firms to agree but usually only works if you have worked with one of the firms previously. The obvious advantage of splitting your summer is that you will likely have two full-time job offers when the summer is over.

## Culture

Make sure that you like the firm's culture. While the word *culture* is overused and somewhat difficult to define, the cultures at various firms are very different and range from stuffy to free-spirited. Some generalizations about a stuffy firm include that it is formal, senior lawyers are addressed using their last names, it is not that diverse, lawyers have a formal dress code, staff are somewhat uptight, face time is required (being there even when there is no work), there are high billable hours, there is not much focus on pro bono work, and there are many type A personalities. Keep in mind that law firms often use the term "good work ethic" to mean long hours.

A non-stuffy firm is usually a bit less formal, but the uptight nature of the lawyers is not that different, as lawyers are generally quite anal (in a good way), so you see this wherever you go. There is a big difference, however, in the diversity of the staff, the dress code, and the fun that the lawyers are willing to have while at work or at play.

Culture may also dictate the demeanor, respect, or professionalism at a firm. Some firms tolerate (and perhaps even encourage) abusive type A personalities. While you may encounter someone who goes off the handle anywhere, you do not want to select a firm that supports or encourages confrontational or unprofessional behavior. There are definitely firms that do not do anything to discourage "screamers" and "throwers." Also, there are some firms that have a reputation for discriminatory acts and low tolerance. This is particularly the case when dealing with women and gay individuals.

A stuffy or more formal firm may also require that you put in "face time." This is the idea that you must stay at the firm until at least 10 P.M. every night even if you do not have much work to do. Some individuals will get very upset if you leave before they do, and these people typically work at stuffy firms.

Another factor that significantly impacts the culture is the compensation system for partners. Some firms adopt a "lockstep" compensation system in which partners are compensated based on how many years they have been partners. The other system is called the "eat what you kill" system, meaning partners are compensated based on the clients that they attract. The two systems breed very different cultures. For most lockstep firms, you will find the partners more relaxed and willing to work with each other. In the other more adversarial system, partners often will not work together since it would mean splitting profits. This will also impact how jobs are staffed and how willing a partner is to put up with errors because the partner will be directly financially impacted by an employee's performance. You can imagine that when it comes to money and the impact on the partner is very direct, some partners can react poorly. This philosophy trickles down and the culture of the firm becomes very much an adversarial one. Make sure you select a firm that is aligned with your personality.

Again, *abovethelaw.com* is a good source for figuring out the reputation of a firm, and you can also get insight from speaking to different lawyers who work or have worked at the particular large firm. Do not be afraid to ask tough questions.

### Salary

While the work at large firms is great, most would not do it if they did not get paid. There is not much of a difference in salary among the large, highly ranked New York law firms—with one exception. Wachtell, Lipton, Rosen & Katz pays almost double what other firms pay. That being said, they have a reputation of working employees to death.

At a large firm in New York, you can expect to earn approximately $160K per year in addition to a bonus of around $15K. As such, at Wachtell, you will earn around $300K. They, of course, only take the best and brightest, and it is very tough to get a job there. Also, it is a smaller firm so there are not as many positions available.

While the salary at large firms is pretty consistent, it differs at smaller and medium-sized firms. You can find the latest salaries by reviewing the ranking websites listed in the "Useful Resources" section. If salary is important to you, be sure to check the latest salary amounts. I have a friend who started at a mid-size firm in New York, and up until recently he was making $15K less than the pay scale at the other large New York firms. Overall, salaries for recent law school graduates vary significantly depending on the size of the firm and the city you are in. For example, the top salary for a small law firm of eleven to twenty-five people in Atlanta is $90K, as compared to $128K in Houston for the same size firm. For large firms (greater than 250 lawyers), starting salaries are $160K, as compared with $130K in Denver. You can find details on starting salaries by city by reviewing the National Association for Law Placement (NALP) website in the "Useful Resources" section.

## Practice Areas and the Assignment System

Pay particular attention to how a firm will assign you to practice areas within the firm. Some firms let you select the practice areas you work in, while others dictate this for you. At Cleary, you can decide whether you want to practice in the litigation, tax, or corporate areas, and it is easy to change groups once you get there. I almost ended up selecting the tax group, and I had not even taken corporate tax in law school. This is NOT the case for many firms. Some firms will not even ask you which areas you would like to work in and will assign you to areas based on their need. Others will ask you to rank your practice areas and put you through a rotation system that is roughly aligned to your selections. Others will make you apply to specialized practice areas and only select a few people. The only thing that will be consistent for each firm is that they will claim their system is the best. If it is important to you to practice in an area of your choice, select a firm that will give you this flexibility. If you would prefer someone else to make the choice because you are not sure, then you should pick a firm that has a rotation system.

*Take some time to understand the staffing and assignment system at the firms you are looking at. It may not seem that important when you are interviewing, but many people are very upset when they start at a firm and find out that they cannot do the type of work they are interested in because the firm has a mandatory rotation system.*

# 7. Work Opportunities Outside the Large Law Firm

There are many students who either before or after their summer experience decide that they do not want to work in a large law firm. They, too, have many options for employment, as a law degree opens many doors. Students may choose to work for a corporation or bank as internal counsel, a judge as a clerk, a not-for-profit organization, as a law school professor, or a sole practitioner in their own practice. There are also many opportunities in the government as a prosecutor or public defender, or in one of the many government agencies.

While there are many options, many students who do not work in large law firms work for either the government or a not-for-profit organization. You should also note that many students clerk for one year with a judge immediately after law school. This is discussed later in this section.

## The Advantages and Disadvantages of Working for the Government or a Not-for-Profit Organization

As a government lawyer, you will probably either work for a government agency, such as the Securities and Exchange Commission (SEC), or in criminal law as a prosecutor or defense attorney. As a not-for-profit or public interest lawyer, you could work in many different areas including an immigration asylum clinic, a legal aid bureau, a center that assists domestic violence victims, a human rights organization, the United Nations, an equal protection or constitutional think tank, or an employment law clinic. Both government and not-for-profit jobs are generally referred to as public sector jobs.

If you select a public sector job, it is likely not for the pay, as the average salary for a public sector employee is between $40K and $50K. This, of course, compares to more than $160K for a large law firm job.

### Advantages of Working for a Not-for-Profit

Although the pay is not great, there are several advantages to working in the public sector. First, you will have a much better work/life balance, as government jobs do not typically require the type of hours that large law firm work does. While you may work some overtime, weekends and all-nighters would not be required or expected. Moreover, there will be a fair amount of predictability regarding your schedule.

Second, a public sector job may also be more secure than a firm job since the government or the organization is not operating for profit. While firm jobs are by no means insecure, law firms are driven by profits and will lay people off in a bad economy. The top twenty firms such as White & Case and Latham, had significant layoffs during the recession, and they are just now recovering. This phenomenon is not as prevalent (although it does exist) in the public sector, and especially not for skilled workers.

Third, a government or not-for-profit job may also attract a certain type of person who may be more relaxed and diverse. For example, a type-A personality will be less likely to get far in the government, so your coworkers may be easier to get along with and less competitive. This, of course, is a generalization. In addition, due to equal protection initiatives, government jobs may attract a more diverse workforce than a law firm. Law firms have a reputation of attracting men to join the "old boys'" network, and this is not so much the case in government. This "old boys'" stereotype is changing in large law firms, but it is a fact that partners at law firms are predominantly non-minority males.

Fourth, while your experience at a large firm will be good, it may be better if you take a public sector job. This is especially the case if you are interested in litigation, as you will end up in the courtroom running your own cases very quickly in some public sector jobs. If you take a prosecutor or defense job, for example, you will very quickly be assigned your own cases and you will have full responsibility for carrying the case through to completion. In a large law firm, you will not see a courtroom for years, and you will typically work on pieces of a case and be subjected to varying levels of review.

I do not want to leave you with the impression that you will not have significant responsibility in a large firm because you will. You can rest assured that if you perform research or give someone an answer to a question, they will take what you say as correct and rely on your work. Keep in mind that senior lawyers and partners will edit your written work significantly and will change it to adhere to their style. Moreover, you will usually be working on a piece of the puzzle in a large firm, as compared to running entire cases in the public sector.

For example, if you work in an immigration asylum clinic, in a few months you would be the person responsible for *all* decisions related to an asylum case that would make the difference between the client staying in the country or being sent back to suffer harm in their country. In a large firm, if you took on an asylum case as a pro bono matter as a first-year associate, you would be one of many lawyers working on the case, your work would be subject to various levels of review, and most major decisions would require a senior lawyer or partner's sign-off.

### *Disadvantages of Working for a Not-for-Profit*

On the other hand, a big disadvantage of public sector jobs is the bureaucracy and pace. If you are a type-A person or you do not like meeting for the sake of meeting, you may not like some public sector jobs. While your day-to-day work may move quite quickly, often public sector jobs function within the context of a vast bureaucracy that moves very slowly. As such, getting approvals for new ideas or trying to effect change in the organization is often very difficult. I worked at the United Nations for my 1L summer, and it was far too bureaucratic an organization for me. I realized after the summer that this type of institution was not for me.

Finally, as mentioned above, the pay for public service jobs is low compared to what you could make in a law firm. Since many students have a vast amount of student debt, this can be a very real consideration that pressures some to take big law firm jobs.

## Judicial Clerkships After Law School

### *What Is a Clerkship?*

Another job choice when you complete law school is a judicial clerkship, a position in which you work as an assistant to a judge. This is usually a temporary position that lasts for one or two years. The law clerk assists the judge with every aspect of trial work. In terms of the day-to-day duties, law clerks read each and every document submitted to the court, perform legal research, and sit in on all court proceedings. In addition, law clerks summarize and synthesize the various reports and documents submitted to the court so that the judge does not have to sift through hundreds of documents. Finally, law clerks actually draft various legal documents, including the first draft of the judicial decisions, and submit these drafts to the judge for final review and correction. The job is great experience, and a clerkship is highly recommended.

## *Can Anyone Clerk?*

In order to work as a clerk, you must have a law degree from a U.S. institution, and for most courts you must be a U.S. citizen. If you are not a U.S. citizen, you will have better luck with state courts, as this requirement is not as prevalent. In addition, clerkships are very competitive, so you typically would have to be in the top twenty-five percent of your class to be considered. If you went to a top law school, however, your class ranking will not be as relevant.

## *How Much Will I Make?*

The salary that you will receive is around $54K but you will also typically receive a bonus of $50K if you join a large firm after your clerkship. (You must, however, typically stay at the law firm for one year after you get the bonus.) Also, if you clerk for the Supreme Court, you will gain a bonus of $250K if you join a law firm after your clerkship. The high bonus ($50K and $250K) law firms are willing to pay if you have a clerkship that shows just how valuable this position is. Believe me when I say that a law firm would not pay this bonus if they did not think having you work for them after you clerked was worth it.

## *How Do I Apply for a Clerkship?*

If you want to become a clerk, the first step is to consider the type of court that you would like to work in and where in the United States you would like to work. In terms of the type of court, you should also decide whether you want to work in a state or federal court and whether you want a trial court or one that handles appeals. In general, federal court clerkships are more prestigious than state court clerkships, and the higher the court (the Supreme Court being the highest), the better.

A clerkship application typically includes a résumé, cover letter, writing sample, transcript, and three or four letters of recommendation. You should include all of these things in one package that is addressed to the judge of that court.

All law schools will do everything in their power to help you get a clerkship, so you should spend a significant amount of time with the career service officer in charge of judicial clerkships. This person will review what each of the requirements (cover letter, résumé, recommendations, etc.) should look like. For example, the advisor will go over the helpful fact that the letters of recommendation should come from professors or someone who is familiar with your legal research and writing skills. Timing of applications depends on the court you are applying to, so you should check with your law school to confirm recruitment schedules.

If a judge likes your application, he or she will invite you to his or her chambers for an interview. The process is very different from the law firm interview and recruitment process, as the flights and hotels are not covered by the court. You will usually be interviewed by other full-time members of the court in addition to the judge, and all members will have input in the hiring decision. As such, it is very important to treat them all with respect.

When you apply and receive an offer from a large firm, you usually have six to eight weeks to think it over, but this is not the case with clerkships. Unfortunately, you are expected to respond almost immediately, and judges will not wait long for your response. If you do not answer quickly (a few days at most), they will simply move to the next candidate.

### Should I Clerk?

If you can get a clerkship, you should certainly accept the opportunity. The job is very hands-on, and you will learn a great deal because clerks gain a significant amount of access and knowledge of the court process and are exposed to a wide number of issues. Moreover, you will be given an enormous amount of responsibility in a very short period of time. A clerkship also allows you to see issues and cases from the court's perspective, which will be extremely valuable once you are practicing law outside of the court.

Clerkships are very well respected in the legal industry and, as such, can be advantageous when looking for employment. Keep in mind that if you have a job offer from a law firm in your third year, the firm will hold the job offer open for you until after you have completed your clerkship. Clerkships are also very helpful when searching for other employment, such as teaching and some government positions. When I spoke to the advisor in charge of teaching positions at Harvard Law School, he said that a clerkship was becoming essential for new law professor jobs.

Clerkships are also fun. Every clerk with whom I have spoken loved what they were doing. They all loved the mix of the court time with legal research and writing, and they felt they gained valuable experience.

# 8. Transferring Law Schools After Your First Year

After you have completed one year of law school, you are eligible to transfer to another law school. If you transfer after your first year, you will get the degree from the new law school that you go to instead of your old school. If you transfer after your second year, you will get the degree from the school that you went to for the first two years. For example, I attended Brooklyn Law School for my first year and then transferred to Harvard Law School. As such, I received a law degree from Harvard Law School that did not indicate that I went to Brooklyn Law School for my first year.

There are two primary reasons for transferring. First, people transfer because they have a personal change in their life, such as a spouse that gets relocated to a different city. The second reason that students transfer is to "upgrade" schools. As discussed in the previous sections, the concept of ranking law schools is very important, and students will often try to move from a second-tier school to a first-tier school. This is what I did when I moved from a school with a rank in the mid-sixties to Harvard Law School, which is ranked number two.

*There are a few (not many) law schools that will review a transfer application after your first term of law school, rather than your first year. You should carefully read the transfer process of the school you want to transfer to in order to see if an early application is an option.*

## What You Need to Transfer

In order to apply for a transfer to another law school, you must go through the same application process that you went through to initially apply to law school. There are some minor differences, but for the most part the process is the same. For most schools, you can use the LSAC process and fill out the transfer application (which is very similar to the original law school application) online. You will require everything that was discussed in "The Law School Application Process," Chapter 1, including a résumé, a personal statement, letters of reference, transcripts, and the completed application. You must also provide your LSAT score, but the schools will not place much weight on the LSAT score for transfer student applications. The most significant factor that the schools will consider is your grades from your first year of law school. Needless to say, the higher the better.

While most schools will want a complete picture, some are only interested in your first-year grades. For example, at New York University (NYU), the personal statement that they request is a mere 500 words, and it does not have to talk about anything specific. Moreover, they do not require (or want) any letters of reference. In contrast, Harvard, Yale, and Columbia all require a comprehensive application, complete with letters of reference, a résumé, and two-page personal statements.

In order to transfer to a top school, you will need top grades. Harvard accepts about twenty-five transfer students a year and boasts that many transfer students could have been admitted if they applied there for their first year or were waitlisted when they applied to Harvard in their first year. If you recall, Harvard's entering class has a GPA very close to an A average and an LSAT score in the top two percent. Yale only admits around ten transfer students, and the competition is very stiff. In fact, many of the transfer students who were admitted to Harvard the year I was accepted were not accepted as transfer students to Yale. (I did not apply to Yale, so I will never know.) Also, a very bright student in my class at Brooklyn Law School applied to Yale, and even though he had top grades and a very strong letter of recommendation from a second circuit judge that he worked for, he was not accepted.

As a rough guide, you should be in the top ten percent of your class if you are applying to a top school. This is by no means a cutoff, and the number could change if you have some other compelling characteristics or you are transferring from a highly or lowly ranked school. The higher the ranking of your school, the lower your grades can be. For example, if you are transferring from Columbia to Harvard, you could likely get away with an A– average (top thirty percent). If you are transferring from Brooklyn Law School, you will generally have to be in the top five to ten percent of your class.

In addition to top grades, most of the transfer students at Harvard had second master's or doctoral degrees or some other significant accomplishment. Moreover, some applicants had significant work experience, were Rhodes Scholars, or worked for Teach for America. Finally, law schools will look at other symbols of excellence that I discussed earlier, such as success in journals or Moot Court competitions. Moreover, work as a research or teaching assistant and participation in student groups during law school demonstrate that you can juggle classes along with other activities. All of these accomplishments will help your application, but again, the main thing the admitting school will look at is high grades.

## Things to Consider When Making Your Decision

There are several factors that one should consider when deciding whether to transfer if your desire to transfer is based on an attempt to upgrade schools. If you are transferring for personal reasons, these reasons may still be relevant, but presumably the personal reason will be the driving force for your decision. Here are some of the things to consider.

### How Significant Does my Jump Have to Be to Make Transferring Worth It?

Many students attempt to transfer to a top school, and this can generally be a smart move as a top school will afford you more opportunity. This advantage is discussed in the section titled "Are Law School Rankings Important?" in Chapter 1. As such, if you attempt to upgrade to a top five school from a second-tier school, you are probably making the right choice.

What about a small jump? I know one student who transferred from a school ranked around number seventy in New York City to a school ranked around number sixty that was also in New York City. This move made absolutely no sense to me. I met him during the summer at Brooklyn Law School (the school he transferred to), and he was not the sharpest tool in the chest and this was evident by more than just his school change.

The point of this story is that you should only change schools if the jump you are going to make is going to put you in a substantially better place than you are. I could have transferred to Fordham Law School (which is ranked in the thirties) from Brooklyn (ranked in the sixties), but I did not even apply because I did not believe that this type of move was worth it.

### Will I Lose Some of my Connections that I Made at my Old School if I Transfer?

When you start law school, you will be assigned to a section along with about eighty other students. Everyone in your section will have the same classes, and you will get to know them quite well. You will all be going through the exact same experience, and as a result, you will form strong bonds and networks. These bonds and networks may result in lifelong friendships, business contacts, and even marriage. Do not underestimate the importance of these connections, and if you transfer, there is a substantial risk that you will lose some or all of these relationships. Moreover, strong bonds have already been formed at the school you will go to, and it may be hard to establish similar connections.

## Will I Be Considered an Outsider at my New School?

As a transfer student, depending on the school and culture, you may be considered one step below the people who started at that school from the beginning. This is particularly the case if you come from a lower ranked school. For example, one day after class, a professor at Harvard took some students for drinks. When he found out I was a transfer student and that I came from Brooklyn Law School, he asked me if the other transfer students looked down on me because I came from a second-tier school. (Most of the transfer students came from other first-tier schools ranked between numbers fifteen and thirty.) If he thought that other *transfer* students would look down on me, you can imagine what he thought (or what other students at Harvard think) about transfers. This is not a reason not to transfer, but it is something to consider. I became used to the facial expressions of other students and professors when I told them I transferred. In fact, after my second year, I intentionally did not mention I was a transfer student unless explicitly asked.

## Will my Grades Fall if I Transfer, and Can I Still Get Latin Honor Awards?

People who get into top schools know how to take exams very well. As such, you will find that the ability to get great grades when you transfer is more difficult. This, of course, depends on which school you are coming from. Generally speaking, if you transfer, your grades will decrease and you will not be at the top of the class. This is especially the case if you are transferring from a second-tier to a first-tier school. Do not get me wrong; it is quite possible to do very well at the new school, and some end up in the top ten or top tirty percent. That being said, most transfer students were in the top one to five percent of their class in the school they transferred from, and some were ranked number one. As such, I am not talking about a significant drop in grades but rather a moderate drop. For some, this is a big deal, and you should consider whether it is important to you to be at the top of the pack or within the top twenty percent.

You should also investigate whether you will be eligible for Latin awards when you graduate and exactly how any class ranking will apply to you. Latin awards are the summa cum laude (top one percent), magna cum laude (top ten percent), and cum laude (next thirty percent).

Some schools do not permit transfer students to be eligible for Latin and other awards because they did not spend all three years at the law school. Moreover, very few schools, if any, will permit the high grades that you obtained at your first law school to count in any calculation. Depending on the law school, the Latin awards or class ranking will be very important, and it may not be obvious to employers that you were ineligible. All they will see is that you were not in the top forty percent and did not receive any awards.

While not as important at a top school like Harvard or Yale, if you are transferring to a school that is, for example, number twenty or thirty, falling within the top levels of your class will be very important.

### Will I Be a Small Fish in a Big Pond if I Transfer?

Depending on the size of your school, as a top student you really stand out. For example, after my first semester when I scored over a 4.0 GPA, the Dean of Student Affairs at Brooklyn Law School called me into her office to discuss my progress. She was very pleasant and told me that she would do everything in her power to assist me. Also, as a top student, I was offered a scholarship in my second year, and it was very clear to me that the eyes of the administration were focused on me.

When I transferred to Harvard, I was one of a class of 550 (plus another 100 LL.M. students), and I was clearly an outsider. I had moved from a big fish in a small pond to a small fish in an ocean. This was not just based on grades but rather the size of Brooklyn Law School and its ability to focus individual attention on top students. Moreover, many students at Harvard were very well connected (sons of judges and senators), so standing out was even more difficult.

## *Other Factors Related to Selection of a Law School*

You should re-read the section "Choosing a Law School," in Chapter 1, as it outlines many different reasons why you may select one law school over another. You should refer to this section now and use it to compare and contrast your current law school to the law school to which you may want to transfer.

# 9. The Part-Time Program

## How the Part-Time Program Differs from the Full-Time Program

In the United States, you may attend law school on a full-time or part-time basis, and up until now we have been discussing primarily the full-time program. The classes for many part-time programs are held in the evening, but there are schools that offer classes for part-time studies during the day. While the term "part-time" might conjure up the image of being relaxed or working at your own pace, it is hardly that. In fact, part-time really only means completing the law school requirements in four years instead of three. Because many people are working full-time while doing this, most part-time students give up a life for four years.

In a part-time program, you will take all of the same first-year courses as the full-time students, but your course load each semester will be four courses instead of five. This is really the only difference between the full-time and part-time programs so you can see how working full-time during your studies would be tough.

In terms of fees, the fees are simply pro-rated based on the number of years of the program, so you can expect to pay around $30K per year for four years instead of $40K for three years. Not all schools offer part-time programs, but it is an option to consider if your life will not permit you the luxury of taking three years off of work. On the opposite end of the spectrum the option of a two-year law school program has been introduced.

## Things to Consider if You Want to Study Part-Time

There are several things you should consider if you sign up for a part-time program. It is very difficult to work while going to law school part-time. Studying part-time is extremely intense and not for the faint of heart. When I started law school, I started in the part-time program at Brooklyn Law School and worked full-time at an investment bank. Instead of taking the fifteen or sixteen credits that the full-time students took, I had twelve credits in my first term and eleven credits in my second. As such, I only had one course less than the full-time students.

A typical day consisted of waking up at 7 A.M. to read cases, going to work from 9 A.M. to 5 P.M., studying at lunch for class, attending class at 6 P.M. for three to four hours, and then going home to study some more. The weekends were completely occupied with studying and this schedule was intensified if, for example, a legal writing memo was due.

I was in the evening session, so most people who started the program had either a full-time or part-time job. Almost everyone I knew had to quit their job because the demands of law school were too great. I quit my job in April in my second semester, as I knew that going through another exam period while working would be impossible. Most other students that I knew quit their jobs after the first semester. One by one, students realized that in order to keep up with the demands of law school, working was very difficult. While there are a few who manage to last the full four years while working, their grades probably suffer and they have many more grey hairs on their head.

### *If I Work Full-Time, Will I Miss Out on What Law School Has to Offer?*

The workload is not the only problem with working full-time while going to law school part-time. Another issue is that you will miss out on much of the law school experience. It is tough to have two significant focuses in your life (school and work), and often one will have to be sacrificed for the other. Since your school schedule is based on your own planning, school will often be the thing that is sacrificed. Moreover, your interactions with other students are clearly different because many are rushing to class immediately after work and most are not willing to stick around to socialize after 10 P.M. when classes are over.

In addition, many interesting law school events are scheduled during the day, and if you are working you will miss them. For example, law schools often have popular speakers who present on a wide range of topics. Also, many of the activities associated with extracurricular activities, such as Moot Court and Law Review, are held during the day, and part-time students are typically not as involved as their full-time counterparts.

Working full-time will also not allow you to participate in clinics or summer legal jobs, and this is another significant loss. Most employers place a significant amount of weight on your legal experience, and these are really the only two opportunities you can get. You will be at a significant disadvantage if you graduate from law school without a day of practical formal legal training.

### Do Part-Time Programs Have as Strong a Reputation as Full-Time Programs, and How Will the Reputation Impact Me?

Although the courses you take as a part-time student are the same as the courses that full-time students take, part-time programs have a reputation for being somewhat less rigorous than their full-time counterparts. This, unfortunately, may have an impact on your job prospects as well as your ability to transfer to another school after your first year.

The lower reputation of the part-time program stems from the fact that in the past, the GPAs and LSAT scores of part-time students were not typically included in the statistical first-year admission information that made up the law school rankings. As such, many feel that people who are admitted to a part-time program generally have lower scores than those admitted to full-time programs. Unfortunately, even if your LSAT and GPA are high, the perception of a part-time program often becomes reality for employers and others you may want to impress.

Some of the blame should be put on the schools; I know students who were not admitted to a school's full-time program but were admitted to the part-time program. They applied to the full-time program but were only accepted to the part-time program because their grades or LSAT scores were not that great. After the first semester, these students were then transferred to the full-time program. This enabled the law school to get the tuition from the students without reporting their poor grades or LSAT scores, which may have reduced their law school's rankings. Unfortunately, this is a game that some schools played and you can see how this policy would really fuel the poor perception of part-time programs. Many schools now report LSAT scores and GPAs from the part-time program, so these perceptions may change over time.

Another reason for the poor perception of part-time students relates to the perception that part-time students are spreading the workload over a longer period of time. This argument may in fact be true for those who are not working, as they will have a lighter course load and no full-time job, but it certainly is not true for those who are working full-time. Unfortunately, the label of "less" has stuck, so it is something that you should consider if you are thinking about a part-time program.

As a result of these perceptions, a part-time program may make it more difficult to get the full-time job of your choice. That being said, it is not an insurmountable obstacle. After all, I started in a part-time program.

Finally, if you would like to transfer to a different law school after your first year, you should not join a part-time program. As stated earlier, part-time programs are not regarded as highly as full-time programs, so you may be at a disadvantage. The more significant problem, however, is that most schools require a minimum number of first-year credits before considering transfer students. At Harvard, transfer students must complete one-third of their law school studies prior to applying. Other schools have similar requirements that would make most part-time students ineligible for a transfer. I was lucky because I had accumulated five additional credits during the summer, which made me eligible.

# 10. What You Should Know About the Bar Examination

When you graduate from law school in the United States, you will have a Juris Doctor degree, which means that you will be a Doctor of Law. This degree, however, does not allow you to practice law in any state, and as such, you cannot yet perform the numerous activities that only lawyers may perform. For example, representing someone in a courtroom when they are sued or drafting a will for someone are activities that only lawyers are permitted to do. The unauthorized practice of law is a very serious offense, so you should be sure not to "act" as a lawyer until a state bar certifies you as a lawyer. When a state certifies you, this is called being "admitted to the bar." If you have any doubts regarding what you can and cannot do either during or after law school, check with the bar association in the state where you live or want to work.

So how do you become a certified practicing lawyer? The first step after law school is to take the bar exam in the state that you plan to practice. Step two is to complete the character certification process and submit your application for admission to that state's bar. Step three is to attend a bar admission ceremony or interview in the state. The order of these steps may vary depending on your state, but you must complete all of these steps before you are able to practice law in any state.

## The Bar Examination

Even though you will not sit for the bar examination until after you graduate, it is a good idea to read this section while you are in law school in order to get a better understanding of what you will be tested on. As I sat in law school classes, I often wondered what the bar exam would be like and how it related to the courses I was taking. If you read this section, you will not have to wonder.

In most states, the bar examination is a two-day exam that you take between approximately 9 A.M. and 4 P.M. each day. (It is a three-day exam in certain states such as California, Iowa, Mississippi, and Louisiana, and two and a half days in other states such as Texas, Ohio, and Idaho.) Check the specifics at the state you are interested in. One day of the exam is made up of a test called the Multi-State Bar Exam (MBE), and this part of the exam is made up of 200 multiple-choice questions. Everyone in the country takes the MBE on the same day, and the exam covers only six topic areas. The other day of the bar exam is a state day on which generally state law is tested. Each state makes up their own state exam, and the exam will fall either on the day before or the day after the MBE depending on which state you reside in.

In the United States, you must be certified to practice law in every state in which you wish to practice. Generally speaking, this means that if your best friend was arrested in Ohio for an offense, you could not represent him or her in court if you were certified to practice law in California. There are exceptions to this rule, but they are beyond the scope of this book.

Given that you must be certified in each state that you want to practice law in, your first step related to the bar examination is to decide which state or states you would like to be certified in. This will usually be the state that you have a job in, but you may also want to be certified in a state that you may move to in the future.

Once you have decided on a state, you should check the bar exam schedule to see when the next exam will be held. For all states, the bar exam is held twice a year—once in February and once in July—and most people sit for the exam in July after they finish law school. If you decide to take two state bar exams (highly recommended), you will have to check to make sure that the state portion of the exam does not fall on the same day. For example, the state portion for New York and New Jersey do not ever fall on the same day. In contrast, you could not take the New York and Florida exams in the same examination sitting because the state portion generally falls on the same day.

You will have to complete an application for each state, so you should review the state application instructions carefully! You should pay particular attention to the application deadlines and any other instructions that you are given. For example, some states, such as New York, require a handwriting sample and a school certification to be sent in with your application. I know of at least two students who went to Harvard and did not send material that the New York Bar examiners required, and they found out at the beginning of July that they were not eligible to sit for the bar exam at the end of July. Do not let this happen to you.

In addition, you should note that when you sign up for your bar exam preparation course, for example, Barbri, you have not signed up for the bar examination. Every year the Barbri instructors say this at the beginning of the Barbri preparation course session, and every year there is at least one student who is ineligible to sit for the bar examination because he or she did not register. To better illustrate the process of registering for the bar exam, I will review the process for signing up for the New York State Bar examination in this chapter. The application process is similar for many other bar exams, so you can use this as a guide for any state bar exam.

Finally, in order to sign up for the bar examination in most states, you must have completed a law degree in the United States.

While this is the case for almost all states, New York does permit some foreign trained lawyers to sit for their bar exam, and if you pass the exam and complete the other requirements, you will be able to practice law in New York. At the law firm that I summered with, there were several Canadian law school trained lawyers who successfully sat for the New York Bar examination in July. You should note, however, that the pass rate for foreign trained lawyers is quite low. In recent years, it was around forty percent for first-time takers as compared to eighty-five percent for first-time takers who graduated with a U.S. law degree.

## How Do I Apply for the Bar Examination?

You should check the specific requirements in the state that you want to practice in, but the general process is the same in all states. Most bar exams are conducted twice a year—in July and February. For the bar examination in July, the New York State Board of Bar Examiners allows registration and signup for a period of one month in April. Once the date is set (usually April 1–April 30), you must sign up online. The signup process is quite straightforward, and you simply follow the instructions and submit payment. (The cost is more for foreign trained lawyers.)

At this point, the Board only asks simple factual information such as name, address, school, and other general questions. Some states (for example, New Jersey) make you complete a comprehensive application at this point on which you are required to get a driver's abstract showing your driving history for the last several years, submit to a criminal background check, answer several character questions, submit finger prints from local police stations, submit references, and answer questions regarding past school conduct. New York and other states ask for similar information, but they ask for it after you have sat for the bar examination rather than before.

The fee for the New York Bar is nonrefundable, and if you miss the signup window by even one day, you will not be able to sit for the exam in July. Do not be fooled and think that the Board of Examiners is flexible. If you miss a date, you will be ineligible.

The price for the New York Bar is the same regardless of when you sign up during the one-month window, but this is not the case for some other states. For example, New Jersey has a sliding scale depending on when you sign up. The application period is open for longer than one month, but the price more than doubles if you apply in the last weeks.

**TIP** *In some states, if you sign up for the bar exam, you are permitted one free withdrawal. After that, if you sign up and then do not sit for the exam, you will have to demonstrate exceptional circumstances.*

State bar exam fees differ; for example, the New Jersey exam is significantly more expensive than the New York exam. It is unclear why there is such a vast difference in price between states, but compared to some states, New Jersey is a bargain. For example, some states charge more than $1,000 to sit for the bar examination.

When applying to sit for the bar, many states will require that you have your law school send a certificate to the Board of Examiners that indicates that you graduated from law school. Also, some states will require that you must submit a handwriting sample that is witnessed by your registrar's office and accompanies the school certification. Finally, all of the Board of Examiners will require a copy of your law school transcripts. All of this material is sent directly by the school, and the Board of Examiners sets a deadline for receipt of the material. As such, you cannot wait until the last day to try to get your school to submit what is required. If your school is late, this means you are late, and the Board of Examiners does not accept excuses.

Once you have submitted all of the required information, you are ready to sit for the bar exam. Some are overwhelmed by the large exam rooms so you should try to select a smaller location if large crowds make you anxious.

You should pay particular attention to the very long list of material that you cannot bring to the exam. While some things are obvious, like a phone, others are not. For example, you are not permitted to bring in a highlighter to the New York Bar exam. Believe it or not, a few years ago, someone had a highlighter that was really a scanner and attempted to scan a copy of the exam. You can find a complete list of the items that are not permitted on the Board's website. Failure to adhere to the Board's guidelines will mean that you will not be permitted to sit for the exam, and the Board could bar you from sitting for future exams. When I sat for the bar exam, an individual's cell phone rang and he was removed from the exam. Do not let this happen to you.

### Can I Use a Laptop?

Essays make up a large part of many bar examinations, and many states allow you to use a laptop as long as the laptop meets certain specifications. In New York, in order to use your laptop, you must follow the registration instructions for the laptop and submit your request along with $100 by a deadline. Again, if you miss the deadline, you will be writing the exam by hand. Although the exam is developed so that you have time to write it by hand, you would be at a significant disadvantage, as the majority of students take the exam with a laptop and most can type faster than they can write. Also, it is easier to edit your answers with a laptop.

## *What Is on the Bar Examination?*

As outlined previously, the examination in most states is a two-day examination: one day is a country-wide exam and the other is a state exam. I will discuss each of these exams in this section, but for the state exam I will only discuss New York and New Jersey. However, the general principals apply to all states.

# The Multi-State Bar Exam (MBE)

The MBE is an exam that consists of 200 multiple-choice questions over a six-hour period. The exam is all done in one day, but it is split between a morning and afternoon session of 100 questions each. After the morning session, you are given a much-needed one-and-a-half hour break to eat lunch and rejuvenate. Since you must complete 100 questions in 180 minutes, you should allocate 1.8 minutes per question. While there is some time pressure, after practice you should find that you are able to finish the exam within the time limit. The key here is to work at a steady pace and to move on when you are stuck on a question.

Although there are 200 questions, only 190 are graded and the remaining questions are test questions. The test questions are indistinguishable from the graded questions, so you must answer everything to the best of your ability.

The MBE covers six topic areas, and you will receive approximately 33 questions in each topic area. The six topics tested are evidence, constitutional law, property, torts, criminal law (which includes criminal procedure), and contracts. As you can see, with the exception of evidence, all of the topic areas are core first-year courses, so this is all the more reason to pay attention during your first year.

For each of the six topic areas, the questions will range from easy to difficult. Of the 33 or so questions that you will get in each area, fifteen percent will be very easy and fifteen percent will be tough. The remaining questions are rated by the examiners as medium difficulty. The questions are not designed to trick you, but they do test whether you understand the material. As such, memorization is often not enough, and you will have to understand how to apply the concepts.

An average passing score on the MBE is approximately sixty-five percent, which translates to 130 correct answers out of 200. Keep in mind that only 190 are graded, so a pass is really around 124 correct answers. Your raw score is then converted to a scaled score, which uses statistical analysis to take into account the difficulty level of the exam. If the exam was particularly difficult one year, the scaled score will be higher than the raw score.

---

**TIP** *During your preparation for the bar exam, you should pay particular attention to the questions that appear on the exam every year. Your exam preparation instructor or the study guide that you use will point out many of these common questions, and you will see them on the exam. As you will already be familiar with these questions, you can usually answer them in a few seconds. I caution you to read the questions and ALL of the answers very carefully because often the examiners will make subtle changes to common questions that may impact the answer.*

---

The MBE is not an easy exam, but it is fair. One reason that the questions are tricky is the fact that the exam is a "best option" exam—that is, you may be given four choices that all are correct, but one is better than the others.

Like anything else, the key to success here is practice. If you study properly for the bar, you will have completed thousands of MBE questions prior to taking the exam. You should also take a few simulated exams to assess areas on which you need to improve.

*There is no easy or fast way to improve your score on the MBE, but your score will significantly improve if you continue studying the material and doing timed practice exams. When you get a question wrong, you should fully review the answer to understand why you got that question wrong. Also, even when you get a question correct, you should review the answer to ensure that your correct answer was not based on luck or flawed logic.*

*In order to ensure success on the bar exam, you should take a preparation course. The key is to take a course from a reputable organization and do what they tell you to do.*

There is one final thing to note about the MBE: You should try to score as high as you can (rather than just try to pass), as your score may impact more than just whether you pass the exam. In some cases, certain states use the scaled MBE score to determine whether a candidate can practice in the state without sitting for an additional examination. For example, Washington D.C. allows you to "motion in" (practice law in the State without sitting for an exam) without any work experience depending on your MBE scaled score. Motioning in is discussed in more detail later in this chapter.

## What Is on the State Portion of the Bar Examination?

The examination that you sit for in a state will depend on the state that you wish to practice in, and each examination will be very different. Bar exams can test state-specific law or very general law that is not really specific to a particular state. New York and New

Jersey have very different examinations, so a look at both should give you a good idea of what the examinations will generally look like in most states.

### What Are the New Jersey Bar Examination Questions Like?

The New Jersey exam consists of seven essay questions, and you are given forty-five minutes for each. The examination covers seven topic areas, and each essay question covers one topic area only. While the examiners indicate that the questions may span across many topic areas, the questions traditionally have just asked about one area and there has been very little overlap between areas. I sat for this exam and did not see any overlap. The topic areas are: contracts, criminal law, property, torts, constitutional law, evidence, and civil procedure.

As you can see, the topic areas are almost identical to the areas covered in the Multi-State Bar Exam, with the exception of civil procedure. As such, the New Jersey examination is an excellent "add-on" if you take the New York or other state exam that tests state-specific topics because you have very little additional areas to study. In addition, the New Jersey essay questions are extremely broad-based and ask about very basic legal principles. Moreover, the New Jersey exam does not test any state-specific topics. I sat for both exams, and if you can pass the New York exam, you should pass New Jersey with ease and with very limited additional studying. Generally speaking, most people who sit for two bar exams either pass both or fail both.

If you sit for the exam in a state that tests civil procedure, do not worry about the fact that topic is not tested on the Multi-State Bar Exam. If you sit for the exam in New York and many other states, you will have to study federal civil procedure for the New York State Bar Exam day, and as such, you will not have to do much additional work for the basic civil procedure question that you will have to answer for that exam. (Most State Civil Procedure is very similar to Federal Civil procedure.) I reviewed a civil procedure handout the night before the New Jersey exam and was able to easily answer the civil procedure questions.

## How Are Bar Exams Graded?

For essay questions on the bar exam, the examiners will usually develop a predetermined grading key that they will follow very closely. Once all of the raw points on a particular exam have been calculated, the scores will be "scaled" to take into account statistical differences over the years. The examiners will then usually combine your scaled score with your MBE score and compare this to a predetermined passing grade for your state. If you are at or higher than that grade, you have passed the exam. Each state will have a similar way of determining what constitutes a passing grade, and the actual passing grade may vary by state. You can see that in some states, the passing rate is quite high (usually over eighty percent in Illinois), while in other states it is quite low (just over fifty percent in California).

## New York Bar Examination

The New York Bar Examination consists of fifty multiple-choice questions, a Multi-state Performance Test (MPT) question, and five essay questions. In the morning, you complete the fifty multiple-choice questions along with three essays. After a lunch break, you complete the remaining two essay questions and the MPT test. In terms of time allocation, the fifty multiple-choice questions should take one hour, the MPT test will take one and a half hours, and each essay question should take approximately forty minutes. There is some time pressure to complete the exam, but in general, the Board of Examiners gives you a sufficient amount of time to answer all of the questions. Time management is key, though, and you should not "borrow" time from any questions, as you will find that you are unable to properly complete the last question. In some cases, that last question could be easy, so you should not take the chance that you will miss these easy points. The New York State Bar exam is a good example of a bar exam on which state-specific law is tested and the majority of bar exams in the country adopt this approach. As such, the New York State Bar exam is pretty representative of bar exams across the country.

## How Is the New York Bar Examination Graded?

The New York day of the bar examination is worth sixty percent of your total bar examination score, and the remaining forty percent is based on your scaled MBE score. Of the sixty percent of the New York day, the multiple-choice and the MPT are each given a weight of ten percent and are graded on a scale of one to ten. An average passing score for the MPT is five, and an average passing score for the multiple-choice questions is twenty-nine out of fifty. The remaining forty percent is divided equally between the five essay questions, so they are worth eight percent each. They are graded on a ten-point scale, and the average passing score is five.

The grading keys for the essays are set by the Board of Examiners, and you get points for mentioning information that is included on the grading key. As such, you will not be rewarded for originality and if you miss what is on the grading key you will not get points. The questions are pretty straightforward, so you should keep your answers simple and always answer the question. This is not the place to discuss policy, and the examiners are looking for right and wrong answers that address the relevant areas of law. Moreover, the questions are quite specific and usually require that you are familiar with very specific points of New York law.

Your scores on the MPT, multiple-choice questions, and essays are all scaled and combined with your scaled score on the

MBE. In order to pass the New York State Bar exam, you must get a combined scaled score of 665. Again, this number does not mean much as it is based on a scaling formula that is not that easy to understand. As a guide, if you get five out of ten on the essays and the MPT, thirty correct out of fifty on the multiple-choice, and sixty-five percent correct on the MBE, you will pass the exam.

You should also note that the Board of Examiners does not set a key or target percentage of the number of people they want to pass. This means that in some years, the pass rate could be ninety percent and in other years it could be forty percent. In fact, for the February sitting of the examination, the pass rate is usually below fifty percent because many candidates are second-time writers, and this group has a low pass rate.

The point to take away here is that the Board of Examiners is not trying to fail you, but they are grading to a minimum standard that you must meet. As such, if you study and listen to what they tell you in your bar preparation course, you should do fine.

## Multi-state Performance Test (MPT)

The MPT portion of the examination is a question that is designed to test your ability to act like a lawyer in a real-life situation. You are given a situation and a set of facts and must complete a task that a first-year lawyer should be able to complete. In order to complete this task, you are given a file that outlines the task, other required source documents, and a library that outlines the black letter law from statutes as well as cases that apply the black letter law. The file may be quite extensive and may contain lawyer's notes, police reports, interview summaries, court documents, newspaper articles, and other pieces of evidence. While most of the information you are given is relevant, the examiners also include irrelevant information that you are expected to ignore.

After reading through everything, you have to follow the instructions and write a short memo or brief.

The Board of Examiners expects you to sort through this material taking note of the relevant parts of the file and library. You must also read the statutes and the cases and understand how to apply the law to the facts that you have just sorted. The law will not be complex and it is not required that you have any knowledge of the subject matter. In fact, if you are familiar with the area of law, you must not use your knowledge and only use what is contained in the library and file.

---

 *The MPT is not tough, but you should complete four or five practice exams prior to sitting for the bar examination. Since it is worth ten percent of your total score on the bar exam, you cannot afford to just wing it; if you practice, it can be an easy way to pick up points.*

---

## Multiple-Choice Questions

The multiple-choice questions on the New York State Bar examination are very specific, detailed questions on various aspects of New York law. The questions are different from the MBE in that only one answer is correct rather than a best answer approach. You should take approximately 1.1 minutes to answer each exam question, and you will be fairly rushed during this part of the exam.

The areas that are most heavily tested are domestic relations, New York civil practice, corporations, and criminal law. While the discussion here is specific to New York, the principles should be applied to any state bar exam that has multiple-choice questions.

The best way to study for this area is to thoroughly review the substantive areas of law and to pay particular attention to the side notes that professors mention during your bar preparation review course. I found at least five things that professors mentioned were actually tested in the multiple-choice part of the examination. Also, prior to studying, you should do ten or more practice questions just to get an idea of the level of detail that the questions ask. It will help you if you look at a few questions before studying as you will understand the level of detail that you will have to go into while studying.

After you have reviewed the substantive areas of law, you should do as many practice questions as you can. By the time exam day comes, you will find that the questions that are asked are actually a bit easier than what you studied, and you should be confident that you obtained a score of at least thirty out of fifty. The preparation course that you take will provide you with several practice questions to do, and you should complete all of them under exam conditions. Also, a good bar exam preparation course will have state-specific options so that the teachers are telling you everything you need to know about a test in a particular state.

### Essay Questions

Many state bar exams consist of essay questions, and in order to do well on the bar examination, you must do well on these questions. The New York State Bar's essay questions are much more difficult than those on the New Jersey Bar because the former covers significantly more subject areas and you are expected to know the topic areas in detail. Moreover, unlike the New Jersey Bar examination, the New York portion of the bar tests mainly New York law and New York distinctions from federal law. Finally, many of the topic areas that you have to study for in New York are not first-year required courses, and as such, you may be seeing them for the first time when you are studying for the bar. For example, the New York State Bar exam (and many other state bar exams) regularly has an essay question related to wills and domestic relations, and many people do not take these courses in law school.

The Board of Examiners publishes a comprehensive content outline that you should review if you plan to take the New York State Bar that you can find in the "Useful Resources" section.

Based on the New York State outline, the following areas are covered: business relationships including agency, corporations, limited liability companies, partnerships and joint ventures; federal civil practice and procedure; future interests; New York civil procedure; conflict of laws; professional responsibility; New York and federal constitutional law; contracts and contract remedies; Criminal law and procedure; evidence; matrimonial and family law; professional responsibility; real property; workman's compensation; personal property; mortgages; insurance; commercial paper; secured transactions; torts; trusts; wills and estates; and UCC Articles 2, 3, and 9. Every state will have similar outlines that show what their exams cover, and you should be able to easily access these from the state bar website.

The link to the content outline for the New York State Bar provides a detailed breakdown of what can be tested in each topic area. While it is possible for all of these areas to be tested, Barbri publishes a frequency chart that can help you narrow down exactly what will be tested; this can be found on their website at *www.barbri.com.*

If you examine the frequency chart, you will see two important things. First, it describes the topic areas that were covered in the last few exams. Some topic areas are tested on almost every exam, so if it is missed in one session, you can rest assured it will appear in the next session. That being said, it should provide little comfort to you to know that there will be a contracts question on the exam, as there are many topic areas within contracts that may appear on the exam.

The chart also shows you how many times each topic area has appeared during the last fifty-five sessions of the examination. For example, based on the Barbri schedule, we can see that there has been a contracts essay question on fifty-five of the last fifty-five exams. Other heavily tested topics are New York civil procedure, wills, and criminal law, which were tested fifty-four, fifty-three, and fifty-two times, respectively, over the last fifty-five sessions. As such, you can almost guarantee a question that at least in part deals with these topic areas. Barbri also publishes similar frequency charts for bar exams in other states.

In contrast, you can see that topics like constitutional law and secured transactions have only showed up around five times in the last fifty-five sessions. Although you have to study for every topic area, you would clearly dedicate more time to contracts than you would to secured transactions. In addition, the Barbri outline displays ten topics that would never make up a complete essay question but would rather be tested as a small part of another essay.

For example, the bar exam I sat for had a commercial paper part of the contracts question that was likely allocated three of the ten points. Also, in the wills question on the bar exam I sat for, there was a small part that related to partnership law. Even though these topic areas make up a small part of the exam, you cannot afford to ignore them. As such, studying for the New York State Bar exam becomes a long and tedious process.

---

*Like other parts of the bar examination, the key to doing well on the essay questions is practice. When I sat for the bar exam, there was at least one question that was almost identical to a practice question I had done while studying. I had gotten the question wrong when I was studying but got it correct during the exam. Also, practice helped me to figure out answers when I was stuck, and review of sample answers illustrated exactly what the board of examiners was looking for.*

---

## The Pass Rates for Bar Examinations

The pass rate on the New Jersey Bar examination for first-time takers is similar to New York and has traditionally been around eighty-six percent for people from ABA-approved law schools. A complete list of statistics regarding pass rates in all states can be found at *http://www.ncbex.org/bar-admissions/stats/*

Pass rates for bar examinations are somewhat confusing, so you should understand what you are reading. First, the pass rates are broken down in a number of different ways. The overall pass rate is not a very good indicator, as it includes people who are second-time takers, and in some states the pass rate includes foreign trained lawyers. For example, for a recent bar examination in July, the overall pass rate for New York was seventy-two percent. When you look at the detail, though, you will see that for first-time takers from law schools in the United States, the pass rate was eighty-eight percent. During that same period, those who repeated the exam in July only achieved a pass rate of thirty-five percent. Similarly, those who sat for the bar examination in New York from law schools outside the United States had a pass rate of thirty-four percent. All of these combined make up the seventy-two percent pass rate.

As you can see, first-time takers from law schools in the United States do very well on the bar exam. In some states, the pass rate for first-time takers is over ninety percent and these high pass rates are the norm. As indicated, second-time takers and foreign lawyers really bring down the state averages so it is best to look at averages from the category to which you belong.

That being said, do not let the high pass rates fool you. You must study for the bar! I know two people from Harvard who failed the New York State Bar examination on their first attempt. Also, I have a friend who failed on his first attempt and passed on his second. When I asked him how he studied the first time, he told me that he had only completed six out of the hundred or so essay questions that Barbri assigned. This was an unusually low amount of practice, so after I heard this I was not too surprised that he did not pass. The key to passing the bar is, of course, preparation.

*If you went to law school in the United States, there is a good chance you are going to pass the bar exam on your first attempt, as most large states have pass rates close to ninety percent for first time takers. Generally, the ten percent who do not pass are the ones who do not study.*

## Preparing for the Bar Exam

The best way to prepare for a bar examination is to take a preparation course. Self-study is a bad option, and you will be at a significant disadvantage if you do not take a preparation course. Barbri offers an excellent course, and if you take it, the course will greatly improve your chances of passing the bar.

*The first step to passing the bar exam is to sign up for a preparation course, such as the one offered by Barbri. Barbri and other organizations have decades of experience with bar examinations and, as such, are experts. During the course, they will hold lectures, give you practice essay questions, give you practice multiple-choice questions, and grade sample exams. This is not the time to self-study, as you will be at a significant disadvantage if you do.*

When you start law school, organizations such as Barbri will approach you to try to get you to sign up with them. They will regularly be at your campus and will try to entice you with T-shirts, candy, and study guides. During your first year, Barbri will lock in your bar examination preparation tuition rate if you pay them a mere $100. (This is applied to your ultimate Barbri tuition amount.) This will also make you part of the Barbri family, which allows you to get various study guides and receive different updates. In addition, the study guides they will provide can be helpful, as they do a decent job spelling out the black letter law.

Typically, you will not have to pay anything else until you are ready to take the MPRE examination (discussed earlier) at the start of your third year. In order to receive the study materials and the lectures for the MPRE, you must pay an additional $150, and this—along with the $100 that you paid in the first year—is considered your "book deposit." Once you take the bar examination and return the various books that Barbri will give you, they will refund the $250 to you. I assume Barbri does this so that their material is not widely distributed to those who have not paid for it. The material is quite good, so I imagine it has some market value.

---

*Do not destroy your Barbri bar exam preparation books, as $250 of the fee that you pay is a book deposit. While you can mark up the books as much as you want, you will only get the money back if all books are returned in one piece. Also, even if you have a law firm job, they will NOT reimburse the $250 deposit even if they pay for your bar exam preparation course. I was not aware of this until it was too late.*

---

In the spring of your final year of law school, you will start to receive all of these bar preparation books, but you will not really start studying until after you graduate. Around April, you (or your firm) are required to pay the remaining Barbri bar exam preparation fee, which is approximately $2,500. The amount depends on the state you plan to take the exam in and you can get accurate information from Barbri's website (*www.barbri.com*).

## *What Is Involved for Bar Exam Preparation?*

Regardless of which state you live in, once you graduate and the official bar preparation course starts, you will attend classes five days a week and listen to lectures that are approximately four hours in length each day. While there is live instruction at one or two sites in a state, most students listen to pre-recorded lectures. You will listen to the same lectures as the live site because the live site occurs one week prior to the taped sessions and the recording is of that live session. For example, I studied for the bar examination in Cambridge and attended the recorded sessions in one of Harvard's large classrooms along with many other students. A Barbri representative would show up each day and pop the disc into the projector, which would project the presentation on a large screen.

Each day the instruction will focus on a different topic area and some topic areas take several days to cover. For example, we reviewed torts for four full days. For each lecture, you are given a comprehensive guide that walks you through what that professor is reviewing page by page. There are blanks that you can fill in, or you may take your own notes. Once you listen to the lectures for a particular session, you must go home and either make or update your notes. In addition, you are assigned both multiple-choice and essay questions that test what you learned that day.

This does not sound too bad at first glance, but it gets very tough once more topics are introduced. In week three, for example, you are required to go to class for four hours a day, review and take notes, do the practice essay and multiple-choice questions, and review the material from the previous two weeks.

You can imagine that this can get very time-consuming in your sixth, seventh, eighth, and ninth weeks. This is especially the case when reviewing a topic that you did not cover in law school. For example, I had not taken domestic relations in law school, so all of the material was new to me.

Barbri also gives you the option of going to the pre-recorded class or watching the lectures online at home. I loved this option, as I found it easier to watch the lectures at home so that I could stop and start as needed. Also, I am not a morning person, so I enjoyed watching the lectures in the afternoon. Moreover, I am a self-starter, so I did not need the structure of a classroom and I kept up with the lectures on my own time. If you do not have that kind of discipline, you should go to the class.

*You will have to listen to three to four hours of lectures daily when you are studying for the bar exam, and you have the option to go to class or watch the lectures online at home. If you are a self-starter and disciplined, you can watch the lectures at home. If not, you should go to class, as it is very difficult to catch up once you have fallen behind.*

For the MBE multiple-choice practice questions you are assigned, you should do them under timed conditions (1.8 minutes per question), and you should review the model answer once completed. For each section, Barbri outlines the scores that you are trying to achieve at that point, and this gives you a good indication of whether you are falling above or below the average so you can focus on trouble areas.

> **TIP** *You should do practice multiple-choice questions under timed conditions and review the model answers for both the questions that you answered correctly and incorrectly. It is important to review the questions that you answered correctly to see if it was just luck. If you are scoring below the average, you should review your notes and the texts and complete more practice questions. If you are doing well in a particular area, you should devote time to the areas in which you are struggling.*

During the process, you are also given practice essay questions and an MPT question that you submit to Barbri for grading. Barbri hires several real lawyers to grade these papers, some of whom have actually graded for the state bar associations. This is an excellent way to see what your essay-writing skills are like, and it helps you to hone in on exactly what the bar examiners are looking for in your answers. There are approximately four questions that are graded for you, but you may also submit additional practice questions to Barbri for grading for an additional fee.

Approximately one month prior to the examination, Barbri also organizes a mock MBE test. This examination is conducted in the same setting where you will sit for the actual MBE, and the 200 questions are done under real exam conditions. When you submit your answer sheet, Barbri will give you information on your raw score and will also give you a detailed breakdown of the areas on which you need improvement. For example, they will break down how you did on the contracts section relative to other students and will also provide you with a breakdown of the sub-areas within contracts and how you did on individual questions relative to other students. This breakdown is extremely helpful and allows you to focus on areas on which you have scored poorly.

I scored 120 out of 200 on this practice exam, and this placed me in the top thirty percent at that point in time. I was able to focus on areas that I needed to improve on (mainly property), and my scaled score on the actual MBE ended up being in the top ten percent. Because you have a month before the real exam when you do the practice test, you have lots of time to improve your performance. Also, I found the actual MBE much easier than Barbri's practice exam. That being said, the Barbri exam was very tough, and while Barbri claims it is a representative exam, I believe they make it a bit harder as a wake-up call to students to motivate them to study.

Barbri also organizes a half day simulated exam of the New York section of the bar in which you sit for an MPT and two essay questions. In addition to finding out your grades on the questions, this simulation will really help you to work on timing and organization.

Finally, Barbri uses something called a paced program to organize and monitor your progress. The paced program sets out what you have to do on each day and breaks this down in terms of morning, afternoon, and evening. All of the lectures are listed out for you, and the program also summarizes each and every multiple-choice and essay question that you are assigned each day. Given the volume of material, it is an essential organizational tool that you should refer to daily. I cannot stress enough how important it is to sign up for a bar preparation course. I cannot imagine passing the bar examination without it.

### How Many Bar Exams Should I Take?

You should try to take bar examinations in at least two states when you graduate from law school. The best time to take a bar examination is immediately after you finish law school, as you will have retained a significant amount of core knowledge that will dissipate over time. This knowledge makes it easier to pass the bar exam, and you are best positioned to do this right after law school.

When you study for one state's bar examination, you will not have to do much additional work to pass another state's exam. There are a few things to keep in mind here. First, the MBE is one part of the bar exam, and it is the same exam for every state. As such, you will not have to do any additional studying for the MBE, and your MBE score will be factored into each state's exam score. Most, if not all, states will allow the MBE score to be transferred to the state if it is taken concurrently but will not permit you to take the MBE one year for one state and then have it count toward the bar examination in a different year. For example, New York used to permit candidates to count their MBE score from a prior year toward a current session, and as such, the candidate would only have to sit for the New York portion of the exam (1 day). New York now only allows candidates to transfer MBE scores from another state if the exam in the other state was taken at the same time.

While some states allow you to transfer your MBE score from non-concurrent sessions, the trend is moving away from this. As such, normally if you want to practice law in another state, you will have to go through the grueling process of restudying for the 200 multiple-choice questions as well as the local day of the exam.

You should also note that many state exams do not contain much state-specific information. For example, as described earlier, the New Jersey exam tests only seven subject areas, so the only additional work you will have to do for that exam is sit for the exam. Other states are similar, and even states where you do have to learn state-specific material, it will almost certainly be in areas such as corporations, wills, and criminal law. As such, you will already have a foundation related to these courses from the work you have done to prepare for the primary state exam.

Another reason to sit for two bar examinations is that you are more marketable. Even if you have a job, your situation may change and you may be looking for one in the future. Being certified in many states not only shows initiative but could give you a practical advantage if a job requires certification in that state.

Finally, some states do not ever permit candidates to "motion in." In many states, when you have practiced law in a different state for five years, you can fill out some forms and pay a fee to have a license in the state. For example, in Washington D.C., you can motion in even without work experience if your scaled MBE score is high enough. Some states, however, do not ever permit this and require candidates to sit for the state bar exam. New Jersey and California are two states that have this requirement.

### What Should I Do While I Am Waiting for Bar Exam Results?

There is a very good chance that you passed the bar exam, so you should not stress yourself out. As I mentioned earlier, almost ninety percent of first-time takers pass the bar, so if you are not used to being in the bottom ten percent, there is no reason for you to believe that you will be in the bottom ten percent this time.

Unlike law school, the bar exams set a minimum standard, and the examiners have not set a specific number of people they expect to pass. If you studied, you most likely will not have anything to worry about, and if you did not, you can always take the exam again. While you are waiting, it may help you to look at the pass rates statistics to reinforce just how high these pass rates are. You should also remember that the average raw scores that you need on each question are very low—that is, fifty percent on each essay and sixty-five percent of the multiple-choice questions. Most people are accustomed to scoring higher than this.

You should avoid talking about the exam with friends. I made the mistake of doing this several times, and every time I did it I left the conversation depressed because I felt that I had made mistakes.

The truth is that no one knows what is on the answer key, and the more confident people are often the ones with the wrong answer. It serves absolutely no purpose to discuss questions, and the downside can be significant.

## How Do I Gain Admission to a State's Bar?

After you complete law school and pass the bar exam, you are still not officially a lawyer. The next and final step involves gaining admission to the bar from the relevant state(s). In order to do this, you must meet the character and fitness requirements of the state and be sworn in. You should check with the specific state to see exactly what they require, but generally speaking, the Board of Examiners wants to make sure that your background meets certain standards and that you are a person worthy of the profession. If the examiners believe that you are unworthy (for example, you lied on your application), they will either require additional investigation or deny you admission.

Either before or shortly after the bar exam, you will receive an admission application that asks questions related to your education, criminal history, employment, civil matter, child support, financial defaults, licenses, and more. Also, you will have to find both personal and professional references to attest to your character. In addition, you will have to get your law school to send information such as a law school certificate and your transcripts. Finally, in most States, you will have to appear for an interview and/or be sworn in before the court at a ceremony.

You can find a comprehensive guide to admission to bars in every state in the "Useful Resources" section.

# Useful Resources

There are a number of websites that will assist you while you are a law student and a lawyer. I've listed these below, with a brief explanation of the content of each site.

| Website | Site Name | Description |
|---------|-----------|-------------|
| http://www.lsac.org/ | Law School Admission Council | Law school application information including the Law School Admission Test (LSAT) and attrition rates |
| http://www.barbri.com/home.html | Barbri | Bar exam preparation information |
| http://www.vault.com/wps/portal/usa/rankings/landing?rankingId=1&regionId=0 | Vault | Law firm rankings and other surveys and rankings |
| http://www.americanbar.org/aba.html | American Bar Association | General information for law students and lawyers as well as law school attrition rates. |
| http://employmentsummary.abaquestionnaire.org/ | American Bar Association | Employment rates by law school |
| http://abovethelaw.com/ | Above the Law | A blog for lawyers and law students with an emphasis on current events |
| http://www.outlinedepot.com/ | Outline Depot | Law school outlines |
| http://law.bepress.com/expresso/ | Expresso | Online journal submission information |
| http://www.nalp.org/ | National Association for Law Placement (NALP) | Career information and salary surveys |

| Website | Site Name | Description |
|---|---|---|
| www.lawschoollowdown.com | Law School Lowdown | A blog with comprehensive tips on law school and law school success |
| http://www.fastweb.com | Scholarship website | Lists various places to look for scholarships |
| http://www.ncbex.org/publications/statistics/ | Bar exam pass rates | Bar exam Pass Rates by state |
| http://www.nybarexam.org/Docs/CONTENT%20 OUTLINE%20(revised% 20May%202010).pdf | New York State Bar Exam Outline | Summary of the content on the New York State Bar Exam |
| http://www.ncbex.org/assets/media_files/Comp-Guide/CompGuide.pdf | Bar Admission | Bar admission information by state |

# Acknowledgments

This book would not have been possible without the love and support of my family and friends. Many people in this world will spend a great deal of time telling you what you cannot do, but I was fortunate to have many people constantly telling me what I could do. I thank the following individuals all from the bottom of my heart:

My mother and father, Peter and Andrea Scott, have always encouraged me and at a very young age taught me that hard work, dedication, and compassion are key ingredients to success. They have made me the person I am today, and I thank them both for providing me with such glowing examples of exceptional human beings.

I would also like to thank Darren Derrick, who has provided me with foundational support and who has always been there for me. I am very fortunate to have his guidance, devotion, and commitment.

I also thank my sister, Naomi Scott, and my cousin, Jamila Poon, who are both shining examples of great parents who have taught me so much about raising my own children.

I would also like to thank Ruben Caceres, who has been the absolute best friend a person could ever have.

I would also like to extend a very special thanks to Laura Nielsen, who is an extraordinary person who has given my family more than she could ever know.

I would also like to extend a special thanks to the many individuals who provided material for this book. Many wonderful friends provided their reference letters, personal statements, and personal anecdotes, and for that I am very grateful.

I would also like to thank friends and family members who have helped and guided me over the years and whose names I have failed to mention. You have all contributed to the person I am today.

# About the Author

Ever since he earned a Bachelor of Arts years ago, Ian E. Scott wondered if he should go to law school. When Mr. Scott graduated from college, he had a strong desire to go to law school, but at the age of 21, he—like many graduating students—did not have a clear picture of what he wanted to do. Instead of going to law school, he applied and was accepted to a Master of Business Administration (M.B.A) program and later became a Certified Public Accountant (CPA).

Mr. Scott went on to have an interesting and lucrative career in investment banking and most recently worked in New York at Credit Suisse, a large investment bank. After several years, his desire to be a lawyer did not go away, and while working full-time as an investment banker, he took the Law School Admission Test (LSAT), completed his law school application, and started law school on a part-time basis (four nights a week) at Brooklyn Law School.

Even though Mr. Scott worked full-time, he was able to obtain top grades. He competed and was selected for Law Review as well as the law school's Moot Court honor society. Also, he conducted research for a professor and joined a few school organizations. After a year of part-time studies, Mr. Scott realized that being a lawyer was his calling. He resigned from his high-paying Wall Street banking job and decided to go to law school on a full-time basis. Mr. Scott applied to some of the "big"-name schools including Harvard, Columbia, and New York University. The day Mr. Scott received a call from Harvard Law School was one of the happiest days of his life, and in July 2008, he accepted Harvard's offer to attend law school and moved to Cambridge, Massachusetts.

After spending the summer of his first year of law school at the United Nations High Commissioner for Refugees, he arrived at Harvard Law School, and almost as soon as he arrived, the on-campus interview process started. This was also right around the time that the economy became very poor and law firms were revoking offers, deferring start dates, and canceling interviews. Mr. Scott was nonetheless very successful during the recruitment process and ended up with multiple offers for summer employment. He decided to accept an offer from Cleary Gottlieb, a large Wall Street corporate law firm in New York and spent his second summer with this firm.

After Mr. Scott graduated from Harvard Law School, he successfully completed the New York and New Jersey bar examinations and started working full-time at Cleary Gottlieb. He worked there in both their litigation and corporate groups and then decided to branch out on his own and opened his own law practice. He currently runs his own law firm, Scott Legal Services, P.C., in New York, specializing in new business setup and business immigration.

Mr. Scott lives in Manhattan, New York, with his spouse and two lovely daughters.

# Index

# Index

# EVERYTHING YOU NEED TO KNOW ABOUT SELECTING A LAW SCHOOL

*20TH EDITION*

This exceptionally useful directory for aspiring law students has been brought up-to-date with the latest information on more than 200 ABA-approved law schools across the United States. Profiles include details on admission requirements, academic programs, the school calendar, a capsule description of the faculty, library facilities, tuition and fees, available financial aid, graduation requirements, professional organizations, and student body composition. Several non-ABA schools get brief summary profiles in a section of their own. The book also offers advice on choosing a law school, getting career counseling, taking the Law School Admission Test (LSAT), and applying to a law school. Added features include sample law school admission forms plus a twenty-page chart that lists major law schools with statistics that will help applicants assess their chances for admission to each school. A sample LSAT with answers and explanations is a bonus feature in this directory.

**Paperback, 7 13/16" × 10 7/8", ISBN: 978-0-7641-4750-0, $24.99, *Can$28.50***

---

### Praise for the previous edition

*From the Reviews:*

"... a practical, straightforward, and useful source of information on the study and practice of law. ... an excellent addition to academic and public libraries, as well as for collections that serve career centers and guidance counselors."

—Sara Anne Hook, *ARBAonline*

---

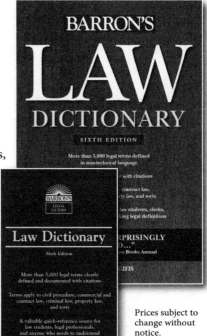